A Reassessment of
D.H. Lawrence's
Aaron's Rod

Studies in Modern Literature, No. 31

A. Walton Litz, General Series Editor

Professor of English
Princeton University

Keith Cushman

Consulting Editor for Titles on D.H. Lawrence
Professor of English
University of North Carolina at Greensboro

Other Titles in This Series

A Reassessment of D.H. Lawrence's *Aaron's Rod*

by
Paul G. Baker

UMI RESEARCH PRESS
Ann Arbor, Michigan

Produced and distributed by
UMI Research Press
an imprint of
University Microfilms International
Ann Arbor, Michigan 48106

Library of Congress Cataloging in Publication Data

Baker, Paul G. (Paul Geoffrey)
A reassessment of D.H. Lawrence's *Aaron's rod.*

(Studies in modern literature ; no. 31)
Revision of the author's thesis—University of
Toronto, 1974.
Bibliography: p.
Includes index.
1. Lawrence, D. H. (David Herbert), 1885-1930.
Aaron's rod. I. Title. II. Series.

PR6023.A93A6533 1983   823'.912   83-9224
ISBN 0-8357-1470-5

Contents

Dedicated, with love
to my parents,
and to Martin, Betty and Nicolas

Preface

Aaron's Rod occupies an extremely interesting and important place in Lawrence's writings. It represents a conscious attempt on the novelist's part to turn away from the aesthetic form of the novel which he had so successfully achieved in *The Rainbow* and *Women in Love* towards a newer kind of fiction: more audacious and aesthetically more freewheeling. This boldly experimental seventh novel would push the previously established limits of the novel even further than his earlier works. *Aaron's Rod* thus stands midway between the earlier masterpieces and the later "leadership" novels. In fact, *Aaron's Rod* was to be the first of three such novels, later described by Lawrence as "thought-adventures." It must seem curious, however, that for years now *Aaron's Rod* has suffered from critical neglect and abuse. The novel has usually been considered an artistic failure or, at best, an uneven work of fiction, far below Lawrence's highest achievements. Most critics have assigned *Aaron's Rod* but a few pages in lengthy critical studies (which nevertheless purport to deal with the entire fiction) choosing rather to devote most of their critical attention and energies to Lawrence's undisputed master-works.

The trend to group *Aaron's Rod* with *The Rainbow* and *Women in Love* was perhaps set in motion by Lawrence's own publishers, particularly Thomas Seltzer who advertised *Aaron's Rod* in the *New York Times* as "the final volume in the monumental trilogy consisting of *The Rainbow, Women in Love,* and *Aaron's Rod.*"[1] In a way this grouping was unfortunate for most other works of Lawrence's fiction pale beside these two superb creations—indeed, few novelists would wish even their finest work placed alongside *The Rainbow* or *Women in Love* for the sake of comparison. Yet surely this cannot account completely for or justify the virtually wholesale ignoring or condemning of *Aaron's Rod* for the past sixty-one years. Oddly enough, even those critics who have seen some good in *Aaron's Rod* have seemed to praise it, not for its artistic merit *per se,* its coherence or importance in terms of Lawrence's entire works, but for curiously "peripheral" aspects: its social comedy or portraiture, its biographical *roman à clef* interest, its scenes of vivid "travelogue," and so on.

This study makes no claim for *Aaron's Rod* as Lawrence's master-work, much less as a work on the same level of artistic achievement as *The Rainbow* or *Women in Love*. Yet it nevertheless attempts to redress the balance through an objective examination of the novel from several new perspectives. It attempts to open up previously neglected or virtually unexplored thematic areas in order to reassess and reestablish better the considerable artistic merit and relative importance of the novel.

The first two chapters of this study are devoted mainly to the important matter of the novel's genesis as well as to the establishing of those aspects of Lawrence's own life which had a direct bearing upon the curious and staggered growth of *Aaron's Rod* from its early stages in November and December of 1917 to its publication in April 1922. Although (as I state in several of the following chapters) the exclusively "biographical" approach to the novel practised so often by critics of Lawrence seems to me an unsatisfactory method of dealing fairly or at all *critically* with *Aaron's Rod,* it still seems necessary to set forth some indication of the events or personages surrounding and affecting Lawrence at the time he wrote the novel. More important it seems imperative to establish a clear sense of the peculiar climate of the later months of the war and its strange aftermath which contributed so directly to Lawrence's emotional outlook, his attitude toward society at this crucial time. While it is tempting to pursue the many biographical strands involving the genesis of the novel, particularly in a novel as close as *Aaron's Rod* is to the *roman à clef* tradition, with its lively, satiric caricatures of various acquaintances—Norman Douglas, "Arabella" Yorke, Richard Aldington, to name but a few—Chapter 1 confines itself strictly to those biographical details which are of immediate relevance.

Chapter 2 deals in considerable detail with the surviving typescript of *Aaron's Rod* (which I examined at the University of Texas), and what it reveals of Lawrence's artistic methods as the novel evolved. Chapters 3, 4 and 5 deal with several larger thematic areas which have heretofore received little attention: the biblical symbolism and analogues of *Aaron's Rod*; music and its importance in the novel; war and its paralyzing after-math as explored in the novel. Chapter 6 devotes itself to a more thorough study of the novel's strange "anti-hero," Aaron Sisson, and his search for identity and "selfhood." Building upon the previous chapters of this study, Chapter 7 addresses several critical problems and was conceived partly in reply to certain perennial misunderstandings of the novel's form or substance. In this chapter, I attempt to establish the considerable artistic achievement of the novel, which unfortunately has been so often overlooked.

The edition of *Aaron's Rod* used throughout this study and in all parenthetical references is Thomas Seltzer's American first edition. This edition follows the single surviving typescript of the novel and, for a variety of reasons outlined in Chapter 2, is superior to either Secker's English first edition or the subsequent Heinemann Phoenix Edition. Unfortunately the American edition is not easily obtained. A paperback version produced by Avon Books once existed but has now apparently passed out of print. The popular Viking Compass Edition is most readily available but simply reproduces Heinemann's text. Nevertheless the American version of *Aaron's Rod* is a more authoritative edition. It provides us with the most complete text of the novel and, according to the evidence offered by the typescript, is considerably more faithful to Lawrence's original artistic intentions.

1

The Genesis of *Aaron's Rod*

"Still I wait for the day when this foul tension of war and pot-bellied world will break, when we can meet in something like freedom and enjoy each other's company in something like decency. Nowadays one can do nothing but glance behind to see who now is creeping up to do something horrible to the back of one's neck."

D. H. Lawrence to Mark Gertler, 16 Feb. 1918[1]

On 14 April 1922, Thomas Seltzer, the relatively unknown American publisher, brought out a two-dollar first edition of D. H. Lawrence's seventh novel, *Aaron's Rod*. This problematic novel had rather fitfully occupied Lawrence's thoughts over a period of almost five years, being continually set aside by its anxiety-ridden author for more pressing and more lucrative literary enterprises. In order for us to grasp fully the reasons for the novel's rather staggered mode of composition, as well as the effect of this upon the form and significance of *Aaron's Rod* itself, it will be useful to retrace briefly the exact chronology of the novel together with the biographical situation of the Lawrences in these crucial years, 1917–22.[2] All of this biographical information is perhaps sufficiently well known to deserve no further comment. My purpose for its inclusion, in considerable detail, in this study of *Aaron's Rod,* is its inherent value as an emotional or artistic *key* to Lawrence himself during the difficult period in which *Aaron's Rod* was begun.

Although critics of Lawrence have frequently assumed that *Aaron's Rod* was first begun by Lawrence in early 1918, in Berkshire,[3] we know for certain that it was begun earlier, in London, as a letter to Koteliansky later affirms:

I have *nearly* finished my novel *Aaron's Rod* which I began long ago and could never bring to an end. I began it in the Mecklenburgh Square days. Now suddenly I had a fit of work — sitting away in the woods. And save for the last chapter, it is done. But it won't be popular.[4]

On 15 October 1917, the Lawrences had arrived in London, officially expelled from Cornwall after months of intolerable harassment at the hands of petty military officials in the area. They sought the protection of friends such as Dolly Radford, and Hilda and Richard Aldington. The embittering effects of the Cornwall episode on Lawrence's already misanthropic outlook cannot be overemphasized. As Frieda later recalled, "when we were turned out of Cornwall something changed in Lawrence forever."[5] Lawrence later recalled vividly this experience in the autobiographical and retrospective chapter of *Kangaroo* entitled "Nightmare":

> But Somers sat there feeling he had been killed: perfectly still, and pale, in a kind of after death, feeling he had been killed. He had always *believed* so in everything — society, love, friends. This was one of his serious deaths in belief.[6]

Mistrusting democracy and its bureaucratic processes more than ever, and with "a sickness" in his "belly,"[7] Lawrence arrived in wartime London which he described as "mad":

> London is really very bad: gone mad, in fact. It thinks and lives and breathes air-raids, nothing else. People are not people any more: they are factors, really ghastly, like lemures, devil spirits of the dead. What shall we do, how shall we get out of this Inferno?[8]

Almost immediately, the Lawrences moved into a room in the Aldingtons' flat at 44 Mecklenburgh Square.[9] It was here that the earliest sections of *Aaron's Rod* were drafted: probably the quasi-bohemian conversations and episodes of *Aaron's Rod* in which Lawrence recalled the restless banter of the cynical London "intellectuals" to whom he had been introduced. Shortly before Christmas of 1917, the Lawrences moved from London to the Radfords' cottage in Berkshire where they lived for the first quarter of 1918, when they were forced to move again. This time they moved to the Midlands, to Middleton-by-Wirksworth,[10] near Lawrence's ancestral home. Here Lawrence soon felt "very lost and queer and exiled."[11]

In this atmosphere of wartime tension and insecurity, *Aaron's Rod* was begun. With the distrustful novelist a seeming-alien in his own country, and shunted from one dwelling to another, Lawrence's early attempts at the composition of his new novel could hardly have been anything but chaotic or staggered. Naturally, the cynical, world-weary, at times irascible tone of the new novel could only reflect the pessimistic mood of the author himself. The projected Rananim of the "east slopes of the Andes"[12] must never have seemed to Lawrence so far removed:

> I have had a sore throat for so long now, that I am getting thoroughly tired of it. Oh my dear, dear Kot, why didn't we go to our Rananim! What a weak-kneed lot we were,

not to bring it off. I do so want something nice — or bit of pleasant world somewhere — nothing but the corner of a cemetery seems to offer. . . [13]

As early as February 1918, Lawrence seems to have set *Aaron's Rod* aside in one of his periods of unsettled inactivity:

> I'm not writing anything — only sit learning songs, which I find a great amusement. I can read well enough to learn a song nicely in about a quarter of an hour. . . . I don't know why it amuses me so much more than reading or writing. [14]

In a letter written to Mark Gertler on 21 February 1918, Lawrence admits with rather forced insouciance that his new novel is progressing with extraordinary slowness:

> I am doing some philosophic essays, also very spasmodically, another daft novel. It goes slowly — very slowly and fitfully. But I don't care. [15]

The use of "daft" is curious, for, like the other adjectives used around this time by Lawrence to describe his "new novel" — "innocent," "blameless" to name a few — it suggests that the novel in its early stages must have seemed an innocuous diversion, a contrast perhaps to *The Rainbow* or *Women in Love*. [16] In a letter to Cynthia Asquith written in March 1918, Lawrence revealed that he had finished "150 pages" of his new novel, definitely *Aaron's Rod*:

> I have begun a novel now — done 150 pages, which is as blameless as Cranford. It shall not have one garment disarranged, but shall be buttoned up like a Member of Parliament. Still, I wouldn't vouch that is is like *Sons and Lovers*: it is funny. It amuses me terribly. [17]

Lawrence's frivolous attitude to the new novel was short-lived. Other more pressing literary (and pecuniary) concerns seemed to occupy his energies almost continuously. At this time he was more and more obsessed with the concept of a violent upheaval of the old world values, a concept which is reechoed particularly in the early chapters of *Aaron's Rod*. Lawrence's letters during this period of artistic and financial crisis reverberate with the sounds of a world cataclysm which he hoped was imminent:

> About the world, I feel that nothing but a quite bloody, merciless, almost anarchistic revolution will be any good for this country; a fearful chaos of smashing up. And I think it will come sooner or later: and I wish it would come soon. [18]

Closely related to this growing obsession was Lawrence's preoccupation with the idea of escape from England with its repressions and outworn values. A letter to Mark Gertler written in March typifies his bleak outlook at this time:

> I don't feel like you about work. I go on working because it is the one activity allowed to one, not because I care. I feel like a wild cat in a cage—I long to get out into some sort of free, lawless life—at any rate, a life where one can move about and take no notice of anything. I feel horribly mewed up. I don't want to act in concert with any body of people. I want to go by myself—or with Frieda—something in the manner of a gipsy, and be houseless and placeless and homeless and landless, just move apart. I *hate* and *abhor* being stuck on to any form of society.[19]

The frustration and humiliation suffered by Lawrence at his third medical examination must have aggravated his already acute paranoia to the point at which work on the "new novel," perhaps all work, became impossible. Many of Lawrence's letters at this time reveal that he was not working at all, or, as in the letter cited above, working only half-heartedly, in order to maintain some feeling of private equilibrium in a world gone mad.

During these dark months, Lawrence turned his attention away from the "new novel" in order to devote his energies to "a set of essays for America,"[20] the *Symbolic Meaning* collection finally entitled *Studies in Classic American Literature.* The final revision and gathering together of these essays seems to have been for Lawrence an annoyingly slow process. In May Lawrence informed Edith Eder that he was still writing his "never-to-be finished *Studies in Classic American Literature.*"[21] Between reading bouts of Gibbon and composing a series of "smallish lyrical pieces," Lawrence was able to complete the last essay (dealing with Walt Whitman), in June 1918.

Shortly after the completion of these major critical essays Lawrence was offered the opportunity (by Oxford University Press) of preparing a history text book, which was to be a "series of vivid sketches of movements and people" as Vere H. Collins later recalled.[22] Lawrence's work on this history book, which he himself entitled *Movements in European History,* appears to have lingered on through summer and fall of 1918, and the text was finally finished early in the new year.[23] In the meantime Lawrence was writing a play, *Touch and Go,* several themes of which were reminiscent of those explored earlier in *Women in Love.* As Lawrence himself informed Amy Lowell, *Touch and Go* was completed by November, 1918.[24]

During the same fall months of 1918, various other literary projects also claimed his attention. The very fine short story, "The Blind Man," was completed in November, and the first version of *The Fox* was apparently being written in November (although, according to E. Tedlock, it was not rewritten until summer 1919).[25] In addition to these shorter works of fiction, Lawrence was involved in producing a series of essays originally intended for the *Times Literary Supplement* entitled *The Education of the People.*[26] Unfortunately these four essays were never published during Lawrence's lifetime. The Lawrences were apparently in London on 11 November 1918, and according to David Garnett attended an Armistice party at Montague Shearman's flat at Adelphi Terrace.[27] Christmas 1918 found the Lawrences still in the Midlands, at their home, "Mountain Cottage" in Middleton. Christmas Day was spent at Ripley in the home of Lawrence's sister, Ada. It was this first Christmas after the Armistice, particularly his visit to a Dr. Feroze, "a Parsee," which Lawrence so vividly recreated in the opening chapters of *Aaron's Rod*. The close of one grim year gave way in Lawrence's mind to a new year of equally bleak prospects:

> Tonight we are going back to Middleton—and I feel infuriated to think of the months ahead, when one waits paralysed for some sort of release. I feel caged, somehow—and I *cannot* find out how to earn enough to keep us—and it maddens me.[28]

In all this confusing assortment of literary projects of nearly every genre, the absence of all mention by Lawrence of any work on *Aaron's Rod* is quite conspicuous. After March 1918 references to *Aaron's Rod* disappear from Lawrence's personal correspondence for a period of two years. Doubtless the virtually penniless novelist was driving himself frantically at this time in an effort to complete more urgent and financially rewarding projects. Thus, the "new novel" which had afforded its author so much amusement in its early stages soon became an expensive luxury which must be relinquished, at least for the time being. Perhaps too, as his letters suggest, Lawrence had momentarily exhausted his ready supply of acquaintances or personal experiences which were to be the "raw substance" for the new novel: materials which might be transformed through his very highly idiosyncratic, novelistic processes into the forms of *fiction*. It was his travels to the Continent, particularly Italy, which would provide Lawrence with a fresh perspective and the new experiences he so urgently required.

In the fall of 1919 the Lawrences had finally left England after annoying passport delays. Frieda preceded Lawrence, departing in October for Germany, where she would be united with her family once again. On November 14, 1919, Lawrence left for the Continent, planning to join Frieda later, in Italy. Travelling alone he passed through such cities as Paris, which he found "nasty," and Turin, where he was the guest of a Sir Walter Becker for a few days.[29] This visit is of special importance for it provided Lawrence with the materials for Chapters 12 and 13 of *Aaron's Rod,* which recount Aaron's brief stay at the estate of "Sir William Franks" in "Novara," as it appears in the final version of the novel. Lawrence and

Frieda were reunited in Florence in December, and subsequently travelled to Rome (which they found "vile") thence to Picinisco, the "Pescocalasco" of *The Lost Girl.* Escaping to Capri from the primitive severity of Picinisco Lawrence seems to have experienced difficulties in attending to his work:

> The days pass rather lazily. I ought really to work. But one loses the desire. Now the weather is sunny again, we think of starting bathing. Italy is a lazy country. One meets people, and lounges till the next meal: But why not![30]

The Lawrences' stay in Capri was predictably short, [31] Capri being for Lawrence "a gossipy, villa-stricken, two-humped chunk of limestone, a microcosmos that does heaven much credit, but mankind none at all...a bit impossible for long."[32] From Capri, the Lawrences travelled to Taormina in Sicily where they remained for two years, their stay broken by occasional trips to the mainland or to nearby islands such as Sardinia and Malta.

Considered in its entirety, Lawrence's "Italian period," as we might refer to it, was uncommonly rich and productive, particularly his stay in Fontana Vecchia, Sicily. After seemingly endless months of postwar deprivation and alienation, the escape to Italy must have seemed to Lawrence a physical and psychological liberation. The early months of Lawrence's self-imposed exile with the usual restless wandering from one city to another, disruptive and exhausting, were hardly conducive to long-range enterprises or literary genres like the novel. Establishing himself at Taormina provided Lawrence with the tranquillity and stability which he so much required at this time, in order to ensure some measure of artistic productivity.

It is also significant that in the months between his departure from England on 14 November 1919, and his taking up residence in early March at Taormina, Lawrence was able to complete only *one* work of any significance, *Psychoanalysis and the Unconscious.* This work was begun in December of 1919 and completed shortly after in January of 1920.[33] Once settled in Taormina, Lawrence could turn his attention once again to the novel. Instead of completing *Aaron's Rod* at this opportune time, Lawrence preferred to direct his energies towards completing another long-neglected manuscript, that of a novel which was entitled *The Lost Girl.* The earliest version of *The Lost Girl* had been left behind in Germany before the war, and, receiving the old manuscript of the novel in February 1920, Lawrence immediately set to work completing it. According to Lawrence's diary in the Notebook containing *Birds, Beasts and Flowers, The Lost Girl* was finally finished on 5 May 1920.[34]

Almost immediately Lawrence seems to have started a new novel, a "hilarious" one, entitled *Mr. Noon.* We may be sure that it is this *new* novel of which Lawrence speaks in his correspondence with Martin Secker in May of 1920:

> I have got ready the ms. of my Studies in Classic American Literature. . . . I have begun another novel.[35]

By July of 1920, Lawrence's initial enthusiasm for *Mr. Noon* had waned somewhat and he was ready to set aside this frivolity for a more serious project. On 18 July Lawrence alludes to *Aaron's Rod* in a letter to Secker:

> Yes, I have another novel in hand. I began it *two years ago.* I have got it ⅓ done, and it is very amusing. But it stands still just now, awaiting events. Once it starts again it will steam ahead.[36]

Despite the optimism of the final sentence, Lawrence was obviously experiencing difficulty in returning to an older manuscript after a "cooling-off" period of over two years. The phrase "awaiting events" reminds us once again of Lawrence's need as novelist to live through the events which he was to transform into fiction, but it also brings to mind the fact that one of Lawrence's greatest challenges as a writer was establishing the proper perspective upon such experience. This narrative objectivity he later described in the Foreword to the *Fantasia,* discussing the relation between his fiction and expository work:

> The novels and poems come unwatched out of one's pen. And then the absolute need which one has for some sort of satisfactory mental attitude towards oneself and things in general makes one try to abstract some definite conclusions from one's experience as a writer and as a man.[37]

Though Lawrence avows, in the sentence which follows, that the "novels and poems are pure passionate experience," I would suggest that most of Lawrence's fiction derives from the double process described above, and that the novels, like the "pollyanalytics" are inferences made afterwards, from the experience."[38]

By this time Lawrence seemed to have exhausted his fund of immediate personal experiences, the events which he had recently included in *The Lost Girl*: the railway trip through Southern Italy and his short stay in "staggeringly primitive" Picinisco, and so on. In the same letter of July 18, 1920, however, Lawrence speaks of his plans for another trip through Italy: "Frieda has promised to go to Germany in August. I shall probably wander about—Rome, Florence, Venice, for some 2 months—returning here in October."[39] No doubt this excursion later inspired some of the chapters required for the completion of *Aaron's Rod*. Lawrence travelled in the next few months through Naples, Amalfi and Rome to Florence, thence to Venice and Northern Italy including Milan. It was from Venice that Lawrence informed Catherine Carswell that he was "still stuck in the middle of *Aaron's Rod,*" adding: "But in Taormina I'll spit on my hands and lay fresh hold."[40]

Unfortunately for the novelist it was still some time before he could make good his promise. The trip through Italy had provided Lawrence with the private experience and relationships which would be necessary ingredients for finishing off the novel *Aaron's Rod*. But the vicissitudes of travel, the abrupt transitions from one social milieu to another, as inevitable as they had seemed, had a distinctly unsettling effect upon Lawrence:

> Am not working—too unsettled yet, and this autumn-winter is my uneasy time. Let the year turn.[41]

When he finally resumed writing, Lawrence seems to have chosen to take up the facetious *Mr. Noon* once again. Through the next winter months Lawrence must have written almost nothing of *Aaron's Rod*. Preparing to leave Taormina for Baden-Baden, the home of Frieda's mother, Lawrence's hopes were set once more upon the completion of his long neglected novel:

> I am leaving Taormina on Saturday. My wife had to go to Baden Baden [sic] her mother ill. So I am alone in the house. I shall go to Palermo and Rome, then perhaps do a walking tour in Sardinia, then to Germany.... I shall try and finish *Aaron's Rod* the summer before finishing *Mr. Noon* II, which is funny, but a hair raiser. First part innocent—*Aaron's Rod* innocent.[42]

In the early part of April Lawrence left Taormina,[43] as usual following Frieda, and working his way slowly up the coast. It was in Capri that Lawrence's memorable meeting with the Brewsters took place, and Lawrence subsequently revealed to these new acquaintances his plans for completing *Aaron's Rod*. As Achsah Brewster later recalled:

> Again in the afternoon Lawrence came swinging up the garden path. We were alone, and he told us that he was writing *Aaron's Rod,* and began outlining the story. It seemed more beautiful as he narrated it in his low sonorous voice with the quiet gesture of his hands, than it ever could written in a book. Suddenly he stopped, after Aaron had left his wife and home and broken with his past, gravely asking what he should do with him.[44]

Shortly after his arrival in Baden-Baden about 26 April, Lawrence wrote the Brewsters an exuberant letter in which he announced that he was finishing *Aaron's Rod,* but in a rather perverse fashion:

> I am finishing *Aaron.* And you won't like it *at all.* Instead of bringing him nearer to heaven, in leaps and bounds, he's misbehaving and putting ten fingers to his nose at everything. Damn heaven. Damn holiness. Damn Nirvana. Damn it all.[45]

By 16 May 1921, Lawrence was able to report to Martin Secker that *Aaron's Rod* was "well under weigh [sic] again."[46] On 27 May, Lawrence informed Koteliansky that the novel was nearly finished, owing to a sudden "fit of work—sitting away in the woods."[47] Lawrence also noted that only the last chapter remained to be written. In another letter, written the same day to Martin Secker, Lawrence informed his English publisher that *Aaron's Rod* was "as good as finished," but expressed concern over the effect which the new novel might have upon its readers:

> You will be glad to hear I have as good as finished *Aaron's Rod,* that is, it is all done except the last chapter—two days work. It all came quite suddenly here. But it is a queer book, I've no idea what you or anybody will think of it. When it is typed, I will let you see it. It is about as long as *Lost Girl,* I presume.[48]

Lawrence's confident calculations that two days' work would be sufficient for completing the last chapter are again over-optimistic, for the novel was in fact not completed until two weeks later. In letters written 12 June 1921, to both Curtis Brown and Martin Secker, Lawrence declared *Aaron's Rod* to be "quite finished."[49] In both these letters he mentions that the first part of *Aaron's Rod* is already in Mountsier's hands. In his letter to Secker, Lawrence mentions that the first part had been typed in England. Although the novel had been finished after innumerable interruptions and lapses, Lawrence's problems were just beginning, as he began preparing the final draft of the novel for publication.

Lawrence had never been optimistic about the reception which would be accorded *Aaron's Rod* by his various publishers and acquaintances. As early as 27 May 1921, he had informed Koteliansky that *Aaron's Rod* "won't be popular."[50] Other letters written soon after to friends like Earl and Achsah Brewster and Mary Cannan all attest to Lawrence's growing uneasiness. His suspicions seemed confirmed by the reactions of his agents to the portions of the novel which he must have sent them. Lawrence was determined to have the novel published, despite all adverse criticism:

> I am going to send *Aaron's Rod* to Curtis Brown. He and Mountsier hate it. Probably you will too. But I want you to publish it none the less. That is to say, I don't in the

least want you to if you don't wish to. But I will have the book published. It is my last word in one certain direction.[51]

Through the fall Lawrence festered with the unfriendly criticisms of his agents, as this diary entry from Lawrence's notebook, dated 26 October 1921, suggests: "...had impudent letters from C[urtis] B[rown] and R[obert] M[ountsier] about Aaron's Rod [sic]: canacci."[52]

Autumn of 1921 also brought Lawrence the news from America that Seltzer was quite enthusiastic about the new novel. From Lawrence's correspondence, we may observe Lawrence's reluctance to accept wholeheartedly such compliments as Seltzer heaped upon the novel. In a diary entry of 13 November, Lawrence wrote: "...feel dubious myself,"[53] and in a letter to Donald Carswell dated November 15, he reported:

Everybody hated *Aaron's Rod* — even Frieda. But I just had a cable from Seltzer that he thinks it wonderful. Maybe it is just a publisher's pat. Anyhow it is better than a smack in the eye, such as one gets from England for everything.[54]

A similar letter to the Brewsters repeats Seltzer's words of approval but Lawrence adds sardonically, "Glad to hear it I'm sure."[55] In another letter to Secker, Lawrence dismissed Seltzer's effusive praise as "an Americanism."[56]

Predictably, Lawrence received no such encouragement from Martin Secker himself. In a letter to Catherine Carswell, Lawrence complained of the animosity with which the novel was treated:

He [Secker] doesn't like my *Aaron's Rod*. That *Rod*, I'm afraid it is gentian root or worm-wood stem. But they've got to swallow it sooner or later: miserable, tonicless lot.[57]

In the meantime Lawrence was preparing his typescript version of *Aaron's Rod* for publication. Originally Lawrence had planned to bring out the English edition with Secker and the American edition with Seltzer simultaneously, as this letter to Secker of 23 November 1921 affirms: "I am sending Curtis Brown the ms. of *Aaron's Rod*. I want it to be published simultaneously with Seltzer's."[58] Yet, Lawrence was particularly concerned that Secker's date of publication should not precede Seltzer's:

I was very glad to get the two copies of *Aaron's Rod* this morning — beautifully typed and bound.... I will return the whole Ms. directly. But *please* see that Secker's date of publication does not precede Seltzer's.[59]

It must be stressed that the rather hasty completion of the novel (and its subsequent revision and preparation for printing) in Baden-Baden was largely due to Lawrence's rather desperate financial straits at this time. Travel had depleted his meager resources, and various other expenditures, such as those in the regrettable Magnus affair, drove him to accelerate his efforts to publish new works. Artistically and, more important, financially it was the appropriate moment to complete and bring out *Aaron's Rod*.

After a few half-hearted and unsuccessful attempts on Lawrence's part to revise the typescript of *Aaron's Rod* for Seltzer, he seems to have sent off the final version for the American edition granting Seltzer full permission to do with the typescript as he pleased.[60] At the same time Lawrence confided to his American agent, Curtis Brown, "I would rather Secker followed the true MS. if he will—and *vogue la galère!*"[61]

It should be noted, however, that the earliest public appearance of *Aaron's Rod* was in February 1922 when Chapter 14, later entitled "XX Settembre" appeared in the *Dial* as "An Episode."[62] Seltzer's publication date in America, actually did precede that of Secker, as Lawrence had intended. Following Seltzer's 14 April publication, Secker brought out his English edition in June. As it turned out, Lawrence's pessimistic forecasts that the novel would initially be ill-received were wrong. The warmest review came from Middleton Murry who wrote enthusiastically in the *Nation and Athenaeum*:

> Mr. Lawrence's sun shines forth after the darkness of eclipse. The exasperation, the storm and stress are gone. He has dragged us with him through the valley of the shadow; now we sail with him in the sunlight. Mr. Lawrence's new book ripples with the consciousness of victory; he is gay, he is careless, he is persuasive. To read *Aaron's Rod* is to drink of a fountain of life....
>
> *Aaron's Rod* is the most important thing that has happened to English literature since the war. To my mind it is much more important than *Ulysses*. Not that it is more important in and for itself than Mr. Joyce's book. No doubt it is a smaller thing. But *Ulysses* is sterile; *Aaron's Rod* is full of the sap of life. The whole of Mr. Joyce is in *Ulysses*; *Aaron's Rod* is but a fruit on the tree of Mr. Lawrence's creativeness. It marks a phase, the safe passing of the most critical phase in Mr. Lawrence's development. He has survived his own exasperation against the war.[63]

Murry's intensely subjective reaction to the new novel may seem today hyperbolic, his claims for its superiority to *Ulysses* wildly extravagant. Certainly his love of *Aaron's Rod* was prompted by a professed personal dislike—for obvious reasons—of *Women in Love*. Most other reviews were favorable and even though Rebecca West could not resist describing it fatuously as a "plum silly book,"[64] the general critical opinion of *Aaron's Rod* was that it represented something innovative and stimulating in British fiction, as well as a new direction for the artistic efforts of one of the most talented and disturbing "young novelists" of the "modern" scene.

2

Aaron's Rod:
The Typescript and the Texts

Unfortunately no manuscript version of *Aaron's Rod* has survived; but a typescript of the novel, used undoubtedly in the preparation of the American edition, is now in the possession of the University of Texas. It consists of 479 typewritten pages, double-spaced.

Lawrence must have had a difficult time revising the novel as this letter written to Curtis Brown, 26 January 1922, suggests:

> I didn't alter the original MS. at all, of *Aaron's Rod*. Or only a few words. I couldn't. Seltzer sent me a clean typed copy of the book, begging for the alterations for the sake of the 'general public' (he didn't say *jeune fille*). I sat in front of the MS. and tried: but it was like Balaam's Ass, and wouldn't budge.[1]

The changes which Lawrence was able to bring himself to make — and there are a great many more than this letter above seems to imply — he entered in ink above the original typescript version through which he drew his pen. This appears to have been Lawrence's customary method of revision, as an examination of other typescripts, as well as letters to agents and publishers, proves. Here is a typical letter written to Martin Secker on 18 September 1920, concerning the typescript of *The Lost Girl*:

> Yes please do correct the proofs in the office, but do them from the typed ms. which *The Queen* had. You will at *once* see my hand-written corrections over the type.[2]

This typescript, of course, represents *Aaron's Rod* in its later form. In this chapter, I should like to discuss what it reveals to us of Lawrence's earlier additions and revisions of the novel, including his extensive reshaping of various important passages as he prepared the novel in its final stages for publication. I shall then proceed to a briefer discussion of the major differences existing between Seltzer's American edition and Secker's English edition of *Aaron's Rod*.

As might be expected many revisions of the original text are decidedly slight: the frequent substitution of synonyms, the occasional reshaping or cancelling of phrases or the alteration of the original syntax and so on. These require little commentary: a few random examples should suffice. Josephine's friend, a dressmaker-decorator, was originally described at the beginning of Chapter 5 as "a man of the greatest chic" (TS62–A54),[3] but this was later revised to "a master of modern elegance." In Chapter 9, "Low Water Mark," Aaron was described as "our old acquaintance" (TS122–A102). For the final version, Lawrence cancelled the word "old." In the original version, Lilly speaks of war as "all foul and unreal," amended simply to "all unreal" in the final version (TS171–A138). As I suggested earlier, such revisions scarcely alter the shape or meaning of passages in which they occur, and some deletions, particularly those in pencil, may even be the work of some conscientious proofreader employed by Lawrence's American publisher.

More interesting are those minor revisions which attest to Lawrence's painstaking efforts to secure the *mot juste* in his final version of the novel. In Chapter 8 where Jim Bricknell's strange visit to the Lillys' cottage in Hampshire takes place, Jim speaks of love as "a great rush of force" in the "solar plexus." Later he strikes Lilly in the solar plexus. Lawrence must have taken considerable pains in choosing "solar plexus." In the title for this chapter, he employed "wind" and the typescript reveals that Lawrence earlier changed "solar plexus" to "middle" but then restored "solar plexus" (TS112–A93). The connection between Lawrence's terminology here and that of *Fantasia of the Unconscious* is obvious.[4] The typescript version also shows a reference, later cancelled, in the same chapter to the Japanese as "aloof little devils" who "don't bother with their solar plexuses" (TS113). In a debate with Lady Franks in Chapter 12, Aaron argues that music is "risky." The typescript reveals that Lawrence took considerable pains to achieve a precise effect here. "Immoral" was first employed, then was amended to "dangerous," finally, to "risky" (TS256–A196).

Even more interesting than these examples of painstaking revision are the revelations provided throughout the typescript of earlier versions of proper names. Josephine Ford was earlier Josephine Hay; the Bricknells apparently were once the Shottles. Sir William Franks was earlier Frank. Lilly's first name was once Wilfred before Lawrence's final "Rawdon." Many place names as well as geographical locations or directions were also revised for the final version. Jim's rooms were originally in Adelphi Terrace: the name was later omitted. In the typescript Aaron and Josephine walk west from Charing Cross Road towards Holborn and the British Museum. Lawrence must have checked the geographical correctness of such a direction for he later amended "west" to "east." Novara, the home of Sir William Franks, was originally Turin and the typescript refers throughout to Torinesi (later changed to Novaresi).[5] Francis' father was originally a highly esteemed barrister and politician of "Cape Town," later revised to "Sydney." The reference to Cape Town seems more appropriate in view of Francis' Afrikaaner-sounding name, Franz Dekker.

The typescript also reveals that the chapter titles were later added by Lawrence and that several of the present titles were originally quite different. Chapter 4 in which Aaron returns home for the first time, a few days after Christmas, was originally entitled, "The House-Breaker," later amended to "The Home Touch." It was finally entitled "The Pillar of Salt," a more appropriate allusion to the biblical parallel of Lot and his obstinate wife. The title of Chapter 6, "Talk" was originally "After the Theatre." The earlier title may perhaps remind us of the similar title assigned to Lawrence's short poem "After the Opera," possibly written at the same time as the London chapters of *Aaron's Rod.* "Talk" is, of course, more appropriate, as it suggests the frivolous chatter of this chapter, and looks forward as well to the title of the final chapter of the novel "Words," an allusion to Lilly's polemical "speech-music." Chapter 7, "The Dark Square Garden," was originally entitled "Love Episode." Chapter 9, chronicling Aaron's recovery from influenza in Lilly's London flat, was originally "Covent Garden"; the final title, "Low Water Mark," is obviously a more appropriate reference to the spiritual and physical nadir to which Aaron sinks in this episode. Chapter 19, "Cleopatra, But Not Anthony" (referring to Aaron's resistance to the feminine will of the Marchesa) was originally entitled simply "Anthony."[6]

It must be admitted that Lawrence's minor revisions on the typescript often bring some puzzlement to the reader. The problem is especially noticeable in dialogues in which Lawrence has not altered the reply of a second character to match the altered question or statement of the first character. An example or two will make this clear. In Chapter 7 in which Josephine and Aaron sit in a Soho restaurant discussing love, marriage, and the future, Aaron's reply to Josephine's statement, "But I often wonder what will become of me," was originally "Does it matter?" (TS93). In the final version Lawrence amended Aaron's reply to "In what way?" Yet Josephine's ensuing reaction, "She was almost affronted," makes very little sense in the final version but much more in the original typescript. Similarly her rejoinder seems more appropriate in the original version: "What becomes of me? I suppose not. And it doesn't matter, not to anybody but myself" (TS94–A78). It may be possibly argued that all of this is fairly minor or inconsequential but I would suggest nevertheless that such details are a necessary part of any examination of a Lawrence manuscript. I would suggest further that the alterations such as those mentioned above may account in some way for the curious obliquity of much of the dialogue in *Aaron's Rod*. Perhaps Lawrence's proof-reading was rushed at this point. A similar ambiguity may be seen later in Chapter 16 when Algy speaks of the Marchesa's strange inability to sing at his tea-party. In the final version Algy asks, "...is it because you don't intend there should be any more song? Is that your intention?" In the earlier typescript version, "intention" was "will" (TS358–A260) which better fits Manfredi's reply a few lines later, "At the present time it is because she *will* not – not because she cannot. It is her will, as you say" (TS359). "As you say," makes little sense in the final version of the exchange because there has actually been no mention of *will* up to this point.

Let us now turn to those areas of more extensive and thematically significant revision. For purposes of this study, I have divided the major revisions to the original typescript into three related categories and will discuss each in turn. The most obvious kind of major revision is that which reveals to us the art of the novelist at work transforming even the plainest descriptions of ordinary actions into the highly charged material of true fiction. This process of intensification or dramatic heightening is particularly evident in the flag incident of Chapter 14. I would therefore like to discuss this important episode in considerable detail.

The flag incident of Chapter 14 displays the greatest amount of rewriting in the entire typescript. The original version has been completely crossed out and a new, more vital version written above. Lawrence's rewriting and reshaping of the entire flag episode provide us with a perfect example of his ability to heighten the dramatic effect of an episode infusing it with tension, vigor and special symbolic significance. On the whole we might say that the flag incident in its final version represents a movement away from realism to a depersonalized account, as well as an increase in effectiveness. In order to facilitate the following discussion of Lawrence's transformation of the flag incident from its original to its final form, I have included as an Appendix to my study of *Aaron's Rod* the original version as it appears in the typescript and have numbered each paragraph. I shall discuss Lawrence's revisions paragraph by paragraph, pointing out the dramatic heightening which the original has undergone. Since the final version as found in the American first edition is not readily available I have also included extensive reference to this *final* American version of the episode.

The first paragraph of the original typescript version is a very general description of a typical "Italian crowd." The final version is infinitely more vivid. The rather lumpy, nondescript opening paragraph of the first version has been transformed into a colorful and intense prelude to the youth's ill-fated climb. The "red flag fluttering from a man's fist"[7] has replaced "They had no flag" while a greater sense of tension and barely suppressed violence is imparted by the addition of such phrases as "calling and vociferating"; "their voices...like a jarring of steel weapons"; "a strange slashing sound," and so on. The closely observed minutiae of the passage suggest a more cinematic approach to the scene, as Aaron's eye picks out various striking details, presented to the reader as a series of "close-ups." A typical example is the vivid description of the "lean strong Italian jaws" of the men which replaces the earlier less vivid description of the crowd. Such details of the final version are more suggestive of the Lawrencean themes of male comradeship and the corresponding themes of leadership and power. The rather burlesque description of the white jacketed man disappearing "like a white rabbit" is replaced by that of the "frowsty-looking man yellow-pale," and the acrid derision which accompanies the hauling in of the national flag. The rather loose and awkward sentence beginning "They had no flag or badge..." has disappeared from the final version. In spite of the fact that Lawrence splits the original paragraph into two more lengthy ones, the final corrected version is obviously more terse and controlled.

The second paragraph of the original version is essentially a rather rambling reiteration of the emotional effects of the first paragraph. In spite of the images of the wave of sound "like a great puff of smoky flame" and other ensuing images of conflagration and boiling, this second paragraph fails to advance the narrative in any significant way. Lawrence has wisely condensed this rather amorphous paragraph into one short transitional passage in the final version, which carries the reader on to the heart of the episode: the climb of the young boy.

At this point in both the earlier typescript and final versions, the scene shifts to the solitary tricolor "which stirred damply in the early evening light." Once again we find a process of intensification, a "tightening up" in the final version. The elaborately repetitive imagery of boiling pitch — the unintentional pun with auditory pitch a few lines later is unfortunate — fusing, hot blood, etc. has been telescoped to Aaron's own view of the crowd "moving like boiling pitch beneath him." Such weak constructions as "the passion was beginning to fuse" of the original have been replaced in the final version with a far more terse and muscular prose which better conveys the feverish intensity of the incident. In the earlier version, Lawrence's abstract description of the "terrible noise" as "unspeakably depressing to the soul" seems needlessly ambiguous as does his rather rambling psychological approach to the mob a few lines later: "The curious hot sound of the rising blood," and "that most peculiar prolonged roaring resonance of a really angry mob." In the final version, all this has again been condensed to a few evocative phrases and transformed into more highly-charged prose. The earlier "loud thuds and crashes" as men "beat and smashed at the great green door" has been replaced with a more energetic description of the knocking and ringing. Lawrence's further addition of the vignette describing the futile protests of the woman in a white blouse is an inspired touch. The cinematic approach of Lawrence focuses our attention on specific colorful figures in the landscape at the same time suggesting, like the incident of the boy's climb later, the helpless involvement of the individual in inexorable political forces.

The fourth paragraph of the original shows comparatively little rewriting, probably because Lawrence has at last reached the heart of the incident, the actual climb, a more decisive action which stimulates him to an outburst of creative energy. Two noticeable departures from the original version are of particular significance. In the final version the climbling youth is described not simply as a black figure, but as "fair haired." This modification suggests the innocent and naive quality of the boy's bravado, and stresses his implication in grim partisan activities which he barely understands and over which he has little control. The original imagery of the boy "cleaving to the house front like a black fly," has been cancelled in the final version as well as the powerfully suggestive description of his climbing "with strange non-human quickness." Instead we find a new and extremely appropriate image of a wriggling lizard applied to the youth, a more ominous and implicit reference to the dehumanizing effect of his involvement. The concluding sentences of the paragraph in the final version seem superior in their vivid description of the youth's ill-fated climb.

In the fifth paragraph of the original version, the youth's name is invoked by the mob as he continues his climb. The focus of the incident constantly shifts back to the crowd's pleased reaction as it swarms "like bees in deep, pleased excitement." In the final version however, Lawrence has tightened considerably the rather loose earlier paragraph. As vivid as the original undoubtedly is—even the first version of the episode displays the stamp of Lawrence's inimitable art—the tension seems rather protracted here, the arrangement of events more random. The great excitement surrounding the boy's climb is dissipated somehow by the rather uninteresting drawing-out of his name syllable by syllable. The chanting of the boy's name disappears in the final version, to be replaced by the succinct phrase "wild, ragged ejaculations of excitement and encouragement." The anonymity of the boy adds further to the symbolic suggestiveness of the episode, as do the mysterious connotations of magic or spell to explain the mesmerized behavior of the lad. Lawrence's prose is firm yet supple and the description of the boy's climb in the final version is brilliantly evocative. The suggestion of the crowd standing "for a second electrically still" underlines the desperate tension of the scene more effectively than the original, relatively plain description of the crowd "standing back from the walls, of the house, so as to watch the progress upwards, and so, also, as to be out of the way if he *did* fall." Once again our attention has been directed in the final version back to the *youth* as he continues his strange quest to seize the flag.

Paragraphs six, seven and eight of the original have been extensively revised and condensed in the final version to a single highly-charged paragraph. The rewriting is entirely consistent with the kind of dramatic intensifying and reshsaping which we have seen so far in detail. The terseness of the final version eliminates the loose "padding" of the final sentence of paragraph seven of the original with its ineffective reiteration of "strange" and the already familiar description of the surging crowd. Likewise the flat rhetorical questions which conclude paragraph eight (examining the reasons for the climb, and so on) have been fortunately omitted in the final version. The effect is more powerful; the causes are left undefined and mysterious. In the eighth paragraph of the original the boy begins his descent "clinging and swarming down the now bare flag-pole" as the crowd responds in very Italianate bravos. In the final version, of course, the youth remains suspended in mindless abstraction, as the tension is deliberately drawn out by Lawrence to suggest that time has momentarily stood still. The unnatural hush acts effectively as a prelude to the stormy onslaught of the carabinieri. The crowd which seems more jubilant in the earlier version of the episode has been transformed into a more surly and vicious mob in keeping with the increased harshness and power of the final version.

The ninth paragraph of both versions focuses on the unexpected arrival upon the scene of the carabinieri. The attack is more brutal in the final version. The defiance which accompanies the fear and rage of the original is gone; the cowardly "frenzy of terror" of the mob seems more pronounced. In the final version, attention is deflected from the youthful climber as he disappears during the sudden fracas, leaving the reader in doubt as to his fate. In the earlier version of the episode, the boy falls from the housefront "as if shot" as the carabinieri rush. The mob disperses, its members bearing off the wounded body of the youth. Lawrence must have cancelled the last half of paragraph nine and the entire tenth paragraph before rewriting the episode in its entirety. The final version of the conclusion to the episode describes the humiliating descent of the youth, the mob's hero a few minutes before, as he is marched away "a prisoner." The flat, anti-climactic ending of the original with its "prosaic carabineers" and its attempts to account for the sudden passing of the incident "like a dream" is replaced in the final version with the milling groups of discontented men and the suggestion added later by Lawrence that they are really prowling and watching "for the next time." The episode ends quite self-consciously with "the scene was ended," which carries the suggestion that this is only one isolated scene in a brutal and continuing drama of political unrest which characterizes the post-war period. Thus the entire flag incident in its final form represents the transformation by Lawrence's genius of the seemingly commonplace or travelogue description of a random incident into an exciting scene of highly dramatic and symbolic proportions. The careful reshaping of the entire episode gives the lie to the facile assumptions, concerning Lawrence's revisions, of earlier critics like Aldington who would have us believe that Lawrence gave *Aaron's Rod* "to the printer in its first draft, without bothering to reconstruct."[8]

A second variety of revision is concerned with the crucial problem of character delineation in the novel. Such revisions provide us with valuable clues to the gradual evolution of such major characters as Aaron and Lilly. An examination of several early chapters of the novel (2 to 4) in the typescript version reveals that Lawrence must have changed his attitude to Aaron's character as his writing and revising of the novel progressed. The numerous revisions to the original text in the early chapters are concerned almost exclusively with the characterization of Aaron. The revisions of this kind begin in Chapter 3, "The Lighted Tree," in which Aaron happens to stumble upon the grounds of the Bricknell Estate, Shottle House, and is immediately "adopted" by Jim. The typescript shows a distinct reshaping of his character by Lawrence, a transformation from an impressionable and naïve member of the proletariat to a more aloof, obstinate, and at times insolent individual with a distinct sense of his own importance. A few examples of Lawrence's revisions of this kind will illustrate better this change in Aaron's character from typescript to final version.

As Aaron approaches the Bricknell party capering in the snow before Shottle House, he is interrogated by Robert Cunningham, enjoying his role as "lieutenant-examiner." In the original version, Aaron stands "mute and stupid" but in the final version "stupid" has been crossed out and replaced by "obstinate" (TS45–A40). The earlier description of Aaron standing "amused and interested" as he gazes at the Bricknell party has been replaced in the final version with the phrase "stubbornly keeping his ground" (TS46–A41) in order to emphasize Aaron's self-control. Similarly the description of Aaron a few lines later as "irresolute, undecided in everything" has been replaced in the final version with "unmoving, static in everything" (TS47–A41). In the original typescript version Aaron allows himself to be "weakly" led off towards Shottle House. In the final version, significantly, he allows himself to be led off "negatively" (TS47–A41).

Once inside the mineowner's home, Aaron in the original version of the scene looks around "with faint wondering," obviously impressed by his wealthy surroundings. In the final version, Lawrence has altered the sentence as follows: "He sat without looking around, a remote abstract look on his face" (TS47–A42). Further, Aaron is described as "handsome but a little coarse" in the earlier typescript version and this has also been amended to "a little obstinate" (TS47–A42). Whereas in the earlier version Aaron seems to smile "impishly" at Josephine's probing inquiries after his wife and children, in the later version he smiles "coldly" (TS50–A44). The adverb "secretly," (TS50–A44), used to describe Aaron's smiling, has been cancelled in the final version of the episode to render the intruder more enigmatic to his questioners. Lawrence's numerous additions to the original typescript version all attest to his change of intention in transforming Aaron into the aloof anti-hero of succeeding chapters. As he sits in the Bricknell living-room we find "He did not wish to be with these people, and yet mechanically he stayed" (TS47–A42) added to the typescript by Lawrence. Similarly Aaron drops his head when asked the whereabouts of his home, and Lawrence adds "as if he did not want to look at them" (TS48–A42).

The same hardening and transforming of Aaron Sisson into enigmatic and aloof anti-hero may be seen in the succeeding London scenes of the novel. In the original version of the scene at Covent Garden in Chapter 5 Aaron seems faintly fascinated by the behavior of the pseudo-bohemians: "They were figures." In the final version however, Aaron's distaste is once again made obvious by Lawrence's revision. "They were figures" has been changed to "He was not really amused" (TS76–A65). Later back at Jim's flat at Adelphi Terrace Aaron sits "smiling wonderingly" in the original but "flickeringly" (TS82–A69) in the final version.

The same kind of revision is obvious in the chapter dealing with Aaron and Josephine, "The Dark Square Garden." Aaron's motives for deserting his family are made more explicit in the original version of Aaron's conversation with Josephine. When Josephine protests "But you couldn't leave your little girls for no reason at all—," Aaron replies:

"Yes I did. For no reason—except I wanted to breathe like Jim Bricknell—"

"You mean you wanted love?" flashed Josephine.

"No I wanted to breathe out."

"Breathe out? A bloody revolution—no!"

"Oh no. A breath of fresh air, by myself. I felt asphyxiated—or something like that. I never asked myself, really."

"Perhaps you wanted more than your wife could give you," she said.

"No I don't think it was that—I've been married nigh twelve years. I wanted to get out."

"A new experience." said Josephine.

"No not particularly. I wanted to be by myself, more. I don't want to be tied."
(TS92–93)

The final version makes the contrast between Jim Bricknell's puerile desire
to be loved and Aaron's rejection of forced love quite obvious. Although
Jim's name is missing from Lawrence's final version, the imagery of
asphyxiation is more subtle yet is made to seem closely connected with the
stifling effects of being "forced to feel." A few lines later, Lawrence has
added to Aaron's outburst, "But I'm damned if I want to be a lover any
more," the bitter avowal, "to her or to anybody that's the top and bottom
of it. I don't want to *care* when care isn't in me and I'm not going to be
forced to it." (A77). To the sense of independence of the original,
Lawrence adds an anti-heroic denial of personal involvement as well as a
faint suggestion of misogyny. Throughout this episode Aaron is rendered
more aloof and misanthropic than Lawrence's original delineation of his
character in this scene suggested.

An examination of the typescript of *Aaron's Rod* reveals further that
at several points Lawrence felt compelled to revise passages describing
Lilly's character. An early example of such revision occurs in Chapter 6 as
Lilly is discussed by Josephine and Aaron in the "dark square garden." The
incident is quite important because it is the first time Lilly has been discussed at length and also the first time the reader is informed of the
impression that Lilly has made upon his new acquaintance, Aaron Sisson.
The original version of this conversation suggests less of Aaron's own
opinion of Lilly but suggests more of Lilly's strange perspicacity:

"You're like Lilly" said Josephine. "He's got that innocence. It isn't innocence with
you though."
"Is Lilly innocent?" asked Aaron.
"Yes, Don't [sic] you think so. Awfully clever as well. He does get one. He sees right
through one, I always feel. It makes me uncomfortable." (TS96)

No doubt in the final version Lawrence wished to render Lilly more mysterious at this point in the novel. Whether or not the "plum-pie-Jack-
Horner" image (A80) is an improvement upon the original is another
question.

Much later, in the final chapter of the novel, Lawrence has made significant revisions to suggest the salutary force of Lilly's increasing influence upon Aaron. Shattered by the exploding of the bomb and the loss of
his flute, Aaron feels compelled to choose "not between life and death, but
between the world and...Lilly" (A336). In the earlier typescript version of
the novel Lilly appears as a much more ambiguous and demonic figure.
Lawrence speaks of him as "more creature than man," "odd, rather

devilish," the "devilish little Lilly" (TS472), and so on. In the final version, however, "more creature than man" has been cancelled, and "rather devilish" has become "uncertain, assertive" (A336). The "devilish little Lilly" has been altered to "the little Lilly" (TS472–A336). Lilly was earlier described in the typescript as "the little violent-souled, indomitable man," but Lawrence has revised this to "the little individual man" for the final version of the novel (TS473–A336). Lawrence has slightly altered Aaron's motivation in turning to Lilly as his last resort. Once again the suggestion of demonic power characterizes the original version: "He believed in Lilly's so-called wickedness, or devilishness, far rather than in people's usual goodness" (TS473). The final revised version of this conveys more Lilly's enigmatic power, and suggests perhaps that Lilly's mentorship may have more positive and salutary effects upon his new "follower":

> But no! If he had to give in to something: if he really had to give in, and it seemed he had: then he would rather give in to the little Lilly than to the beastly people of the world. If he had to give in, then it should be to no woman, and to no social ideal, and to no social institution. No! — if he had to yield his wilful independence, and give himself, then he would rather give himself to the little, individual *man* than to any of the rest. For to tell the truth, in the man was something incomprehensible, which had dominion over him, if he chose to allow it. (A336)

It is therefore appropriate that Lilly should find Aaron lying in bed "like a woman who's had a baby" rather than "like a skulking rabbit" as in the earlier version of the episode (TS473–A337). The imagery of childbirth suggests that Aaron has reached a turning point in his life. Just as he was massaged and nourished back to life in Lilly's flat, so here Aaron is reborn to a new phase of existence under the aegis of the enigmatic Lilly.

A third source of interest provided by a detailed study of the typescript is the discovery of numerous passages which have presumably been omitted from the final version for reasons of censorship. Obviously Lawrence had less control over this type of revision and one suspects that the novelist has often been at the mercy of his publishers and contemporary rules of censorship. In this segment, I shall discuss only those passages which have been omitted for reasons of censorship from *both* American and English editions of *Aaron's Rod*. The disparate approach of each editor to these "problem passages" will be later discussed in an examination of differences between the American and English editions of the novel.

Several such passages are connected with the jovial and high spirited Argyle, a portrait based, by Lawrence's own admission, upon Norman Douglas. One such censored passage may be found in Chapter 16, during a rather tedious discussion in which Argyle warns Aaron not to be "led

astray by the talk of such people as Algy...you've a soul to save" (A252).
The conversation turns facetiously to souls:

> "You are in need of enlightenment. A set of benighted wise virgins"..."What about
> the bridegroom, Algy, my boy? Eh? What about him? Better trim your wick, old man,
> if it's not too late—"
> "We were talking of souls, not wicks, Argyle," said Algy.
> "Same thing. Upon my soul it all amounts to the same thing. Where's the soul in a
> man that hasn't got a bedfellow—eh?—answer me that! Can't be done you know. Might
> as well ask a virgin chicken to lay you an egg." (A252–53)

Following the reference to the virgin chicken Argyle puts in the following
comment, later censored:

> "I don't know what cock-bird committed adultery with the holy dove, before it laid
> the Easter egg, I'm sure. But there must have been one. Ha! Ha! Ha!—I'd give a lot to
> have seen him at it. Soul is born of ——, believe me. Of nothing but ——."
> We cannot print the word used by Argyle, though it is a quite common one often
> chalked on walls by little boys. (TS349)[9]

A few lines later Argyle denounces the hypocrisy of "impotence set up in
the praise of chastity": "Ha-ha! Saving their souls! Why they'd save the
waste matter of their bodies if they could. Grieves them to part with it." As
might be expected the euphemistic "waste matter" was earlier "urine"
(TS349–A253).

In a later scene in Chapter 17, which takes place in his own flat,
Argyle and his all male party gaze down on the Cathedral square. In a
passage later censored, Argyle humorously refers to Rossetti's Blessed
Damozel:

> "...The Blessed Demosel [sic] looked down—what? Lucky thing for her she wasn't on
> my balcony. I'd have turned up her skirts while she was looking down. Ha-ha-ha! Oh
> you never know, she might have enjoyed it. Never believe a woman when she says she's
> chaste, nor a man when he says he's a ____." (TS382)

The passage then continued as we now have it, "Yes I had a charming show
of flowers" (A275), and so on. Bustling about trying to boil water for his
guests' tea, Argyle deplores the "damned filthy methylated spirit" sold in
post-war Italy (A276) adding, in a passage later censored:

> "...I asked the man if he peed in it. Ha-ha-ha!"
> "Probably does. It seems the chief occupation of the Florentines," said Lilly.
> "Without a doubt! Without a doubt! I tell them they can do nothing more violent
> than make water. Give them a corner, and they're at it. Town of Peabody's and pis-en-
> lits—" (TS383)

The omission of these relatively harmless passages seems a shame, because they seem so typical of the robust libertine Argyle, so much a part of his boisterous good spirits. In spite of this censorship, Argyle remains one of the most fascinating and vivid of the many minor characters of the novel. It must be admitted that none of these censored passaged in any way alters our reading of the novel as a whole. I present these passages simply as a part of a detailed examination of the *Aaron's Rod* typescript, and also in preparation for a later discussion of how the English and American publishers of the novel have approached these supposedly "dangerous" passages.

A far more important occurrence of literary censorship which I have discovered occurs, predictably, in several passages dealing with the sexual relations of Aaron and the Marchesa. One such passage occurs shortly after the sexual consummation of their affair as Aaron admits ruefully to himself, "This is not my woman." In the final version this important passage is cut (Aaron supposedly sleeps on until he awakes with "that click of awareness which is the end"):

> But afterwards her fingers traced him and touched him with a strange fine timidity, and a strange, strange curiosity. And he felt somewhere beyond himself—as it were ship-wrecked. He was acutely sensible to the delicate, inordinate curiosity of her finger-tips, and the stealth and the secrecy of the approach of her power. —Nay, nay, was this the woman he had known as Cleopatra, with the rouge on her lips and the fard on her face, and the elegant, frightening Paris gown?
>
> He slept for a very little while and woke suddenly, and his desire had an element of cruelty in it: something rather brutal. He took his way with her now, and she had no chance now of the curious opposition because of the way he took her. And afterwards she clung suddenly to his breast, and curled her head there as if hiding, and as if suddenly convulsed with shyness or shame of what had been: but still pleased. And so curled, with her hair on his breast and her hair tangling about his throat, it was she who slept now. And after a long while, he slept too.
>
> And when he woke, and still the desire came back, with something dogged in its persistence, she seemed to wince a little. But perhaps she was pleased too. But this time she took no part, really. (TS427)

Both printed versions of the novel pick up the episode again at this point: "When he came fully to himself..." (A306). The omission of this further qualification of the sexual union of Aaron and the Marchesa is unfortunate. The passage makes the connection once again between the attractiveness of this modern woman with "fard on her face" and the notorious emasculating power of Cleopatra. The "approach" of the Marchesa's deadly power is sensed by Aaron as she explores him with her fingertips. The passage is also important for its suggestion of the thinly disguised brutality which is an essential element in the sexual relationships of Aaron and the Marchesa. Similarly the element of lust is more pronounced in this censored passage as Aaron takes "his way" with the Marchesa. The actions of the Marchesa here are suggestive of what Lawrence referred to constantly in *Women in Love* as the mindless progression in sensual knowledge which can end only in destruction. The passage is thus quite explicit about the sexual egocentricity which blights the love relationship from the very beginning.

In a later sexual episode, the suggestions of the violent male orgasm have been censored:

> And again, this night as before, she seemed strangely small and clinging in his arms. And this night he felt his passion drawn from him as if a long, live nerve were drawn out from his body, a long live thread of electric fire, a long, living nerve finely extracted from him, from the very roots of his soul. A long fine discharge of pure, bluish fire, from the core of his soul. It was an excruciating, but also an intensely gratifying sensation. As his passion broke from him to her, he felt the long live fire thread drawn downwards through him, terribly down his legs and through his heels, leaving his heels feeling bruised, and himself feeling vacant. It was like a discharge of lightning, but longer, more terrible — And this night he slept with a deeper obliviousness than before. But ah, as it grew towards morning, how he wished he could be alone. And then immediately she crept to his breast again. (TS 445)[10]

Once again the ultimately destructive nature of the sexual relationsh is conveyed in sado-masochistic imagery.

Further censoring of supposedly "inflammatory" passages is si   ar. The Marchesa later touches Aaron with a strange fear — "fetish afr   and fetish fascinated":

> Or was her fear only a delightful game of cat and mouse? Or was the fear genuine: and the delight the greater: a sort of sacrilege? The fear, the phallic fear: and the dangerous, sacrilegious power over that which she feared. (TS445)

The uncensored version reveals to the reader the deeper source of her mixed fear and delight, a peculiar "phallic fear." In the final printed versions of the novel "phallic fear" has been removed. A few lines later Aaron realizes that he has been appropriated by the Marchesa as god and victim, but his soul resists her power:

> ...And he looked back over the whole mystery of their love-contact, and his soul saw himself, saw his own phallic God-and-victim self there lying, with her on his breast. Only his soul stood apart.
>
> She lay curled on his breast, with her wild hair tangled about him. And he was aware of the strength and beauty and godlikeness that his breast was then to her, the magic male breast with its two nipples. But himself he stood far off, like Moses [sic] sister Miriam. There lay the phallic God, the phallic victim, twined round utterly with his

priestess. The breast, the limbs — and then she would drink the one drop of his innermost heart's blood, and he would be carrion. As Cleopatra killed her lovers in the morning. Surely they knew that death was their just climax. Accept then.

There was a lust and a temptation: the phallic Godhead. The lust and loveliness of his flesh, his godlike phallic power in the flesh. And the inevitable consummation, the drinking of his innermost drop of heart's blood. Lust and temptation. — And then carrion. (TS446-A31)

In the final printed version of the novel these passages have been heavily censored by both of Lawrence's publishers.[11] It is still difficult to ascertain where Lawrence's revision might have ended and that of the publisher (afraid of official censorship) has begun. Obviously the above third paragraph omitted is loose and repetitive, its cancellation justifiable on purely aesthetic grounds. Yet the omission in the second paragraph above is serious because this paragraph vividly continues the imagery of destructive sexuality in the serpentine twining of the Marchesa about her phallic God-victim. The references to the male breast were obviously too graphic for Lawrence's editors. The omission of such passages as those above seems more grave to me than the censoring of the Argyle passages. Because the sexual relationship with the Marchesa plays such an integral part in Aaron's quest for self-realization, such passages are linked inextricably to his ultimate discovery of the Marchesa's destructiveness and Aaron's decision to reject such false forms of love. These censored passages thus bear close examination and would constitute an important part in reconstructing an authoritative or variorum edition of *Aaron's Rod*: one which might be consistent with Lawrence's clear intentions in respecting his original text of the novel.

A number of important differences may be observed between the American Edition of *Aaron's Rod* published by Thomas Seltzer (April 1922) and the English Edition published by Martin Secker (June 1922). No doubt many such differences may be attributed to the fact that after minor revisions Lawrence surrendered his typescripts of *Aaron's Rod* to both the discretion and the individual approach of his respective publishers, as the conclusion of this crucial letter to Curtis Brown suggests:

> . . . So I sent it [the typescript] back to Seltzer to let him do as he pleases. I would rather Secker followed the rule MS. if he will — and *vogue la galère!*[12]

Lawrence's hopes that Secker would not tamper with the original text of *Aaron's Rod* were, however, to be disappointed. Though the typescript of Secker's English edition has not survived and many of our observations concerning Secker's treatment of Lawrence's original text must, therefore, be hypothetical, nevertheless a close examination of the American type-script version as well as a comparison of the final printed versions by both Seltzer and Secker leads us to the definite conclusion that Secker altered Lawrence's typescript a considerable amount. Secker probably feared another outcry such as that which *The Rainbow* and *Women in Love* had met. Recalling the suppression of *The Rainbow*, Secker was anxious to remove from *Aaron's Rod* those passages of a libellous or inflammatory nature. He pruned *Aaron's Rod* for the English public and what Lawrence called the *jeune fille*. It must be assumed however that several discrepancies are owing to Lawrence's own whims, his preferences at the time he was preparing the final version for each of his publishers. We know definitely that he had at least two typescripts from which to work as his letter to Curtis Brown of 7 July 1921 makes clear.[13] Possibly he changed his mind about certain constructions or passages, etc. as he proof-read and corrected each typescript. In any case we can never be certain where Lawrence's revisions ended and Secker's fastidious editing began, since the English typescript has not survived.

It seems incredible, however, that readers and critics of Lawrence should have been unaware for so many years that two distinctly different editions of *Aaron's Rod* exist, each bearing authorial approval. In *D. H. Lawrence and The* Dial, a study by Nicholas Joost and Alvin Sullivan of Lawrence's important contributions to the *Dial,* we find the following curious footnote dealing with the flag incident of Chapter 14 as it appeared in the *Dial,* in February 1922:

> The excerpt in the *Dial* begins with the paragraph that opens, "As he lay thinking of nothing": *Aaron's Rod,* Compass Books (New York, 1961), p. 179. Several words in the *Dial*'s excerpt are different from those of the Compass Books edition. In the first line of the last paragraph (p. 182), the *Dial*'s passage substitutes "dispersed" for "disappeared," and in this case, the *Dial*'s word seems more appropriate, suggesting an error in the Compass Books edition. In the same paragraph, after the phrase "Let themselves foolishly be taken" (p. 183), the *Dial* has a colon, and after the word "prisoners" it has a semi-colon. Moreover, this paragraph is not separated from the one that follows, as it is in the Compass Books edition. For the phrase "in cautious dejection" at the end of the first paragraph on p. 183, the *Dial* reads "in humiliation." In the first sentence of the second paragraph on p. 183, the *Dial* substitutes "surrounded" for "seized." And in the magazine the last sentences of the second paragraph on p. 183 have been altered and combined to read, "And away they marched, the dejected youth between them." The next two paragraphs are not reprinted in the *Dial* except for the last sentence of paragraph four on p. 183, which is also the last sentence of the excerpt, "The scene was ended."[14]

What Joost and Sullivan have stumbled upon is the fact that the Compass edition actually reproduces the text of Secker's English edition. As such, the Compass edition would naturally differ noticeably in several places from the *Dial* version. The *Dial* episode submitted by Thomas Seltzer was undoubtedly taken from the American typescript version, the one used in the preparation of the American edition of the novel which was to appear later in April of the same year. It is, therefore, not simply a question of "an error in the Compass edition" but a matter of differences in edition. The business of this segment of my study will be an examination of these significant discrepancies.

The differences between the American and English editions may be arranged under three related headings: a) minor or simple differences; b) major variants, often involving lengthy omissions in the English edition; and c) differences arising from censored passages, largely the result of a different attitude of each publisher to such "problem passages."

The minor differences in punctuation in the two texts are quickly dispensed with. More often these are the result of a publishing house format than deliberate revision on Lawrence's part. The English use of more paragraphs; spaces instead of the American 'dash'; the English use of two separate words where the American prefers a hyphenated one, e.g., well-nourished; and so on, are all quite minor. The spelling in the English edition especially of foreign names tends to be more haphazard: San Trinita for San Trinità, Lugarno for Lungarno, Curaçou for Curaçao. In the English edition there are also a few peculiar differences in usage, as for example "front hill of war" for the obviously more correct American "front hell of war." All of these are fairly minor points but they do contribute to the overall impression that Seltzer's American edition is the more careful and authentic of the two first editions.

Other minor differences need not occupy us for long. Many are of simply routine interest and in no way alter our reading of the particular episode or chapter in which they appear. The English edition prints the description of Tanny as "a fine blond" (E67), while the American edition prints "strong and fair" (A85). At the conclusion of Chapter 8, Tanny admonishes Lilly in the English edition: "You shouldn't try to make a little Jesus of yourself" (E80) whereas in the American edition she tells Lilly "You shouldn't play at little Jesus" (A99). The minor differences continue throughout in this fashion, particularly in the flag incident which I shall discuss more fully later.

Several minor discrepancies are of interest, however, as they affect our reading of certain passages. A few examples should suffice. The English edition is more explicit about Aaron's relationship with Mrs. Houseley, the landlady of the "Royal Oak" in Chapter 2, substituting "He disliked her at her tricks. He had come to her once too often" (E18) for the vaguer American version, "He saw her once too often" (A27). Possibly the English version is meant to suggest a sexual affair which Aaron has once had with the Jewish landlady, since he does admit later, in Chapter 14, that he has turned to adulterous affairs as a protest against Lottie's domineering. Mrs. Houseley with her deadly will is linked to Lottie and later in the novel to the Marchesa in her sexual affair with Aaron. In the English edition, Chapter 9, the pseudo-bohemians of the Bricknell set are condemned by Lilly, as "this little gang of wastrels" (E92), a denunciation which seems more appropriate than "this little gang of Europeans" (TS137–A113), as the phrase appears in the American edition. In the American edition the Marchesa's father is spoken of as having once been "ambassador to Paris" (A283), but in the English edition this has been changed to "a famous figure in Europe" (E219). Perhaps Secker altered the original to avoid any possible reference to an actual person, since the novel was already full of thinly disguised (and often unflattering) caricatures of actual acquaintances. The English edition similarly alters the location of the former del Torre home in Paris to Rome. One final minor difference is of particular interest. The American edition prints the title of Chapter 17 as "High up over the Cathedral Square," but the English edition prints this as "Nel Paradiso."

A comparison of the American and English editions reveals also that the conclusion of Chapter 10 is significantly different in each edition. The American edition prints the conclusion as:

> Aaron did not find his friend at home when he called. He took it rather as a slap in the face. But then he knew quite well that Lilly had made a certain call on his, Aaron's soul: a call which he, Aaron, did not at all intend to obey. If in return the soul-caller chose to shut his street-door in the face of the world-friend — well, let it be quits. He was not sure whether he felt superior to his unworldly enemy or not. He rather thought he did. (A141–42)

The conclusion in the English edition is slightly longer:

> Aaron did not find his friend at home when he called. He felt it was a slap in the face. But then he knew perfectly well that Lilly had made a certain call upon his, Aaron's, soul: a call which he, Aaron, did not intend to obey. Rather he curled his fine nose, worldly-wise. People who make calls on other people's souls are bound to find the door shut. If in return the soul-caller chooses to shut his worldly house-door in the face of the world-caller, well, it is nearly quits. Aaron accepted the *quid pro quo.* He was not sure whether he felt superior to his unworldly enemy or not. He rather felt he did. (E116)

The English version makes more explicit Aaron's physical and emotional reaction to Lilly's "slap in the face." It presents us with a more balanced view of Lilly and Aaron's "*quid pro quo*" relationship at this point and suggests the annoying aspect of Lilly's spiritual hectoring, to which Aaron refuses to submit. Yet this version obviously sacrifices the terseness and enigmatic quality of the American edition, in the interests of psychological realism.

One other major discrepancy deserves our close attention, a lengthy omission, almost four pages long in Chapter 17, during the scene of Argyle's male symposium. In a moment of pathetic seriousness Argyle admits that the sum of his experience has been "the search for a friend." To this admission Lilly replies "And never finding?", whereupon the dialogue becomes an inquiry into the necessity of love and this search for a lifelong friend. Because the American edition of *Aaron's Rod* is no longer readily available I shall quote in full this important exchange between Lilly and his acquaintances:

"I look a fool, do I, when I'm playing?" said Aaron.

"Only the least little bit in the world," said Lilly. "The way you prance your head, your know, like a horse."

"Ah, well," said Aaron, "I've nothing to lose."

"And were you surprised, Lilly, to find your friend here?" asked del Torre.

"I ought to have been. But I wasn't really."

"Then you expected him?"

"No. It came naturally, though. — But why did you come, Aaron? What exactly brought you?"

"Accident," said Aaron.

"Ah, no! No! There is no such thing as accident," said the Italian. "A man is drawn by his fate, where he goes."

"You are right," said Argyle, who came now with the teapot. "A man is drawn — or driven. Driven, I've found it. Ah, my dear fellow, what is life but a search for a friend? A search for a friend — that sums it up."

"Or a lover," said the Marchese, grinning.

"Same thing. Same thing. My hair is white — but that is the sum of my whole experience. The search for a friend." There was something at once real and sentimental in Argyle's tone.

"And never finding?" said Lilly, laughing.

"Oh, what would you? Often finding. Often finding. And losing, of course. — A life's history. Give me your glass. Miserable tea, but nobody has sent me any from England — "

"And you will go on till you die, Argyle?" said Lilly. "Always seeking a friend — and always a new one?"

"If I lose the friend I've got. Ah, my dear fellow, in that case I shall go on seeking. I hope so, I assure you. Something will be very wrong with me, if ever I sit friendless and make no search."

"But, Argyle, there is a time to leave off."

"To leave off what, to leave off what?"

"Having friends: or a friend, rather: or seeking to have one."

"Oh, no! Not at all, my friend. Not at all! Only death can make an end of that, my friend. Only death. And I should say, not even death. Not even death ends a man's search for a friend. That is my belief. You may hang me for it, but I shall never alter."

"Nay," said Lilly. "There is a time to love, and a time to leave off loving."

"All I can say to that is that my time to leave off hasn't come yet," said Argyle with obsinate feeling.

"Ah, yes, it has. It is only a habit and an idea you stick to."

"Indeed, it is no such thing. Indeed, it is no such thing. It is a profound desire and necessity: and what is more, a belief."

"An obstinate persistency, you mean," said Lilly.

"Well, call it so if it pleases you. It is by no means so to me." There was a brief pause. The sun had left the cathedral dome and the tower, the sky was full of light, the square swimming in shadow.

"But can a man live," said the Marchese, "without having something he lives for: something he wishes for, or longs for, and tries that he may get?"

"Impossible! Completely impossible!" said Argyle. "Man is a seeker, and except as such, he has no significance, no importance."

"He bores me with his seeking," said Lilly. "He should learn to possess himself—to be himself—and keep still."

"Ay, perhaps so," said Aaron. "Only—"

"But my dear boy, believe me, a man is never himself save in the supreme state of love: or perhaps hate, too, which amounts to the same thing. Never really himself.—Apart from this he is a tram-driver or a moneyshoveller or an idea-machine. Only in the state of love is he really a man, and really himself. I say so, because I know," said Argyle.

"Ah, yes. That is one side of the truth. It is quite true, also. But it is just as true to say, that a man is never less himself, than in the supreme state of love. Never less himself, than then."

"Maybe! Maybe! But what could be better? What could be better than to lose oneself with someone you love, entirely, and so find yourself. Ah, my dear fellow, that is my creed, that is my creed, and you can't shake me in it. Never in that. Never in that."

"Yes, Argyle," said Lilly. "I know you're an obstinate love-apostle."

"I am! I am! And I have certain standards, my boy, and certain ideals which I never transgress. Never transgress. And never abandon."

"All right, then, you are an incurable love-maker."

"Pray God I am," said Argyle.

"Yes," said the Marchese. "Perhaps we are all so. What else do you give? Would you have us make money? Or do you give the centre of your spirit to your work? How is it to be?"

"I don't vitally care either about money or my work or—" Lilly faltered.

"Or what, then?"

"Or anything. I don't really care about anything. Except that—"

"You don't care about anything? But what is that for a life?" cried the Marchese, with a hollow mockery.

"What do *you* care for?" asked Lilly.

"Me? I care for several things. I care for my wife. I care for love. And I care to be loved. And I care for some pleasures. And I care for music. And I care for Italy."

"You are well off for cares," said Lilly.

"And you seem to me so very poor," said del Torre.

"I should say so—if he cares for nothing," interjaculated Argyle. Then he clapped Lilly on the shoulder with a laugh. "Ha! Ha! Ha!—But he only says it to tease us," he cried, shaking Lilly's shoulder. "He cares more than we do for his own way of loving.

Come along, don't try and take us in. We are old birds, old birds," said Argyle. But at that moment he seemed a bit doddering.

"A man can't live," said the Italian, "without an object."

"Well—and that object?" said Lilly.

"Well—it may be many things. Mostly it is two things—love and money. But it may be many things: ambition, patriotism, science, art—many things. But it is some objective. Something outside the self. Perhaps many things outside the self."

"I have had only one objective all my life," said Argyle. "And that was love. For that I have spent my life."

"And the lives of a number of other people, too," said Lilly.

"Admitted. Oh, admitted. It takes two to make love: unless you're a miserable—"

"Don't you think," said Aaron, turning to Lilly, "that however you try to get way from it, if you're not after money, and can't fit yourself into a job—you've got to, you've got to try and find something else—somebody else—somebody. You can't really be alone."

"No matter how many mistakes you've made—you can't really be alone—?" asked Lilly.

"You can be alone for a minute. You can be alone just in that minute when you've broken free, and you feel heart thankful to be alone, because the other thing wasn't to be borne. But you can't keep on being alone. No matter how many times you've broken free, and feel, thank God to be alone (nothing on earth is so good as to breathe fresh air and be alone), no matter how many times you've felt this—it wears off every time, and you begin to look again—and you begin to roam round. And even if you won't admit it to yourself, still you are seeking—seeking. Aren't you? Aren't you yourself seeking?"

"Oh, that's another matter," put in Argyle. "Lilly is happily married and on the shelf. With such a fine woman as Tanny I should think so—*rather*! But his is an exceptional nature, and an exceptional case. As for me, I made a hell of my marriage, and I swear it nearly sent me to hell. But I didn't forswear love, when I forswore marriage and woman. Not by *any* means." (A279–83)

The omission of this crucial portion of the original typescript points to a serious flaw in the English edition, and demonstrates clearly the superiority of the more complete American edition. Lilly's denial of the love-urge and the self-possession necessary to self-knowledge is once again placed before Aaron and the reader. The passage shows clearly that Aaron is undergoing a profound psychological transition towards self-knowledge. He has begun to question his escape and his directionless freedom. He is able to articulate his compulsion to seek out new relationships, to express his awareness that aloofness and isolation can only be a temporary state. An exposure to this passage, missing in the English edition, makes it clear to the reader that Aaron is moving closer to Lilly. The passage further justifies Aaron's ambivalent attitude to Lilly's remote and strange power and makes more understandable Aaron's musings on Lilly's influence which conclude the chapter.

A glance at the flag incident of Chapter 14 reveals once again a series of minor textual differences, which point at the same time to the superiority of the more terse and tightly woven American version which appeared in the *Dial*. The English version was apparently later but is decidedly not as fine as the American version. It is difficult to account for these discrepancies. The English version at every turn seems more padded, probably as a result of Lawrence's last minute tampering with his original, more concise version before submitting the typescript to Martin Secker. In the English edition, the noise of the crowd is "like a scraping of steel and copper weapons" (E179), an elaboration of the American version, "like a jarring of steel weapons" (A215), while the phrase "and sharp will" is added to the description of the crowd's "demon-like. . .purpose" (E179). In the English version, the "head of the procession" advances "clustering thick before the shop," (E180) a departure from "swirling like a little pool" in the American edition (A215). The description of the clamor outside the shop door is different in each edition. The American, "There had been a great ringing of a door-bell and battering on the shop-door" (A216), is more concise than the English version, "There had been a great banging on the shop door and a ringing of the bell of the guilty house door" (E180). In the English edition the description of the carabinieri rushing like "a posse of foot-soldiers" (E182) has been added to the American description of the rushing carabinieri. An explanation for the fierceness of the attack is also added to the simpler American description:

> In utmost amazement he saw the sturdy, greeny-grey carabinieri, like a posse of foot-soldiers, rushing thick and wild and indiscriminate on the crowd, with a *frenzied excitement which must have been based on fear*: a sudden, new, excited crowd in uniform attacking the civilian crowd and laying about blindly, furiously, with truncheons. (E182; italics mine)

The omission of such a psychological explanation in the American edition makes the carabinieri seem more like automaton-like dispensers of a brutal and impersonal civil punishment.

In the English version of the episode, the youthful climber descends "in cautious dejection" (E183); yet in the American, he descends "in humiliation" (A219). The ignominious conclusion of his bravura feat as he is led away seems more detailed or "padded out" in the English edition:

> Once in the street he was seized by the grey uniforms. The soldiers formed up. The sergeant gave the order. And away marched authority, triumphant and thankful to have got off so lightly. The dejected youth was marched away between them. (E183)

The American version seems more terse:

> Once in the street he was surrounded by the grey uniforms. The soldiers formed up. The sergeant gave the order. And away they marched, the dejected youth a prisoner between them. (A219)

The focus here seems more upon the youth than in the English edition with its satiric sneer at civil authority.

The third and final area of discrepancy between American and English editions is concerned with literary censorship, the omission of various passages either sexual or political which might prove offensive to the reading public. One typical example is the exclusion from Chapter 10 in which Herbertson demeans the Royal Family:

> But I like the children. Very different from the Battenbergs. Oh! — he wrinkled his nose. "I can't stand the Battenbergs."
> "Mount Battens," said Lilly.
> "Yes! Awful mistake, changing the royal name. They were Guelfs, why not remain it? Why, I'll tell you what Battenberg did. He was in the Guards, too —" (A132)

Such an unflattering allusion to the royal family was obviously unacceptable to Secker.

References to bodily functions have obviously created problems for Lawrence's publishers, especially Martin Secker. The many episodes in which Argyle appears have been altered in different ways, which reflect the varying disposition of Lawrence's respective publishers. In the sacrilegious and rather dispensible discussion in Chapter 16 concerning the Holy Ghost, the virgin chicken and so on, cited earlier, the English edition omits Algy's reply to Argyle's randy references to the soul being "born of ——" [sic], and further omits Argyle's elaboration of his theory:

> "Of what? Of soul? There ought to be a good deal of soul about? — Ah, because there's a good deal of ——, you mean. — Ah, I wish it were so. I wish it were so. (A253)

The American edition, of course, prints both passages. Both editions substitute "waste matter" for "urine."

Later in Chapter 17 which features Argyle's strange all male tea-party, the host's remarks that "respectability...argues a serious diminution of spunk" (A274), have been omitted in the English edition. Likewise his subsequent confession (concerning the required alterations on his suit) "seems I've grown in the arsal region" (A274) has been struck from the English edition. Argyle's speculation that the Italians have urinated in his methylhydrate has been cancelled by both publishers, but the American edition has retained part of his curse: "Damned filthy methylated spirit they sell" (A276). Argyle's rather harmless schoolboy joke about the Blessed Damozel is censored by both editions. The English edition preserves the literary aspect of the reference, yet omits Argyle's randy "I'd have turned up her skirts while she was looking down" (E249). A later passage of homosexual implications is also omitted by the English edition.

Lilly describes another form of love which man seeks as an alternative to the destructive passion of the terrible "modern woman":

> Then man seeks other forms of loves, always seeking the loving response, you know, of one gentler and tenderer than himself, who will wait till the man desires, and then will answer with full love. — But it is all *pis-aller,* you know." (A288)

Perhaps Secker was troubled by the over-resemblance to Norman Douglas of Lawrence's Argyle, and wished to avoid another libel suit such as that involving Heseltine and *Women in Love.*

A few more humorous lines of Argyle's robust speech are omitted later as Argyle and friends sit in the Florentine café in Chapter 20. The English edition omits Argyle's reference to "that befouled Epictetus" (A325) and Argyle's harsh reply to an appeal to logic, "Use logic as lavatory paper" (A325).

Similar differences between the English and American editions are apparent in those episodes dealing with the sexual affair of Aaron and the Marchesa. The approach of each publisher to such problem passages as those outlined earlier in this chapter (in a discussion of the major differences between typescript and final versions) are particularly fascinating. The description in Chapter 19 of sexual orgasm is more explicit in the American edition which prints:

> And this night he felt his passion drawn from him as if a long, live nerve were drawn out from his body, a long live thread of electric fire, a long, living nerve finely extracted from him, from the very roots of his soul. A long fine discharge of pure, bluish fire, from the core of his soul. It was an excruciating, but also an intensely gratifying sensation. (A317)

The English edition stops the description at "electric fire" (E264). However, the English edition seems more permissive a few lines later because the phrase "the magic feeling of phallic immortality" is allowed to remain as Aaron questions the nature of his desire for the Marchesa and her peculiar gratification:

> He only knew it had nothing to do with him: and that, save out of complaisance, he did not want it. But did he not want it? — the magic feeling of phallic immortality. But at the same time it simply blasted his own central life. It simply blighted him. (E264)

The phrase "of his actual male physique" is also omitted in the American edition. Later, in Chapter 20, Argyle playfully inquires if Aaron has "been going to the dogs." Aaron's reply, "or the bitches" has been omitted in the English edition as has Argyle's sympathetic "Oh! but look here, that's bad!

That's bad!" (A322). Argyle's remarks have been simply run together in a single paragraph and thus seem typical of his usual humorous rambling.

Although, as I have demonstrated above, the English edition surprisingly includes a few explicit details which the American edition omits, it would be accurate to state that the approach of the English edition to "sensational" or "inflammatory" passages is more stringent. This may understandingly be attributed to the zealous efforts of Secker. Recalling the problems of *The Rainbow* and *Women in Love* Secker was no doubt anxious to remove all passages which might be judged libelous or pornographic, and so might lead to a simple suppression of *Aaron's Rod.*

3

Biblical Analogue and Symbolism in *Aaron's Rod*

Lawrence's considerable debt to the Holy Bible as a source of literary inspiration has long been critically acknowledged. Indeed, it might be difficult to name one English novelist — aside from Bunyan — whose creative imagination has been more profoundly stirred by the literature of the Bible. From his earliest acquaintance with the familiar Bible stories told in the Non-Conformist Chapel at Eastwood, the style and thought of the Bible must have quickly become part of Lawrence's youthful subconsciousness. Years later Lawrence recalled this process of unconscious absorption in his "Introduction" to Frederick Carter's *Dragon of the Apocalypse*:

> I was brought up on the Bible, and seem to have it in my bones. From early childhood I have been familiar with Apocalyptic language and Apocalyptic image: not because I spent my time reading Revelation, but because I was sent to Sunday School and to Chapel, to Band of Hope and to Christian Endeavour, and was always having the Bible read at me or to me. I did not even listen attentively. But language has a power of echoing and reechoing in my unconscious mind....And so the sound of Revelation had registered in me very early, and I was as used to: "I was in the Spirit on the Lord's day, and heard behind me a great voice, as of a trumpet, saying: I am Alpha and the Omega" — as I was to a nursery rhyme like "Little Bo-Peep"![1]

Still later, in *Apocalypse*, the work which grew out of his "Introduction" to Carter's *Dragon*, Lawrence recalled in similar terms the utter saturation of his young imagination by the great myths of the Bible:

> From earliest years right into manhood, like any other nonconformist child I had the Bible poured every day into my helpless consciousness, till there came almost a saturation point. Long before one could think or even vaguely understand, this Bible language, these 'portions' of the Bible were *douched* over the mind and consciousness, till they became soaked in, they became an influence which affected all the processes of emotion and thought. So that today, although I have "forgotten" my Bible, I need only begin to read a chapter to realise that I know it with an almost nauseating fixity.[2]

In view of such conclusive autobiographical testimony, it seems strange that critics of Lawrence should have consistently neglected Lawrence's pervasive use of biblical sources. Commenting upon the lack of critical attention to this crucial aspect of Lawrence's art, George M. Ford writes:

> In a useful study of the ways in which the Bible has affected twentieth-century novelists, *The Prophetic Voice in Modern Fiction* (1959), William Mueller discusses novels by Joyce, Camus, Kafka, Silone, Greene, and Faulkner. It is curious that he says nothing of *Aaron's Rod* and other novels by a writer who, more than any of these named, reflects Biblical influences and correspondences on almost every page.[3]

Unfortunately Ford also declines to discuss at any length such important biblical parallels in *Aaron's Rod*. Nevertheless, in his discussion of "*The Rainbow* as Bible" he draws our attention to the special problems facing most readers of Lawrence, lacking such a ready knowledge of Biblical myth. Though critics have devoted pages to explication of Joyce's constant use of Homeric parallel in *Ulysses*, so much that "readers can readily see the Odyssean shadows looming as counterparts behind every scene in his novel," still

> *The Rainbow* oddly enough has received less attention of this kind, perhaps because the old assumption dies hard that all educated readers will be thoroughly familiar with the minutiae of every page of the Bible. Lawrence himself, "soaked" in Biblical reading to the saturation point...,certainly makes such an assumption in his writings. His allusiveness takes a great deal for granted.[4]

This chapter proposes to be a study of Biblical analogue and allusion in *Aaron's Rod,* involving a detailed reading and study of relevant episodes and passages of the Old Testament. With such episodes or passages Lawrence would have been familiar from an early age. He would have recalled them automatically at the time he was writing *Aaron's Rod.* In many ways, then, this chapter is an exploration of one neglected aspect of *Aaron's Rod.* Taking its hint from Mr. Ford's astute yet incomplete remarks, the following discussion might be said to begin where Mr. Ford and other critics of the novel have been disposed to leave off. It should be pointed out that the very subtle matter of adjustment between two related but differing genres causes special critical problems in approaching Lawrence's use of Old Testament narrative. What the Old Testament provided Lawrence with was a kind of loosely constructed mythic chronicle of events from which he might choose, according to his artistic requirements. Lawrence transposes some elements of the Old Testament narratives, adapting them, with varying degrees of success, to the novel form.

His method is idiosyncratic yet highly selective: he fixes exclusively upon those elements which are of use to the concerns of his own work and his artistic "scheme." The oft quoted remark by Lawrence that the Bible is "a great confused novel" is much to the point. In writing *Aaron's Rod* Lawrence more than often simply took his inspiration for certain scenes with biblical echoes from his own intuitions or personal inferences from what was merely *suggested* in a line or two in the Old Testament narrative. The hints which Lawrence took for the aloofness of Sisson are much in this vein and will be discussed later.

The familiar story of Lot and his disobedient wife provided Lawrence with a biblical analogue for the early chapters of *Aaron's Rod* which depict the troubled married life of Aaron and his wife. As it appears in Genesis, the biblical narrative is a brief but vivid chronicle of the destruction of the wicked cities of Sodom and Gomorrah. From these cities Lot, one of the few remaining "righteous within the city," flees with his wife and his two daughters who "have not known man." Warned by two visitant-angels to flee the city which God has marked for destruction "because the cry of Sodom and Gomorrah is great and because their sin is very grievous," Lot and his family are set upon the road to Zoar by the mysterious angels, and are forbidden to look behind them at the terrible destruction of the cities of the plain:

> Then the Lord rained upon Sodom and upon Gomorrah brimstone and fire from the Lord out of heaven;
> And he overthrew those cities and all the plain, and all the inhabitants of the cities, and that which grew upon the ground.
> But his wife looked back from behind him, and she became a pillar of salt. (Gen. 19: 24-26)

In *Aaron's Rod* the biblical scene of the doomed cities has been shifted to a mining town in the English Midlands—a fictionalized Eastwood—where Aaron is employed as a miners' checkweighman. The mining village and his strife-torn home are the Sodom and Gomorrah which Aaron must flee. With remarkable subtlety, Lawrence has suggested the parallel between the destruction of Sodom and Gomorrah, with its rain of fire and brimstone, and the modern mining village with its colliery and burning pit hill. In Genesis Abraham gazes towards the destruction of Sodom and Gomorrah, and "toward all the land of the plain," and sees that "the smoke of the country went up as the smoke of a furnace" (Gen. 19:28). In Chapter 3, "The Lighted Tree," the narrator notes that the ever-burning pit-hill "glowed, fumed, and stank sulphur in the nostrils of the Bricknells" (31). Later the pseudo-bohemians gathered around Jim Bricknell at Shottle House gaze at the "red light" of the "pit-bank on fire" which "has been burning for years" (36). Again the night air is described as reeking of sulphur.

In these early episodes of the novel Lawrence is suggesting that the mines, and everything connected to them, the mine machinery, the mine-owners themselves, are all symptomatic of a society as confirmed in its iniquity as the ancient Sodom and Gomorrah, and therefore equally doomed. This impression of imminent doom which threatens the modern social structure gone rotten is sustained in the narrator's description (in the first chapter) of the "neurasthenic haste for excitement" of the villagers, stirred by "the violence of the nightmare [of war] released now into the general air" much like a poison gas. It is not difficult to grasp the parallel in Lawrence's mind between the destruction of a wicked Old Testament World and the much needed holocaust which would destroy and, hopefully, purify the infected modern world. In April 1917 Lawrence had prophesied to Lady Cynthia Asquith that there would "fall a big fire on the city before long, as on Sodom and Gomorrah... But when the bust-up is made and the the place more or less destroyed we can have a new start."[5] In the early chapters of *Aaron's Rod*, the greedy impulse to lay hold of non-existent luxuries on Christmas Eve, the increased wrangling of the colliers, the exploitation of worker by mineowner, — all are part of Lawrence's view of the modern world as a Sodom and Gomorrah in need of destruction and rebirth. It is from such a society that Aaron is compelled to flee.

Yet, it is for the spectacular metamorphosis of his nameless wife that Lot is most remembered. Lawrence has made full use of the symbolic overtones of such an episode in his portrait of Aaron's marriage. The name of Aaron's wife, Lottie, obviously recalls her biblical antecedent and the titles of two chapters, "The Pillar of Salt" and "More Pillar of Salt," refer directly to the transformation of Lot's wife. In both chapters, though, it is *Aaron* who looks back. His return to the scene of domestic strife parallels the fatal backward glance of Lot's wife towards the burning Sodom.

Aaron's first turning back occurs in Chapter 4, only a few days after he has deserted his family on Christmas Eve. Lottie's bitter outbursts and accusations overheard by Aaron have the effect of transforming Aaron into a motionless "pillar of salt" (52). In Aaron's second turning back, months later (in Chapter 11), there is even a suggestion that *psychologically* the destruction of Sodom is taking place within Aaron himself as he confronts Lottie for a final time:

> Curious sensations and emotions went through the man's frame, seeming to destroy him. They were like electric shocks, which he felt she emitted against him. And an old sickness came in him again. He had forgotten it. It was the sickness of the unrecognised and incomprehensible strain between him and her. (145)

Later, in Novara, Aaron recalls the deadly opposition of wills in his marriage to Lottie in images which indirectly echo the transformation of Lot's wife:

> So...it reached a deadlock. Each will was wound tense, and so fixed. Fixed! There was neither any relaxing nor any increase of pressure. Fixed. Hard like a numbness, a grip that was solidifying and turning to stone.... He realized somehow that...[Lottie's] fixed female soul, her wound up female soul would solidify into stone...whereas his must break. (190)

Lottie has also become a pillar of salt in her fiercely over-protective motherhood, as Aaron in Novara later reflects:

> It had taken him years to realise that Lottie also felt herself first and single: under all her whimsicalness and fretfulness was a conviction as firm as steel: that she, as woman, was the centre of creation, the man was but an adjunct. She as woman, and particularly as mother, was the first great source of life and being, and also of culture. The man was but the instrument and the finisher. She was the source and the substance. (186)

Lilly and Aaron sum up the entire syndrome earlier, though more bitterly:

> "Sacred children, and sacred motherhood, I'm absolutely fed stiff by it. That's why I'm thankful I have no children. Tanny can't come it over me there."
> "It's a fact. When a woman's got her children, by God, she's a bitch in the manger. You can starve while she sits on the hay. It's useful to keep her pups warm." (116)

In a poem probably written in 1912, and published in the collection *Look! We Have Come Through,*[6] entitled "She Looks Back," Lawrence invoked the figure of Lot's wife, using her transformation as an image of the fatal gaze backwards at her children of one mother (Frieda), who has left her children to follow her "Lot" (Lawrence) Her willful longing has transformed their marital relationship to bitter salt:

> I have seen it, felt it in my mouth, my throat, my chest,
>   my belly,
> Burning of powerful salt, burning, eating through my
>   defenseless nakedness.
> I have been thrust into white, sharp crystals,
> Writhing, twisting, superpenetrated
> Ah, Lot's Wife, Lot's Wife!
> The pillar of salt, the whirling, horrible column of salt,
>   like a waterspout
> That has enveloped me!
> Snow of salt, white burning, eating salt
> In which I have writhed.
>
> Lot's Wife! — Not Wife, but Mother.
> I have learned to curse your motherhood,

> You pillar of salt accursed.
> I have cursed motherhood because of you,
> Accursed, base motherhood![7]

The poem ends with a reiteration of the curse against "all mothers who fortify themselves in motherhood, devastating the vision," and the extension of the blight of modern motherhood to the poet himself, in whom "the curse...burns within...like a deep, old burn." In still another "biblical" poem, "Lady Wife," the poet speaks of the offspring of a selfish separateness which has been substituted for a proper relationship of servitude, as "apples of Sodom":

> Bring forth the sons of your womb then, and put them
> Into the fire
> Of Sodom that covers the earth; bring them forth
> From the womb of your precious desire.
> You women most holy, you mother, you being beyond
> Question or diminution,
> Add yourself up, and your seed, to the nought
> Of your last solution.[8]

The indictment of the modern woman's *magna mater* complex, and her assumption of the selfish rights of womanhood, is particularly harsh in *Aaron's Rod.* It is a charge which had been levelled against the female sex in Lawrence's earlier novels, as the trait revealed itself in various willful feminine figures: Annable's wife (*The White Peacock*); Siegmund's shrewish wife (*The Trespasser*); Mrs. Morel (*Sons and Lovers*); also in Hermione Roddice and Gudrun (*Women in Love*). All are possessed to varying degrees of a deadly female will which supposedly opposes and attempts to destroy the male principle in their husband or lover. In later novels Lawrence would become even more preoccupied with this exploration of the relationship between man and woman, and with the theme of positive subservience of the female to the authority of the male principle. The latter theme was to be further developed in such relationships as that of Harriet and Richard Lovat Somers in *Kangaroo,* or more significantly in those of Kate and Cipriano in *The Plumed Serpent* and Constance and Mellors in *Lady Chatterly's Lover.*

In order to understand the type of "sterile" motherhood in which Lottie turns away from Aaron to her children, we might look a little beyond the novel itself, to the description of Anna's role of *magna mater* in *The Rainbow.* Anna's role is one which forcibly excludes Will, and provokes a profound hostility between husband and wife, finally destroying the masculine soul of her husband:

In the house, he served his wife and the little matriarchy. She loved him because he was the father of her children. And she always had a physical passion for him. So he gave up trying to have the spiritual superiority and control, or even her respect for his conscious or public life. He lived simply by her physical love of him. And he served the little matriarchy, nursing the child and helping with the housework, indifferent any more of his own dignity and importance. But his abandoning of claims, his living isolated upon his own interest, made him seem unreal, unimportant.[9]

On both occasions of his return Aaron enters his home through the bottom of the garden, experiencing feelings of nostalgia mingled with morbid fascination and, ultimately, revulsion as he gazes at his own home and those beside it as if "through the wrong end of a telescope." The entire prospect of the doomed world of domestic triviality and failure is set before him.

It is significant that the autumnal decay of the Sisson's garden at the time of Aaron's September visit coincides with the final disintegration of Aaron's marriage. In a biblical context, the withered garden suggests the Garden of Eden after the Fall as well as the marital strife and discord which befell Adam and Eve and their descendants. The biblical antithesis of the garden is a wilderness or desert, and it is in this type of withered garden that fallen man finds himself. It was only natural that the compilers of Old Testament history would liken those periods of moral decay involving a falling away from Jehovah — periods which preceded such apocalyptic purges as the Flood or the destruction of the cities of the plain — to a metaphorical desert or withered garden. In the autumnal decay of Aaron's garden, the sin of Adam is invoked as well as those biblical periods of depravity from which a few remaining good men — Noah, Lot, Abraham — were rescued.

It is interesting to note that the Eden imagery is further sustained in the later description by the Marchese of the antipathetic female will as the "Eve" principle:

This desire which starts in a woman's head, when she knows, and which takes a man for her use, for her service. This is Eve. Ah, I hate Eve. I hate her, when she knows, and when she *wills*. I hate her when she will make of me that which serves her desire. (285)

The Marchesa and Lottie are, of course, linked thematically in the novel as possessors of an unyielding and cunning female will and, as destroyers of the male principle, modern counterparts of Eve, mother of mankind. At one point, it is even implied that the female will is to be equated in its wiles with the serpent of Eden, which has led to man's destruction:

Her will, her will, her terrible, implacable cunning will! What was there in the female will so diabolical, he asked himself. . . . The female will! He realised now that he had a horror of it. It was. . . cunning as a snake that could sing treacherous songs. (185)

All of this "Adam-Eve" imagery is of course indirect (though obvious enough) and occupies a place of secondary importance to the more explicit "Lot" imagery, particularly in those scenes of domestic conflict.

It is interesting that Aaron's return visits both culminate in his fleeing the domestic scene without once looking back. Revolted by the bitterness of his wife's attitude toward him as she pours out her complaints to the local doctor, Aaron flees, driven to the point of hating his musical instrument, an indication of the profoundly damaging effects which the struggle with Lottie has produced:

> He felt sick in every fibre. He almost hated the little handbag he carried, which held his flute and piccolo. It seemed a burden just then—a millstone around his neck. He hated the scene he had left—and he hated the hard, inviolable heart that stuck unchanging in his own breast. (53)

After his second return to Lottie, one filled with harsh recrimination, emotional and physical violence, Aaron flees his wife's terrible will without looking back:

> His soul went black as he looked at her. He broke her hand away from his shirt collar, bursting the stud-holes. She recoiled in silence. And in one black, unconscious movement he was gone, down the garden and over the fence and across the country, swallowed in a black unconsciousness. (149)

It is this final meeting with Lottie which plants the seal of absolute doom upon the marriage of Aaron and Lottie, their private Sodom and Gomorrah. Aaron's last visit leads naturally to his resolution that "the illusion of love" between him and Lottie is gone forever and that henceforth he will live "a life single, not a life double." Ostensibly liberated from the restrictions of "life double" in a sterile marriage of opposed wills, Aaron now sets out in search of "sheer, finished singleness," and eventually, is reunited in Florence with the novel's "Moses" figure, Rawdon Lilly.

Lawrence clearly refers us to the biblical Aaron in both his title for his seventh novel and the name he assigns his strange new anti-hero. The biblical narrative of the prophet Moses and his brother Aaron provided Lawrence with a framework of biblical allusions ideally appropriate to his presentation of the mysterious, ever-changing relationship of the novel's two central characters, Aaron Sisson and Rawdon Lilly. Allusions to the story of Moses and the wandering chosen people abound, and are so skillfully interwoven into the central narrative of the novel that one can scarcely scan a single page of *Aaron's Rod* without encountering some reference, however oblique, to the biblical legend. Lawrence must certainly have reread the entire biblical narrative as it appears in Exodus, Leviticus and Numbers, stirring that "instant recall" which he later described in *Apocalypse.*

Moses' ministry as prophet and (eventually) liberator of his enslaved people really begins in the third chapter of Exodus. Moses first encounters the presence of God in the form of a burning bush which miraculously "burned and was not consumed," and is informed of his divine mission:

> Now therefore, behold, the cry of the children of Israel is come unto me: and I have also seen the oppression wherewith the Egyptians oppress them.
>
> Come now therefore, and I will send thee unto Pharaoh, that thou mayest bring forth my people the children of Israel out of Egypt. (Ex. 3:9–10)

Lawrence has incorporated his own version of the burning bush episode into the narrative structure of *Aaron's Rod.* In the third chapter, "The Lighted Tree," the biblical incident is invoked as Sisson [10] catches sight of his own "burning bush" and encounters the Bricknell set for the first time. It is Christmas Eve. Sisson has just left "The Royal Oak," at closing time. In a moment of symbolic choice he takes a third way which leads him far from the homeward path, towards the "mouth of Shottle Lane" and the estate of Alfred Bricknell, owner of the New Brunswick Colliery.

In the meantime, the occupants of Shottle House have drifted out of doors to set up a lighted tree: a Christmas evergreen with attached candles which at first flicker weakly in the sulphurous night atmosphere. The entire scene becomes a parody of the familiar biblical episode. Julia's clumsy dance, her "worship" of the tree, parodies the reverence paid to the biblical burning bush and to the ground on which the bush stood, consecrated by the presence of the Deity.[11] Aaron seems to be mysteriously drawn like Moses to the blazing spectacle of the lighted tree:

> The beam of the bicycle-lamp moved and fell about the hands and faces of the young people, and penetrated the recesses of the secret trees. Several little tongues of flame clipped sensitive and ruddy on the naked air, sending a faint glow over the needle foliage. They gave a strange, perpendicular aspiration in the night. Julia waved slowly in her tree dance. . . .
>
> The party round the tree became absorbed and excited as more ruddy tongues. . . pricked upward from the dark tree. Pale candles became evident, the air was luminous. The illumination was becoming complete, harmonious. (39)

Sisson's aloofness, as he stands "mute and obstinate" before the tree and the occupants of Shottle House contrasts sharply with Moses' terror and awe before the burning bush of Exodus, as does the resentful interrogation of the interloper by Robert Cunningham. Jim Bricknell's hysterical whooping and writhing at the ridiculous irony of the whole situation is set sharply against the hushed solemnity of Moses' first encounter with God.

This early scene of *Aaron's Rod* is crucial, both in terms of Sisson's own destiny and as a revelation of Lawrence's characteristic methods of presenting the Moses legend and incorporating it into the central narrative. For Sisson himself, the occasion marks a significant turning-point in his personal destiny, for it is on this particular Christmas Eve (and at Jim Bricknell's ensuing suggestion that he spend the night at Shottle House) that Sisson chooses to abandon Lottie and his ruined marriage. This grotesque and irreverent parody of the biblical burning bush scene suggests also that the sacred and mythic qualities of other such biblical scenes invoked in *Aaron's Rod* will frequently be undercut by the acute irony or naturalism of the actual narrative situation. The burning bush incident marks for Moses the beginning of a heroic mission to liberate the Israelites from their bondage in Egypt, Moses evolving from humble servant to divinely inspired leader. No such heroic transformation takes place in Sisson. His desertion appears at this point to be more of a negative escape than a positive commitment to a new vision. The incident as it appears in *Aaron's Rod* has thus been secularized and trivialized by Lawrence. Of course we must recall that in Exodus Aaron is the priest, Moses the leader. In Northrop Frye's terms we might say that Lawerence has here deliberately provided a "displacement" of the original biblical scene in an ironic context.

Lawrence's use of Sisson in this scene suggests that it would be an oversimplification to think of him exclusively as the biblical Aaron, or to see Lilly simply as Moses-Lawrence. Lawrence is asking us to recall of course that Moses was the inarticulate brother who frequently required the assistance of his eloquent brother Aaron in fulfilling the tasks assigned to him by God. Moses' reply to God's calling is typical of his humility. "And Moses said unto God, Who am I that I should go unto Pharaoh and that I should bring forth the Children of Israel out of Egypt?" (Ex. 3:11). Later God promises the aid of Aaron:

> Is not Aaron the Levite thy brother? I know that he can speak well. And also, behold, he cometh forth to meet thee: and when he seeth thee, he will be glad in his heart.
>
> And thou shalt speak unto him, and put words in his mouth: and I will be with thy mouth, and with his mouth, and will teach you what ye shall do.
>
> And he shall be thy spokesman unto the people: and he shall be, even he shall be to thee instead of a mouth, and thou shalt be to him instead of God.
>
> And thou shalt take this rod in thine hand, wherewith thou shalt do signs. (Ex. 4:14–17)

Aaron's eloquence is thus to be employed in the extraordinary confrontations designed to move the stubborn heart of the Egyptian Pharaoh.

> And the Lord said unto Moses, See, I have made thee a god to Pharaoh: and Aaron thy brother shall be thy prophet.
>
> Thou shalt speak all that I command thee: and Aaron thy brother shall speak unto Pharaoh, that he send the children of Israel out of his land.
>
> And I will harden Pharaoh's heart, and multiply my signs and my wonders in the land of Egypt. (Ex. 7:1-3)

In *Aaron's Rod,* however, it is Lilly who seems to do most of the talking and preaching. His eloquence is employed to move the stubborn hearts of his listeners, particularly that of Sisson, especially in the novel's important final chapter, "Words." Sisson's inability to articulate his innermost feelings and desires is evident throughout the novel and becomes the focus of Chapter 18, "Wie Es Ihnen Gefaellt," in which the role of the narrator as intermediary between Sisson and reader is defined. Sisson's taciturnity, which seems at times to be an insulting aloofness, is also conspicuous in his relations with the Bricknell set, at Shottle House and at Covent Garden.

Lawrence has thus transferred several important characteristics which we might normally expect to find in the novel's "Aaron figure" to the "Moses figure," Rawdon Lilly. Indeed, the roles of the two characters will be frequently reversed, often for ironic effect. Yet the biblical parallel helps to clarify for the reader the peculiar but close bond between Aaron and Lilly, at the same time drawing attention to the strangely "dual" relationship of the two characters.

It is interesting that Sisson and Lilly first meet each other in an "Egyptian" context: at a performance of *Aïda* at the Royal Opera House, Covent Garden, where, in an amusing allusion to the flight of the children of Israel from their Egyptian bondage, Lawrence depicts the hasty departure of the opera audience, particularly of the Bricknell set. But is is not until later in the novel, after Aaron collapses, with symbolic appropriateness, outside the Opera house at Coven Garden and near to Lilly's flat that Lilly begins to exert his influence upon Sisson. At this point, Lilly's self-conceived mission as a prophet like Moses really begins, as, nursing his patient back to health, Lilly performs the strange ritual of anointment as an effort to revive Sisson's will to live:

> Quickly he uncovered the blond lower body of his patient, and began to rub the abdomen with oil, using a slow, rhythmic, circulating motion, a sort of massage. For a long time he rubbed finely and steadily, then went over the whole of the lower body, mindless, as if in a sort of incantation. He rubbed every speck of the man's lower body—the abdomen, the buttocks, thighs and knees, down to the feet, rubbed it all warm and glowing with camphorated oil, every bit of it, chafing the toes swiftly, till he was almost exhausted. Then Aaron was covered up again... (112)

Lilly's actions in this crucial scene of the novel are a deliberate parallel to Moses' anointing of Aaron his brother as high priest, following the behest of the Lord:

And thou shalt anoint Aaron and his sons, and consecrate them, that they may minister unto me in the priest's office (Ex. 30:30)

The investiture of Aaron as High Priest defines more clearly his relation to God's prophet, Moses. Aaron will be interpreter of God's word to the people of Israel, and Aaron's social sense, his eloquence, is thus formally consecrated to the task of intercession and explication of God's holy ordinances. In Exodus, Leviticus and Numbers, Aaron stands between Moses and the people and is frequently called upon to defend God's grand design for Israel against the murmuring of the rebellious chosen people. At other times, he intercedes on Israel's behalf: in times of drought and threatening famine, as in Exodus 16, in which God provides the children of Israel with life-sustaining manna; or in Numbers 16, in which Aaron appeases God's wrath, thus atoning for Israel and averting the destruction of the tribes of Israel by a terrible plague.

All of this biblical account has been ironically transformed in the novel in the refusal of Sisson to surrender his soul to the prophet, Lilly. Sisson's constant vacillation parallels that of his biblical namesake, and he thus becomes an ironic high priest, or anti-priest of Lilly's new philosophy of living and self-possession. Sisson's inability to articulate his mistrust of love and any social relationship, indeed, the profound misanthropy of the novel itself, all undercut Aaron's biblical role as "eloquent intercessor," creating a bitterly ironic effect. Lilly seems painfully aware of Sisson's resistance to his doctrines, and recalls at the same time the brutal defection of a former potential apostle, Jim Bricknell:

"I wonder why I do it. I wonder why I bother with him.... Jim ought to have taught me my lesson. As soon as this man's really better he'll punch me in the wind, metaphorically if not actually, for having interfered with him. And Tanny would say, he was quite right to do it. She says I want power over them. What if I do? ...Why can't they submit to a bit of healthy individual authority? The fool would die, without me: just as that fool Jim will die in hysterics one day. Why does he last so long!" (112)

Aaron Sisson's reaction to Lilly's absence from home a few days later indicates his disaffected attitude towards Lilly and his preaching at this point in the novel:

Aaron did not find his friend at home when he called. He took it rather as a slap in the face. But then he knew quite well that Lilly had made a certain call on his, Aaron's soul: a call which he, Aaron, did not at all intend to obey. If in return the soul-caller chose to shut his street-door in the face of the world-friend — well, let it be quits. He was not sure whether he felt superior to his unworldly enemy or not. He rather thought he did. (141–42)

In the Old Testament narrative it is Pharaoh who hardens his heart against Moses' appeal to liberate Israel. In *Aaron's Rod,* Sisson himself plays a stubborn Pharaoh to Lilly's Moses. Like Pharaoh, Sisson also demands signs or proofs of the authenticity of Lilly's authority. Not until he has followed Lilly beyond his English home to Italy, and has been reunited with him in Florence, does Sisson begin to turn towards Lilly for spiritual guidance. Sisson's own restless wanderings from one social milieu to another as he leaps across the gulf separating one social class from another, parallel the lengthy wandering of Israel in the wilderness in search of the Promised Land.

The title of the novel *Aaron's Rod* is, of course, a direct reference to the miraculous staff with which Moses is provided by God at the time of his calling. The staff is endowed with wondrous powers enough to astonish the Egyptian Court. In the hands of his brother Aaron the rod is employed in the preliminary stages of the contest with Pharaoh. The rod turns into a serpent, a feat which the magicians of Pharaoh are able to match; whereupon Aaron's serpent swallows up all the others (Ex. 7:12). Later, Aaron's rod transforms the waters of the land into blood (Ex. 7:20–21) and brings the dreadful plagues of the frogs and the lice (Ex. 8:6,17) upon the kingdom of Pharaoh. The miracles worked by Aaron's rod thus defeat the magicians of the Egyptian court. They act as a revelation to Pharaoh of the seriousness of Israel's plea for freedom and the authenticity of Moses' claim to be the leader of his people. As well they act as a dark warning of other disasters which will befall Egypt if Pharaoh still refuses to yield. Pharaoh's heart is of course more hardened than ever, and the situation requires the powerful miracles effected by the rod in the possession of Moses himself. Moses stretches forth the staff at God's command and various plagues rage throughout the land: deadly hail and thunder-storms (Ex. 9:23); swarms of locusts (Ex. 10:13) and darkness (Ex. 10:22); and so on, until God is forced to smite the firstborn of every Egyptian family, including that of the Egyptian monarch. Symbolically Aaron is succeeded by Moses and the greater power with which Moses' rod is invested.

The explicit revelation of Aaron's calling as high priest and of the pre-eminence of his family occurs much later, in Numbers, in the miracle of the blossoming rod of Aaron. The incident occurs, significantly, after the rebellious Korah challenges the supremacy of Moses and Aaron. To stay the wrath of Jehovah, Aaron intervenes and averts the wholesale destruction of the children through plague:

> And Moses said unto Aaron, Take a censer, and put fire therein from off the altar, and put on incense, and go quickly unto the congregation, and make an atonement for them, for there is wrath gone out from the Lord; the plague is begun.
> And Aaron took as Moses commanded, and ran into the midst of the congregation; and, behold, the plague was begun among the people: and he put on incense, and made an atonement for the people.

> And he stood between the dead and the living: and the plague was stayed. (Num.
> 16:46–48)

The ensuing tale which describes the miraculous blossoming of Aaron's rod
is important enough to quote in its entirety:

> And the Lord spake unto Moses, saying,
>
> Speak unto the children of Israel, and take of every one of them a rod according to
> the house of their fathers, of all their princes according to the house of their fathers
> twelve rods: write though every man's name upon his rod.
>
> And thou shalt write Aaron's name upon the rod of Levi: for one rod shall be for the
> head of the house of their fathers.
>
> And thou shalt lay them up in the tabernacle of the congregation before the testi-
> mony, where I will meet with you.
>
> And it shall come to pass, that the man's rod, whom I shall choose shall blossom: and
> I will make to cease from me the murmurings of the children of Israel, whereby they
> murmur against you.
>
> And Moses spake unto the Children of Israel, and every one of their princes gave him
> a rod apiece, for each prince one, according to their fathers houses, even twelve rods:
> and the rod of Aaron was among their rods.
>
> And Moses laid up the rods before the Lord in the tabernacle of witness.
>
> And it came to pass, that on the morrow Moses went into the tabernacle of witness;
> and, behold, the rod of Aaron for the house of Levi was budded, and brought forth
> buds, and bloomed blossoms, and yielded almonds. (Num. 17:1–8)

Sisson's "rod" is his flute, the instrument by which he is able to make
his living and which guarantees for him a certain amount of independence.
Lilly himself first draws attention to the biblical parallel of Aaron's blossoming rod when Sisson is recovering from influenza and takes up his flute
once again:

> "Aaron's rod is putting forth again," he said, smiling.
>
> "What?" said Aaron, looking up.
>
> "I said Aaron's rod is putting forth again."
>
> "What rod?"
>
> "Your flute, for the moment."
>
> "It's got to put forth my bread and butter."
>
> "Is that all the buds it's going to have?"
>
> "What else!"
>
> "Nay—that's for you to show. What flowers do you imagine came out of the rod of
> Moses's brother?"
>
> "Scarlet runners, I should think if he'd got to live on them."
>
> "Scarlet enough, I'll bet."
>
> Aaron turned unnoticing back to his music....
>
> "It's all one to you, then," said Aaron suddenly, "Whether we ever see one another
> again?"
>
> "Not a bit," said Lilly, looking up over his spectacles. "I very much wish there might
> be something that held us together."

"Then if you wish it, why isn't there?"
"You might wish your flute to put out scarlet-runner flowers at the joints."
"Ay—I might. And it would be all the same."
The moment that followed was extraordinary in its hostility. (126)

This is one of the most crucial dialogues in the novel. The incident points not only to the biblical parallel of Aaron's miraculous staff, but also to the strangely ambivalent relationship between Aaron and Lilly. Although Lilly seems convinced that Sisson is marked for a special destiny, like his biblical counterpart, Sisson's unwillingness to follow in the footsteps of Lilly-Moses is obvious. Sisson's intended role as "high priest" seems ironically far-removed from the reality of his hostility toward Lilly at this stage of their relationship. This episode also introduces the concept of *Blutbrüder-schaft* into the novel, a theme strengthened by the biblical parallel of the brothers Moses and Aaron.

A few minutes later, in tones which border on puerile resentment, Lilly draws the connection between Sisson's flute and the social facility or self-dependence which the flute provides (127). Lawrence thus prepares the reader for his later elaboration of the flute as symbol of the male sexual power. Aaron's musical talent first provides him with the necessary means of access to higher social circles which would normally be closed to a member of the working class, like Aaron, a miners' checkweighman. Later, through the connection between Aaron's flute music and his sexual charm, the flute provides a means of access to the Marchesa's bed-chamber.

In its initial stages, Aaron's affair with the Marchesa appears to restore a measure of the virility which his sterile relationship with Lottie has destroyed. The rod is revealed here as the instrument of phallic con-sciousness:

And now came his desire back. But strong, fierce as iron. Like the strength of an eagle with the lightning in its talons. Something to glory in, something overweening, the powerful male passion, arrogant, royal, Jove's thunderbolt. Aaron's black rod of power, blossoming again with red Florentine lilies and fierce thorns. He moved about in the splendour of his own male lightning, invested in the thunder of the male passion-power. He had got it back, the male godliness, the male godhead. (301–302)

Lawrence has substituted red Florentine lilies for the white almond blossoms of the Old Testament narrative, and further invokes the rising phoenix, to suggest Sisson's awareness of his male power: "He felt his turn had come. The phoenix had risen in fire again, out of the ashes" (302). The imagery of regeneration is, however, savagely ironic in view of the Mar-chesa's subtle but deadly sexual aggressiveness and her resistance to Aaron in this episode, indeed her aggressive sexual will power employed through-out the relationship:

> But as he played, he felt he did not cast the spell over her. There was no connection.
> She was in some mysterious way withstanding him. She was withstanding him, and his
> male super-power, and his thunder-bolt desire. She was, in some indescribable way,
> throwing cold water over his phoenix newly risen from the ashes of its nest in flames.
> (303)

As Sisson succinctly sums up his frustrated sexual dilemma earlier, the rod
contains both the blossom and the thorn of desire:

> As he laid his flute on the table he looked at it and smiled. He remembered that Lilly
> had called it Aaron's Rod.
> "So you blossom, do you? —and thorn as well," said he. (301)

Aaron's brief but destructive intimacy with the Marchesa del Torre
also takes its place within the structure of the Moses-Aaron imagery of the
novel. Although the biblical Aaron is invested into the priesthood and the
supremacy of his line is established by the budding of his rod, he is still
prone to frequent disobedience and vacillation in the face of God's ordinances, the most notorious of which is his fashioning a golden calf during
Moses' sojourn on Mount Sinai: a graven image to worship as a substitute
for the true God in the absence of His prophet. When Moses returns from
his long vigil he discovers the treachery of the people of Israel and accuses
Aaron of misleading them into idolatry. Aaron's replies to Moses are
rather interesting:

> And Aaron said, Let not the anger of the Lord wax hot: thou knowest the people,
> that they are set on mischief.
> For they said unto me, Make us gods, which shall go before us: for as for this Moses,
> the man that brought us up out of the land of Egypt, we wot not what is become of
> him.
> And I said unto them, Whosoever hath any gold, let him break it off. So they gave it
> me: then I cast it into the fire, and there came out this calf. (Ex. 32:22–23)

I would suggest that from this biblical episode Lawrence took a
considerable hint for Sisson's nature. Lawrence probably looked upon this
exchange as particularly illustrative of Aaron's character; to him there was
an evasiveness and coolness in Aaron's treatment of Moses. What was only
at most hinted at in the Old Testament chronicle Lawrence with his highly
idiosyncratic and eclectic method has adapted, selecting certain details of
the narrative in order to draw a parallel between the behavior of the
biblical Aaron and the aloof indifference so often displayed by Sisson,
especially in his encounters with Lilly-the-prophet. And yet it is also true
that Sisson's aloofness or taciturnity also owes something to earlier
Lawrencean figures such as Siegmund and Tom Brangwen. The relation of

Sisson to earlier Lawrencean protagonists will be discussed in a later chapter.

In *Aaron's Rod,* the love urge is the golden calf which the world worships. The temptation to possess and control; the thirst for absolute love-knowledge together with the impulse to search after social relationships based only upon intimacy and self-sacrifice; all these are aspects of the golden calf idolatry of modern society, which Lilly consistently attacks. In terms of Sisson's own personal fate, his worship of the golden calf of love is represented by his repeated falling away from Lilly-Moses' teachings particularly in his substitution of the love urge for the superior power urge. Lilly himself sums up Sisson's (and society's) "idolatry" in the final chapter of the novel, "Words":

> "I told you there were two urges — two great life-urges didn't I? There may be more. But it comes on me so strongly, now, that there are two: love and power. And we've been trying to work ourselves, at least as individuals, from the love-urge exclusively, hating the power-urge, and repressing it. And now I find we've got to accept the very thing we've hated."
>
> "We've exhausted our love-urge, for the moment. And yet we try to force it to continue working. So we get inevitably anarchy and murder. It's no good. We've got to accept the power motive, accept it in deep responsibility, do you understand me? It is a great life motive. It was that great dark power-urge which kept Egypt so intensely living for so many centuries. It is a vast dark source of life and strength in us now, waiting to issue into true action, or to burst into cataclysm. Power — the power urge. The will-to-power — but not in Nietzsche's sense. Not intellectual power. Not mental power. Not conscious will-power. Not even wisdom. But dark, living, fructifying power." (345)[12]

Sisson's search for the "Promised Land" of a "life single not double" which begins on a frosty Christmas Eve leads him through a series of moral wildernesses in which the erring protagonist enters upon a succession of misguided attempts to achieve a satisfactory love relationship: a brief but ultimately revolting affair with Josephine Ford; a return to Lottie which ends in psychological torture for both parties; and finally a potentially soul-destroying sexual relationship with the Marchesa del Torre. The Marchesa is herself the supreme "golden calf" of *Aaron's Rod,* and the novel itself has been carefully structured to lead up to this final destructive relationship, the failure of which urges Sisson towards the influence and teaching of Lilly. Notice Lawrence's carefully detailed descriptions of the Marchesa on the occasion of Sisson's dinner-visit:

> She seemed like a demon, her hair on her brows, her terrible modern elegance. She wore a wonderful gown of thin blue velvet, of a lovely colour, with some kind of gauzy gold-threaded filament down the sides.... He thought her wonderful, and sinister. She affected him with a touch of horror. She sat down opposite him and her beautifully

> shapen legs, in frail, goldish stockings, seemed to glisten metallic naked, thrust far out
> of the wonderful, wonderful skin, like periwinkle-blue velvet. She had tapestry shoes,
> blue and gold: and almost one could see her toes: metallic naked. The gold-threaded
> gauze slipped at her side. Aaron could not help watching the naked-seeming arch of her
> foot. It was as if she were dusted with dark gold-dust upon her marvellous nudity
> (291)[13]

The suggestion of the Marchesa as a modern Cleopatra stresses the connection between Sisson's new mistress and the Egyptian flesh-pots. Sisson's near enslavement both to over-powering desire for his new mistress as well as to the Marchesa's possession of his selfhood parallels the bondage of the chosen people in the demonic kingdom of Egypt. At his most vulnerable moment, when enslavement to the Marchesa's feminine will appears imminent, Sisson suddenly experiences a sharp repulsion, a sense of withdrawal. Lawrence's image for this process of withdrawal to heightened objectivity is indeed curious:

> He was aware of the strength and beauty and godlikeness that his breast was then to
> her—the magic. But himself, he stood far off, like Moses' sister Miriam. (318)

The allusion is certainly difficult to explain. Most likely Lawrence is referring to the incident along the journey to Kadesh-barnea in which Miriam and Aaron draw away from Moses, challenging his divinely appointed authority as well as his marriage to an "Ethiopian woman" (Num. 12:1–2). Miriam's defection is severely punished, for shortly thereafter she is stricken with leprosy and can only be healed by the prayers of Moses himself. Perhaps Lawrence is also thinking of a parallel between the resistance of Miriam to Moses and that of Sisson to Lilly-Moses. Sisson's relationship with the Marchesa, as I have previously indicated, is a step away from Lilly-Moses and the "Promised Land" and is thus part of Aaron's continual resistance to Lilly's authority. Of course, Sisson saves himself just in time from being fatally stricken by the Marchesa's "cunning sexual will."

The Old Testament narrative of the Israelites' quest for the promised land contains one further reference to the magical rod of Aaron and Moses. In the desert, the thirsty people of Israel rebuke the brothers for bringing them out of fertile Egypt into the wilderness, crying "And why have ye brought up the congregation of the Lord into this wilderness, that we and our cattle should die there?" (Num. 20:4). Once again God appears to his prophet and high priest, bidding them assemble the people together before a large rock:

> Take the rod and gather thou the assembly together, thou, and Aaron thy brother, and
> speak ye unto the rock before their eyes; and it shall give forth his water, and thou shalt

bring forth to them water out of the rock: so thou shalt give the congregation and their beasts drink. (Num. 20:8)

In their anxiety to appease the rebellious people, Moses and Aaron disobey God's command. Taking up the miraculous staff which was once used to perform awe-inspiring miracles before Pharaoh, Moses twice taps the rock sharply with the staff. Although water issues from the rock and the people drink abundantly and are saved from perishing, nevertheless Aaron and Moses pay dearly for their momentary mistrust of God's word. Both are denied entrance to the promised land.

In spite of the disobedience and punishment of Moses and Aaron at Meribah (literally, "strife"), the people of Israel are once more saved from destruction. The incident illustrates perfectly the salutary and life-giving properties of Aaron's rod as it draws water from stone. The use of the rod in this incident, itself an Old Testament prefiguration of the Resurrection, contrasts with its former use as a weapon of destruction employed against the kingdom of the Egyptian Pharaoh.

In *Aaron's Rod* the supposed life-giving or reviving properties of Sisson's flute, his "rod," are demonstrated in the scene of the Marchesa's recovery of her singing voice (Chapter 18). This episode parallels the striking of water from the rock at Meribah described above; and like its biblical counterpart, this scene initially carries some suggestion of spiritual regeneration by the water of life, or as in the Marchesa's case, by a stream of music, "a bright, quick sound of pure animation" (266). The Marchesa's renewed power to sing also has distinct overtones of a renewal of feminine sexual powers of the flute. Significantly, the Marchesa herself registers the sound of the flute as a sexual, male call upon her:

And the music of the flute came quick, rather brilliant like a call-note, or like a long quick message, half command. To her it was like a pure male voice—as a blackbird's when he calls: a pure male voice, not only calling, but telling her something, telling her something, and soothing her soul to sleep. It was like the fire-music putting Brunnhilde [sic] to sleep. But the pipe did not flicker and sink. It seemed to cause a natural relaxation in her soul, a peace. Perhaps it was more like waking to a sweet, morning awakening, after a night of tormented, painful tense sleep. Perhaps more like that. (296-97)

Sisson sees himself as a "miracle worker" and glows with triumph over the Marchesa's husband, in the scene following her vocal regeneration:

The two men also sat quite still. And in the silence a little drama played itself between the three, of which they knew definitely nothing. But Manfredi knew that Aaron had done what he himself could never do, for this woman. . . . And so, he was displaced. Aaron, sitting there, glowed with a sort of triumph. He had performed a little miracle, and felt himself a little wonder-worker, to whom reverence was due. (300)

Once again Lawrence draws a connection between music and sexuality as Sisson's masculine power soars along with the Marchesa's liberated feminine soul:

> Ah what a woman to enjoy! And was it not his privilege? Had he not gained it?
> His manhood, or rather his maleness, rose powerfully in him, in a sort of mastery. He felt his own power, he felt suddenly his own virile title to strength and reward. Suddenly, and newly flushed with his own male super-power, he was going to have his reward. The woman was his reward. So it was, in him. (301)

Lawrence thus uses music and its potent effects as a means of uniting two symbolic aspects of Sisson's flute and presenting his own version of both the biblical anecdote of Aaron's blossoming rod, as well as the episode at Meribah. Like the misguided action of his biblical namesake at Meribah, Sisson's affair with the Marchesa is presented clearly as a step in the wrong direction, away from the "promised land" and the proper relationship with Lilly as high priest of Lilly's design for a "life single, not double." The collapse of his sexual attraction to the Marchesa propels Sisson towards Lilly's mentorship once more. Rather than *producing,* like its biblical counterpart, a restorative or life-giving stream, Sisson's rod, his flute, is drowned in the muddy Arno.

Soon after the incident at Meribah God reveals that Aaron is shortly to die. Accordingly Moses strips Aaron of his priestly garments, transferring them to Aaron's son Eleazer, and Aaron thereafter dies on top of Mount Hor (Num. 20:23–29). The biblical death of Moses' brother is symbolically represented in *Aaron's Rod* by the shattering of the flute in the chapter entitled "The Broken Flute." In the midst of a discussion concerning the nature and limits of power, both political and individual, the verbal conflict between Lilly and the others at his table is reinforced externally by the terrifying crash of a bomb outrage which destroys the flute. Sisson registers the destruction of his instrument as a "death" to himself:

> He felt at once for his flute.... He pushed and struggled, caught sight of a section, and picked it up. But it was split right down, two silver stops were torn out and a long thin spelch of wood was curiously torn off. He looked at it, and his heart stood still. No need to look for the rest.
> He felt utterly, utterly overcome—as if he didn't care what became of him any further. He didn't care whether he were hit by a bomb, or whether he himself threw the next bomb, and hit somebody. He just didn't care any more about anything in life or death. It was as if the reins of his life slipped from his hands. (330)

In a symbolic moment of surrender to the command of the Moses figure, "Let us go," Sisson follows Lilly out towards the river and the Ponte Santa Trinità. At Lilly's bidding he drops the shattered flute into the river:

"Is that your flute?" asked Lilly.
"Bit of it. Smashed."
"Let me look."
He looked and gave it back.
"No good," he said.
"Oh no," said Aaron.
"Throw it in the river, Aaron," said Lilly.
Aaron turned and looked at him.
"Throw it in the river," repeated Lilly. "It's an end."
Aaron nervelessly dropped the flute into the stream. The two men stood leaning on the bridge-parapet, as if unable to move. (331)

The dialogue above has all the stylization of ritual. This impression is sustained a few lines later by Sisson's interpretation to himself of the event as a symbolic turning point in his private destiny:

Aaron was quite dumbfounded by the night's event: the loss of his flute. Here was a blow he had not expected. And the loss was for him symbolistic. It chimed with something in his soul: the bomb, the smashed flute, the end. (331)

Immediately Sisson recalls the biblical parallel to which Lilly once drew his attention so long ago:

"There goes Aaron's rod, then," he said to Lilly.
"It'll grow again. It's a reed, a water-plant — you can't kill it," said Lilly, unheeding.
"And me?"
"You'll have to live without a rod, meanwhile." (331)[14]

For Sisson the smashing of his flute symbolizes a death of the old self, the end of what Lilly sees as a feverish and fruitless search for love. The breaking of the flute supposedly represents the beginning of a new life, and is accompanied by ritual of symbolic baptism in the waters of the river. Ostensibly Sisson's new life will assume a new direction under the aegis of the prophet Lilly. In the Old Testament the death of the high priest Aaron, which follows closely upon the Lord's repudiation of his rod at Meribah, signifies the end of Israel's wanderings in the desert. Though Israel will march in the future she will never again wander aimlessly. The metaphorical "death" of Sisson's former self through the destruction of his instrument, and his subsequent release into Lilly's protection both seem to indicate the end of Sisson's own wandering which has occupied the central action of the novel. Yet Moses himself never reaches the Promised Land. True to God's word he is given a view of the Promised Land from Pisgah but dies on the summit of Nebo:

And the Lord said unto him, This is the land which I swore unto Abraham, unto Isaac, and unto Jacob, saying, I will give it unto thy seed: I have caused thee to see it with thine eyes, but thou shalt not go over thither.

> So Moses the servant of the Lord died there in the land of Moab, according to the word of the Lord. (Deut. 34:4-5)

In view of the fate of Moses and Aaron, the conclusion of the novel seems bitterly ironic as both men strive for understanding, and Lilly attempts to convince Sisson of the truth of his power-doctrine. Lawrence uses the fact that neither Moses nor his brother Aaron is permitted to enter the promised land in order to call into question the ultimate validity of Lilly's teachings which aspire to lead Sisson towards a private "promised land" of power and self-possession. The recollection that the biblical Aaron was denied entrance to the promised land leads us to wonder if Sisson really will ever be prepared to embrace Lilly's doctrine of self-possession. Will he ever become high priest, apostle even, of the fretful and tenacious little prophet, Lilly?

In the final chapters of the novel, Lawrence has skillfully prepared, through careful use of biblical allusion, for Sisson's entrance into the "promised land" of Lilly's sphere of influence and the salvation offered by Lilly's philosophy. Nevertheless, Lawrence leaves his unheroic Aaron figure ironically suspended, misgiving and mistrustful, between the extremes of love and power. Lawrence is perhaps suggesting that Sisson must indeed await the soul-call which Lilly has promised will reveal the true leader to whom he should submit. The conclusion hints strongly that the dark little man before Sisson, his face seeming to Sisson "dark and remote" as a "Byzantine eikon," is decidedly *not* the destined leader of men, certainly not one to whom Sisson will freely submit. Perhaps Lawrence is suggesting with bitter irony that there are hidden flaws in Lilly's new philosophy of power. In view of the fate of his biblical counterpart, perhaps Lilly turns out to be something of a latter-day prophet who somehow fails. The novel seems to ask whether Lilly's doctrine of self-possession and selfhood is a feasible design for living or simply the idiosyncratic remedy of one highly erratic and speculative mind.

4

The First Wild Natural Thing:
A Study of Music in *Aaron's Rod*

—and there isn't any thought behind music, but the music is behind the thought, music behind the idea, music the first wild natural thing, and the thought is the words writ to music, the narrow rows of words with little meanings.... And all that is sayable let it be said, and what isn't you may sing it, or act it, or even put it in poetry. I don't care a damn about the technique and technicalities of music.

D. H. L. to Blanche Jennings, 1908

From the earliest childhood hours spent in Eastwood's Congregational Chapel or at the parlor piano, music seems always to have commanded a very special place in Lawrence's life. Although in no sense what we would think of as a "professional" musician, certainly not skilled in the performance of any particular instrument, Lawrence must always have impressed his acquaintances with his ready sensitivity to a variety of musical forms: German *Lieder,* Grand Opera, symphony, and later the primitive dance rhythms of Sicily and New Mexico.

A clear impression of the wide scope of Lawrence's musicality, even at this early stage, is provided by the memories of his younger sister Ada:

Some of our happiest hours were spent at our old piano with its faded green silk front. It had to be touched gently to bring out the tinkling notes. Bert bought me Chopin waltzes, music by Tschaikowsky and Brahms, Boosey's song books, and opera selections. He could not play but sat by my side for hours at a time encouraging me to practice [sic] difficult pieces. Sometimes they seemed beyond me and I was often on the verge of tears, begging to be left alone, but he insisted that I should persevere and hummed the air while I struggled with its complications. We sang duets—Mendelssohn's *Maybells and Flowers, The Passage Bird's Farewell,* and Rubenstein's *Song of the Birds,* but no one else heard them. There were sing-songs at Hagg's Farm but our duets were never given there. He only sang them for his and my amusement.[1]

After a few impatient attempts to teach himself, Lawrence seems to have given up the notion of playing the piano himself, content to supervise Ada's musical activities.[2] The Chambers family has also left us interesting reminiscences of Lawrence's early musical talent and interest. Jessie Chambers' brother, later Dr. J. D. Chambers, recalled the extraordinary effect which Lawrence with his musical enthusiasm must have had upon the entire household:

> Besides charades, he introduced whist, chess, dancing, singing.... In regard to singing, he contrived to make my brothers and sisters learn their parts from tonic sol fa, and even went into the cowshed to teach them while they were milking. We sang *Friars of Orders Grey, Two Grenadiers, Caro Mio Ben, Larboard Watch* and a host of others which I can never hear even now without an echo of these family sing-songs with Bert conducting and singing all parts as required although he had by far the poorest singing voice of us all. And when he left us to start out on his two and a half mile walk through fields and woods...we gathered outside and sang in full-throated family chorus what would now be called our signature tune—*A Tavern in the Town* or shattered the midnight stillness by a final crashing rendering of *Larboard Watch.*[3]

Jessie's own accounts of sing-song activities at the Lawrence home are similar, but contain the further revelation of "an undercurrent of hostility running strong beneath it all," doubtless caused by Mrs. Lawrence sitting in her chair "like a little figure of fate, coldly disapproving."[4] Lawrence's continuing love and discovery of music is suggested in Jessie's rather touching recollections of Lawrence during his college days:

> The subject he enjoyed most of all in college was music, which of course was singing. He liked the Folk songs, particularly the ballad of 'Henry Martin' and 'I sowed the seeds of love.' We bought the song book in use at College, *A Golden Treasury of Song,* and had great times singing 'I triumph, I triumph,' 'The Lay of the Imprisoned Huntsman,' 'Vulcan's Song' and practically everything in the book. I have seen Lawrence standing in the open doorway of the cowshed while my brother was milking, humming a tune from the sol-fa notes by the light of the hurricane lamp for the latter to learn. And he once persuaded my brother to cycle the twelve hilly miles into Nottingham to listen to a rehearsal of the College concert. But we often sang without the piano, just sitting round the parlour fire, from the National song-book, sometimes taking two and even three parts, and in all this Lawrence was the moving spirit.[5]

Lawrence's ensuing years at Croydon were crucial in the formation of a more sophisticated critical response to an increasing variety of musical exprience. Through his friendship with Helen Corke, Lawrence was introduced to the world of opera, a musical genre which will be discussed in detail later, in its relevance to *Aaron's Rod*. Lawrence's letters during this period to his fiancée, Louie Burrows, abound in musical references, from the mawkish declaration that his "days are spent in uttering that mournful lament "meine Ruh is [sic] hin, mein Herz ist schwer,"[6] to the more interesting accounts of a considerable range of operatic and symphonic performances.

Aside from the very frequent mention of such standard operatic items as *Trovatore, Bohème, Samson* and so on, Lawrence mentions specifically that he has been attending symphony concerts. He writes to Louie Burrows during the interval at a concert of 17th December 1910, at the Public Hall, Croydon, that he has just heard Debussy, declaring, "I love Debussy."[7] On 29 December he writes that he will attend that evening a "Tchaikowsky concert in the Dome [Brighton Pavilion]."[8] It is entirely characteristic of Lawrence's impetuous emotional response that only a few days later he should comically denounce Debussy and Wagner after attending an energetic provincial performance of *Cavalleria Rusticana.*[9]

I will later have much more to say of Lawrence's curious relationship with Helen Corke during this important period, but at this time it seems sufficient to observe that the impetus for a great deal of Lawrence's musical activity was provided by his association with Helen Corke at Croydon. Somewhat an amateur musician herself, Helen was quite obviously an admirer of Grand Opera, particularly of the musical dramas of Wagner. It was from Miss Corke's account of her brief idyll with Herbert B. MacCartney[10] and its tragic *finale* that Lawrence's second novel, *The Trespasser,* evolved. *The Trespasser* represents Lawrence's single attempt at a fiction almost exclusively Wagnerian in texture. As such, this novel is of special interest, not only as a stylistic experiment, but as an important stage in the development of a critical attitude to Wagnerian opera by a discerning *amateur.* Henceforth, music plays an increasingly crucial role in Lawrence's development. One would be justified in considering music to be the "basso continuo" — as the Baroque Masters would have called it — of Lawrence's existence. Music contributed considerably toward the achievement of an emotional equilibrium during periods of extreme stress or mental depression.

It should also be emphasized that in spite of his humble origins as a miner's son in a quite ordinary and comparatively impoverished mining village, Lawrence had spent his early manhood in an unusually intellectual or "cultured" home environment. It was the curious juxtaposition of the refined and the ordinary, the artistic and the pragmatic, which most impressed Ford Madox Ford, who claimed to have visited Lawrence at his home "in Nottingham":

I visited him in Nottingham and was astonished at the atmosphere in which he lived though less astonished by then as to the great sense of culture in his work.... [Y]oung people from down the pit or from schools and offices drifted in and out of the

Lawrences' house with the sort of freedom from restraint that I have only seen elsewhere in American small towns. I have never anywhere found so educated a society.
Those young people knew the things that my generation in the great English schools
hardly even chattered about. Lawrence, the father, came in from the mines on a Saturday evening. He threw a great number of coins on the kitchen table and counted them
out to his waiting mates. All the while the young people were talking about Nietzsche
and Wagner and Leopardi and Flaubert and Karl Marx and Darwin and occasionally
the father would interrupt his counting to contradict them. And they would discuss the
French Impressionists and the primitive Italians and play Chopin and Debussy on the
piano.[11]

During the grim days of the seemingly interminable war, music
became for the despairing Lawrence a source of artistic stimulation as well
as a pleasurable diversion. During their troubled stay in Cornwall
(1915–17) the Lawrences entered into a short-lived friendship with the
notable musician, Philip Heseltine, who with his mistress, Puma, provided
the model for the artist Halliday and his promiscuous Pussum in *Women
in Love*. Heseltine was one of the most important and spirited musical
figures of the twenties in London, an admirer of Delius. Under the
pseudonym of Philip Warlock, he left to posterity many song-settings generally considered to be among the finest ever produced in England.
Lawrence, however, seems to have taken very little account of Heseltine's
esteemed musical reputation, regarding him merely as "one of those people
who are transmitters, and not creators of art."[12] Lawrence, however, seems
to have been familiar enough with Heseltine's close connection with Delius,
for at one point he had cast his eye towards Florida, where an old estate
still belonging to Delius was to provide the setting — at least, initially — for
the utopic Rananim.

Another acquaintance of the Cornwall period was the music critic
Cecil Gray, who inadvertently "sat" for the portrait of the effete Cyril
Scott in *Aaron's Rod*. Ironically the musical evenings spent with Gray
proved to contribute to the growing suspicion of the local authorities of the
belligerent, subversive novelist and his militant *Frau* — a mistrust which led
eventually to the Lawrence's expulsion from Cornwall in October 1917.
Catherine Carswell's colorful account of the Cornwall incident confirms
Cecil Gray's[13] and might seem quite hilarious, if we were not aware of what
tragic implications the expulsion from Cornwall would later have for
Lawrence:

Frieda was not only German but loudly provocative and indiscreet. In the spring
Lawrence had committed the extravagance of buying for five guineas a worn cottage
piano "with an old red silk front and a nice old musty twang": and with its help he had
set himself to increase his already considerable repertoire of songs. Some of
these — especially as rendered in Frieda's loud, fresh voice — could not have been

mistaken for anything but German. Others must have sounded equally blood curdling to the curious or the hostile, who took to iying beneath the garden wall to listen. Through Cecil Gray, Lawrence had recently become acquainted with the researches of Mrs. Kennedy Fraser. And he had some Hebridean numbers which he howled in what he ingenuously supposed to be the Gaelic, at the same time endeavouring to imitate the noise made by a seal! [14]

Crushed by his Cornwall ordeal, mistrustful of all personal contacts, Lawrence found himself continually distracted, as I pointed out earlier, by the threat of poverty, police persecution, and above all, by "the foul tension of war." He naturally turned to such diversions as music as an attempt to alleviate the burden of suffering which he was experiencing, emotionally and artistically. In her memoirs, Cynthia Asquith suggests that in this dark period, "the one thing which seemed able temporarily to take Lawrence's mind off the war was going to the opera. . . ." [15] It was during his brief second stay in London that Lawrence became connected with the intellectual atmosphere of the Mecklenburgh Square, the semi-bohemian circle which consisted of such figures as Richard Aldington, Arabella York, Jack White, Cecil Gray and Brigit Patmore. All these friends were transformed by Lawrence's satiric pen into the rather superficial, pseudo-bohemian characters encountered by Aaron Sisson in the early chapters of *Aaron's Rod.* As noted earlier, it was during this brief stay in London that *Aaron's Rod* was begun. The vivid London early episodes of the novel could really only have been written while Lawrence was experiencing life in London. They register the effect upon Lawrence of his recent exposure to the musical scene (professional and otherwise) of wartime London as well as the frenetic activities of the young intellectuals and semi-bohemians. Together with those scenes involving Halliday in *Women in Love,* these episodes constitute a unique aspect of Lawrence's work, displaying a satiric tone and intention all their own. At the same time they suggest Lawrence's growing dissatisfaction with the London milieu, and his urban acquaintances' superficial attitude to the tragic reality of war.

Shortly after his move to Hermitage, Berkshire, Lawrence wrote this rather wistful letter to Cecil Gray:

> I'm not writing anything—only sit learning songs, which I find a great amusement. I can read well enough to learn a song nicely in about a quarter of an hour—so I have already got off twenty or thirty. I don't know why it amuses me so much more than reading or writing. So perhaps your opera will amuse you. [16]

This important letter reveals not only that Lawrence was depending more and more upon music during this period of restless inactivity when he felt his artistic energies flagging, but also that he had temporarily set aside work on *Aaron's Rod* so recently begun at Mecklenburgh Square. This letter to Gray also reveals that Lawrence was a quite proficient sight-reader of music and indicates the impressive knowledge of folksong and *Lieder* which he must have been accumulating at this time. As Brigit Patmore wryly observed, "They [Lawrence and Frieda] both had an enormous repertory of song and could find an appropriate one for almost any event."[17]

In these war months and the ensuing years of "savage pilgrimage," often far from the cultural or musical centers of the world, musical evenings around the piano became one of the few stable features of the Lawrences' existence. Such sing-songs invariably consisted of a strange medley of operatic arias, folk tunes and familiar *Lieder,* and have been vividly recalled by those who knew the Lawrences at various stages of their relentless wanderings. One typical recollection is the following, by Rosalind Thornycroft Popham, who was friendly with the Lawrences during their stay in Dollie Radford's cottage at Hermitage:

> In the summer of 1919. . .we picnicked in the woods together, and Lawrence and Frieda sang German Folk songs—*"Wo has du Die schönes Töchterlein?"*—in shrill, penetrating, unforgettable voices. Back in the house at the spinet by the French windows we sang Mozart arias from *Figaro.*[18]

Hilda Brown Cotteral (who occupied the other half of Chapel Farm cottage at the time the Lawrences were occupying the left side), the Brewsters, even Dorothy Brett—all have similar recollections of the importance of music and singing to Frieda and Lawrence in these years.[19] Frieda herself must have been a fairly proficient amateur pianist, whose musical knowledge, especially of German *Volkslieder,* was naturally considerable. Frieda seems to have been happiest when she had access to a piano and could thus entertain herself. In 1927 Lawrence reported:

> Frieda has a piano again, now she wants to play Handel, the "Messiah", but she hasn't arrived at the alleluia [sic]![20]

As late as November 1929 Lawrence writes that:

> Frieda is happy. She is now singing Schubert at the piano: but the gramophone—"Kiss your hand, Madame"—I only allow in the kitchen, with the doors shut. I do mortally hate it.[21]

It seems entirely typical of Lawrence's general hatred of the machine (as an encroachment upon all that is natural or healthy in human life) that he should banish the gramophone so decisively. One other musical experience worth noting in Lawrence's later years was his scoring of the original music for the production of *David* in 1926. In a letter written on 16 October 1926 to Robert Atkins, the London theatrical producer, Lawrence was quite specific in his musical requirements for the play:

> I enclose the music I have written out for *David.* It is very simple, needs only a pipe, tambourines, and a tom-tom drum. I hope it will do. . . . If one can only get that feeling of primitive religious passion across to a London audience. If not, it's no good.[22]

To conclude this brief introduction, it is obvious that though he knew a great deal about music, Lawrence's approach to music *per se* was rarely strictly "musical" in the sense that we might understand the term. His fondness and his preferences were instinctive and in his earlier Croydon years, his reactions quite emotional. As will be further demonstrated in the remainder of this chapter, Lawrence's responses to music, especially Grand Opera, became increasingly arbitrary and moralistic. It was for precisely this reason that music, particularly that of the opera and concert hall, could never be a satisfactory alternative to literary enterprise. Rather, music remained to the end for Lawrence a secondary diversion, which, however pleasant, or urgently required in times of unbearable stress, invariably yielded its place to the more important demands of literary creativity. In any case, as this brief introduction to Lawrence's early exposure to music hopes to have demonstrated, Lawrence's knowledge of music was far from scanty. The statements by biographers or gossips like Joseph Foster that "Lawrence had no appreciation of music"[23] may be utterly discarded.

At both a literal and symbolic level, *Aaron's Rod* is Lawrence's most "musical" novel. At every turn, it seems, we find characters engaged in musical activities, discussing specific composers, urging their preferences or airing their dislikes, often participating in amateur *musicales.* A few of these characters, those of the Bricknell set, actually attend a performance of *Aïda* at Covent Garden. A current of musical symbolism runs throughout *Aaron's Rod,* drawing the many disparate strands together and imposing its own distinctive unity upon the novel. This musical framework is associated thematically with Aaron's developing consciousness and provides the reader with a means of assessing, in musical terms, Aaron's central role as artist and protagonist. At times we are even permitted a glimpse of the world as it is perceived by Aaron-the-musician. However, Aaron's role as musician-hero must first be discussed, if we are to understand Lawrence's "musical" methods which contribute to the unique texture of *Aaron's Rod.*

The creation of Aaron Sisson does not, of course, represent

Lawrence's first attempt at a musician-hero who is required to function simultaneously in a realistic environment and a more private musical world. The first creation of such a complex artist-protagonist was the doom-ridden Siegmund of *The Trespasser,* Lawrence's second novel (1912). A brief comparison of Siegmund and Aaron Sisson suggests that Lawrence's powers of characterization were considerably more developed at the time he created Aaron Sisson. Whatever the shortcomings of *Aaron's Rod* might be when it is compared with the major fictions of Lawrence's highest achievement, it cannot be denied that the subtlety of Lawrence's characterization of the mysterious Aaron owes a great deal not simply to his experiments with an earlier musician-hero, Siegmund, but also to the richness and profundity of characterization in *The Rainbow* and *Women in Love.*

It would not be an oversimplification to state that whereas Lawrence fails in Siegmund to present the reader with a convincing musician-hero, he succeeds admirably in the creation of Aaron Sisson. In *Aaron's Rod,* the male protagonist as musician has moved more to the center of the novel, exulting in the mastery of his instrument and its miraculous sound. The recurrent music of the flute bears directly upon the rhythm and structure of the novel. In *The Trespasser,* however, Siegmund's violin, far from assuming the importance of a unifying symbol, remains outside the central narrative. In the first scene of the novel, the "Prologue," the violin merely recalls the dead musician and provides Lawrence with the means of a cleverly maneuvered flashback. Siegmund's violin is relegated to a position of secondary importance, its music overpowered, like its owner, by the obsessive Wagnerism of Helena. Significantly, there is no mention of Siegmund's taking his violin along on his vacation with Helena, much less of his violin music operating in a salutary or regenerative manner upon the relationship of the lovers. Perhaps part of the problem with Siegmund is that he is in a sense *too* articulate—that he is able to express himself without his violin.

The operatic milieu of Covent Garden in *The Trespasser* and the contrasting shabbiness of Siegmund's home life anticipate remarkably similar settings in *Aaron's Rod.* Yet the increased powers of Lawrence's later creation are seen vividly in Aaron's ability to transcend through his art his domestic surroundings, and the repressions which they embody. Siegmund is trapped and destroyed by the stifling pettiness of his bourgeois surroundings. Aaron escapes this deadly atmosphere and is presumably free to grow artistically and spiritually, enjoying the newly discovered power which his music exerts upon his listeners, particularly the upper classes of society. The chief reason for the failure of Siegmund to emerge as a strong musician-hero may be traced to Lawrence's inadvertent failure to present us with Siegmund's awareness of himself *as a musician.* Nor is Siegmund ever aware that, as a musician, he has the power to shape for himself a separate sphere of artistic existence, one divorced from both Helena's neurosis, or Beatrice's scolding. Dominated to the very end by Helena's often hysterical Wagnerian fantasies, in which, ironically, "passion exhausts itself at the mouth," Siegmund remains sexually and artistically unfulfilled. His suicide removes him from the equally destructive influences of Beatrice and Helena, but fails to mitigate the moral and artistic debasement which his return home effects:

> The body of life for him meant Beatrice, Helena, the Comic Opera, his friends of the orchestra. How could he set himself again into joint with these? It was impossible. Towards his family he would henceforward have to bear himself with humility. That was a cynicism. He would have to leave Helena, which he could not do. He would have to play strenuously, night after night, the music of *The Saucy Little Switzer,* which was absurd. In fine, it was all absurd and impossible.[24]

His one act of self-determination comes pitifully late.

Aaron, who is more aloof and enigmatic than weak, tastes physical passion and, denying providence or fate, consistently acts upon the strength of his own decisions. I am aware that it may be argued with some success that Aaron fails at love, but would contend that, unlike Siegmund, he is not destroyed by it. Within the musical symbolism of the novel, he is a fully developed figure in the exercise of his musical powers and the sexual energies which they convey. The shattering of his flute is by no means a surrender of his artistic powers, but a turning point in his life. In another context, his "rod" is supposed to blossom again, under the mentorship of Lilly.

In the early stages of *Aaron's Rod,* Lawrence carefully establishes Aaron's musical nature and suggests the very special part which music plays in his daily life. The early descriptions of Aaron's rapt flute-playing are quite explicit:

> He tried his flute. And then at last, with the odd gesture of a diver taking a plunge, he swung his head and began to play. A stream of music, soft and rich and fluid, came out of the flute. He played beautifully. He moved his head and raised his bare arms with slight, intense movements, as the delicate music poured out. It was sixteenth century Christmas melody, very limpid and delicate.
>
> The pure, mindless, exquisite motion and fluidity of the music delighted him with a strange exasperation. There was something tense, exasperated to the point of intolerable anger, in his good-humoured breast, as he played the finely-spun peace-music. The more exquisite the music, the more perfectly he produced it, in sheer bliss; and at the same time, the more intense was the maddened exasperation within him. (16)

Note that Aaron's "rich and fluid" playing follows closely upon the dissonance of the half-hearted carollers, the music providing a sharp contrast to the sordidness, the "unspeakable familiarity" of Aaron's home which he must soon reject. The simple harmony and control in Aaron's skilled playing of an exquisite sixteenth-century carol suggests an order and a radiance which are noticeably lacking in Aaron's domestic and communal surroundings. Significantly, Millicent, the most aggressive (and thoroughly unlikeable) of Aaron's three daughters, resents her father's playing. "The music was a bug-bear to her, because it prevented her from saying what was on her own mind" (16). Aaron picks up his piccolo in reply to Millicent's insistent pleas for Christmas candles, and begins again:

> Then suddenly the piccolo broke forth, wild, shrill, brilliant. He was playing Mozart. The child's face went pale with anger at the sound. She turned, and went out, closing both doors behind her to shut out the noise.
>
> The shrill, rapid movement of the piccolo music seemed to possess the air, it was useless to try to shut it out. The man went on playing to himself, measured and insistent. In the frosty evening the sound carried. People passing down the street hesitated, listening. The neighbours knew it was Aaron practising his piccolo. He was esteemed a good player: was in request at concerts and dances, also at swell balls. So the vivid piping sound tickled the darkness. (17)

The child's adverse reaction to the delicate music of her father suggests that she is somehow emotionally blighted, even at an early age; at least, quite insensitive to the art which makes her father unique. Millicent's badgering of her father here is used by Lawrence as a parallel to Lottie's habitual nagging, her bitter resentment as Aaron leaves her for the comforts of the pub on Christmas Eve. Lawrence is also suggesting through music that the aggressive child will closely resemble her mother in maturity, thus perpetuating a line of wilful women who deprive the male of his essential manhood.

I have dealt in some detail with this "miniature drama," because I think it is important in establishing the musical proficiency of Aaron at home, at the same time preparing for Aaron's seemingly effortless transition to the professional music-circles of London. Aaron is revealed in this episode as feeling uncomfortable and restless in mining village surroundings. We notice the sense of alienation which haunts him in the following scene at the "Royal Oak," indeed, throughout the novel. Lawrence's method of characterizing persons by their attitude towards certain kinds of music is here evidenced for the first time and will hereafter be employed in the various portraits of musical *cognoscenti,* encountered at various stages of Aaron's travels.

A careful reading of the novel reveals that Lawrence has taken considerable pains to establish the sensitivity of Aaron's musical ear, as it reacts to external stimuli. Lawrence suggests that as those of an artist's, Aaron's sensory responses will be more profound and instinctual, perhaps therefore, more inexpressible than those of ordinary characters. This particular sensitivity on Aaron's part is clearly demonstrated in the first chapter as the hiss of the fir boughs; the "little splashing explosion" of the treasured blue ball; the hum of the boiler; the "dissonant voices of boys pouring out the dregs of carol-singing"—all register themselves on Aaron's auditory awareness. In the fourth chapter of the novel Aaron returns home for the first time and stands outside listening to the "trickle of the rain in the water-butt" (48). Aaron's musical ear is particularly stressed in the scene. The acuteness of sound provides a notable contrast to the "windy darkness" of the nocturnal landscape:

> A motor-car was labouring up the hill. His trained ear attended to it unconsciously. It stopped with a jar. There was a bang of the yard-gate.... He stood by the climbing rose of the porch, listening. He heard voices upstairs. Perhaps the children would be downstairs. He listened intently. Voices were upstairs only.... So Aaron quietly entered on the parlour. He could hear footsteps passing outside on the asphalt pavement below the window, and the wind howling with familiar cadence. (48-49)

Much later in the novel, when leaving behind Novara and the home of Sir William Franks, Aaron notes the hum of the "soft-running automobile" as it makes its way to the train station (210). Soon after, in Milan, the strange "flag incident" is presented, specifically from Aaron's point of view. The shock and horror of the episode are presented in terms of Aaron's acute awareness of the sounds of civil strife: the noise of voices "like a jarring of steel weapons"; the murmur of the crowd rising "ragged and ironical"; the "tremendous long yell, touched with a snarl of triumph" as the boy tears the flag down; finally the "startling challenge" of the Carabinieri trumpets," and so on (215-18). Afterwards, Lawrence draws our attention once again to the sensitivity of Aaron's "fine sharp ears," as he overhears Francis and Angus discussing his appearance (221). After he has arrived in Florence, Aaron responds with obvious relish to the early morning sounds of the bustling community:

> And through the open window was the sound of the river's rushing. But the traffic started before dawn, with a bang and a rattle of carts, and a bang and jingle of tramcars over the not-distant bridge. Oh, noisy Florence! (247)

When he first meets the Marchesa at Algy's flat, Aaron seems attracted to her "slow contralto" manner of speech (259), and later is aware of her "sing-song lapsing voice" which sounds "almost like one in a trance" (265). The strained attempts of the Marchesa to regain her singing voice are vividly conveyed to the reader through Aaron's auditory awareness: "She had a beautiful, strong, sweet voice but it was faltering, stumbling, and sometimes it seemed to drop almost to speech. After three verses she faltered to an end, bitterly chagrined" (298). Aaron plays the tune, "Derrière Chez Mon Père" for her and attempts "to catch the lilt and timbre of her voice" (299).

In the penultimate chapter of the novel, Aaron sits in a café in Florence and the sudden terrifying explosion of an anarchist's bomb is conveyed directly in an agony of sound:

> CRASH!
> There intervened one awful minute of pure shock, when the soul was in darkness.
> Out of this shock Aaron felt himself issuing amid a mass of terrible sensations: the fearful blow of the explosion, the noise of glass, the hoarse howl of people, the rushing of men, the sudden gulf, the awful gulfing whirlpool of horror in the social life. (329)

Throughout the novel we are aware of Lawrence's attempts to translate the ordinary world into a series of vivid musical images. These images create for the reader an illusion of seeing the phenomenal world *directly* through Aaron's eyes. In its simplest form, the musician's point of view is presented by means of an ingenious comparison in which, as in the conceits of the metaphysical poets, "the most heterogeneous elements are by violence yoked together" to suggest the uniqueness of the musician's response to his surroundings. An early example of this is Aaron's musical interpretation of the Jewish landlady's unusual features:

> He glanced at her profile—that fine throwback of her hostile head, wicked in the midst of her benevolence; that subtle, really very beautiful delicate curve of her nose, that moved him exactly like a piece of pure sound. (26-27)

A few days after Christmas, Aaron returning home stands at the bottom of his garden and envisions like a keyboard the familiar panorama of "back premises":

> So he saw a curious succession of lighted windows, between which jutted the intermediary back premises, scullery and outhouse, in dark little blocks. It was something like the keyboard of a piano; more still like a succession of musical notes.... So the long scale of lights seemed to trill across the darkness, now bright, now dim, swelling and sinking, the effect was strange. (46)

In Chapter 10, "The War Again," Lilly and Aaron compare the strange compulsion, with men and women, to take new lovers. In an image perhaps more startling than felicitous, women are spoken of as sexual musicians: "A woman is like a violinist: any fiddle, any instrument rather than empty hands and no tune going" (125).

A further refinement of this musical technique is Lawrence's attempt to express the inexpressible through metaphors of music. In the extensive *"dialogue intérieur"* of Chapter 13, the reader is permitted to follow Aaron's complicated thought processes as he struggles towards a greater degree of self-realization. Yet Aaron's nature has so far been clearly established as a singularly taciturn and incommunicative one. Lawrence obviously feels that he is required to justify this sudden articulation. In what must be considered one of the most audacious "sleight of hand" manipulations in the history of the English novel, the narrator slyly informs us that he has merely assumed a role as translator of the *musical thoughts* of Aaron Sisson. Though usually silent or withdrawn in social company, Aaron is profoundly eloquent at this subconscious level of musicalized ratiocination. I shall discuss such an intrusion in a later chapter of this study. As far as a study of the nature and function of the music of *Aaron's Rod* goes, this incident provides us with a perfect example of Lawrence's attempts at a musicalization of normal experience. The novelist creates for the reader the sensation of entering the musician's mind. It is no accident that Aaron should conceive of Lilly's earnest polemic later in Chapter 21 as "speech music." Just as music has brought Aaron to one decisive turning point of his life, the understanding and renunciation of his tormented relationship with Lottie, so again in this final scene music operates at the subconscious level of Aaron's deepest instincts. The strange speech-music seems to be drawing him closer to Lilly, the prophet, though perhaps not quite to a submission of his soul to Lilly's enigmatic power.

Such symbolic scenes as those above are constantly juxtaposed throughout the novel with other scenes which satirize the abuses of music in the hands of socialites and dilettantes. Such debased forms of music as the dissonant carolling or the tawdry *Aïda* at Covent Garden gradually give place to the truer, regenerative forms of music expressed chiefly by Aaron's flute. In order to understand fully this life-restoring function achieved by music at its highest form, it is necessary to examine first several contrasting examples of a lesser, often false, musical expression.

During his extensive wandering Aaron is lionized by society hostesses, pseudo-bohemians, dilettantes, and other music amateurs. The decidedly second-rate performance of Verdi's *Aïda* at Covent Garden is the first extended scene of the novel in which a kind of false music is revealed. Significantly, Jim Bricknell's set of pseudo-bohemians attend this performance (Lilly and Tanny are present also) and seem particularly taken in by the sham splendour of the occasion. Only the artistic Josephine objects strenuously[25] to the falsity of the operatic situation:

> The sham Egypt of *Aida* hid from her nothing of its shame. The singers were all colour-washed, deliberately colour-washed to a bright orange tint. The men had oblong

dabs of black wool under their lower lip; the beard of the mighty Pharaohs. This oblong dab shook and wagged to the singing.

The vulgar bodies of the fleshy women were unendurable. They all looked such good meat. Why were their haunches so prominent? It was a question Josephine could not solve. She scanned their really expensive, brilliant clothing. It was nearly right — nearly splendid. It only lacked that last subtlety which the world always lacks, the last final clinching which puts calm into a sea of fabric, and yet is the opposite pole to machine fixity.

But the leading tenor was the chief pain. He was large, stout, swathed in a cummerbund, and looked like a eunuch. This fattish, emasculated look seems common in stage heroes — even the extremely popular. The tenor sang bravely, his mouth made a large, coffin-shaped, yawning gap in his orange face, his little beard fluttered oddly, like a tail. He turned up his eyes to Josephine's box as he sang — that being the regulation direction. Meanwhile his abdomen shook as he caught his breath, the flesh of his fat naked arms swayed. (55–56)

This effect of triviality and falsehood is not dispelled by the continuous chit-chat of the spectators in Josephine's opera box. Julia's idle speculation upon the possibility of a love affair with Cyril Scott is a grim parody of the lofty love interest and intrigue of *Aïda*. The incessant stage-whispering of Struthers, the artist, and the petulance of Jim Bricknell, demanding to be loved, continue throughout as an ironic counterpoint to the performance on-stage.

The opera incident is of course the fictionalization of an actual performance of *Aïda* which Lawrence and Frieda must have attended in early 1918. Lawrence's harsh opinion of the performance, transmitted in the novel through the scornful eyes of Josephine, indicates that at this point of his life his musical tastes had changed significantly, enough to reject the emotional experiences of Grand Opera which he had previously welcomed. Augustus John's version of the opera incident suggests Lawrence's growing dissatisfaction with the conventions of Grand Opera:

> ...Lady Cynthia treated us to a box at the Opera that evening.... On leaving what Sir Edwin Lutyens used to call the "uproar," D. H. L. announced that he would like to howl like a dog.[26]

However, none of this quite explains Lawrence's curious reaction to the performance of *Aïda* in 1918, or to Grand Opera in general. I have previously mentioned that Lawrence's earlier reactions to music during the Croydon years, especially to opera were chiefly emotional, and usually based upon vivid first-impressions. His enthusiasms were genuine, though; the variety of his operatic expriences impressive. The letters to Louie Burrows are a valuable key to Lawrence's developing attitude toward many of the operas he was hearing with Helen Corke during these crucial years.

On 1 April 1911 he writes rather impetuously of a colorful Italian production of *Cavalleria Rusticana* and *Pagliacci*:

> I went to Cavalleria Rusticana & Pagliacci at Croydon last night — one shilling in the
> pit. It's an Italian company from Drury Lane — Italians of the common class — opera in
> Italian. But I loved the little folk. You never saw anything in your life more natural,
> naive, inartistic, & refreshing. It was just like our old charades.
>
> I love Italian opera — it's so reckless. Damn Wagner, & his bellowings at Fate & death.
> Damn Debussy, and his averted face. I like the Italians who run all on impulse, & don't
> care about their immortal souls, & don't worry about the ultimate. . . .
>
> But if you were here tonight we'd go to Carmen, & hear those delicious little Italians
> love & weep. I am just as emotional & impulsive as they, by nature.[27]

This letter illustrates perfectly Lawrence's typically emotional response to
Grand Opera and the beginnings of a reaction against any art form (such
as Wagnerian music-drama) which presumed to take itself too seriously.

Lawrence's exposure to Italian opera was evidently considerable, his
early reactions enthusiastic. Why then his later disenchantment? Although
it must be conceded that any answer might be considered hypothetical, I
would speculate that Lawrence's increased despair during the period
following the expulsion from Cornwall had somehow carried over to his
musical experiences in London. Although Cecil Gray could dismiss the
persecutions of the local authorities as the comic gestures of a Verdi
opera,[28] Lawrence obviously could not. The profound contempt which he
felt during this period for what he considered the hypocrisy of personal
relationships, indeed his bitter condemnation of all idealistic faith in love,
humanity, and brotherhood — which the interminable war seemed horribly
to refute — Lawrence had somehow extended to his experience of music at
this time. An opera like *Aïda,* which to Lawrence dealt in sentimental and
melodramatic terms with the interrelated themes of love and war, could
only rouse his angry protest. Yet Lawrence's curious ambivalence toward
Grand Opera and its social milieu shows plainly in the way in which he
seems split in his presentation of the opera scene between the outrage of
Josephine Ford and the amused detachment of Lilly whose *sang froid* is
very close to the satiric tone of the narrator himself waggishly observing
the operagoers' foibles.

It is interesting that after the performance, when the pseudo-
bohemians return to Jim's rooms in Adelphi, Robert Cunningham plays
Bach on the piano: "They needed the Bach to take away the bad taste that
Aïda had left in their mouths" (67). The use of Bach here as a "musical
mouthwash" seems frivolous and quite typical of the Bricknell set.[29]

From all this it is evident that somehow Lawrence's initial emotional
enthusiasm for opera (cultivated during the Croydon years) had cooled a

great deal, probably as a result of the hardship of war and the human treachery which he felt he had lately discovered. He had also become impatient with the conventions of opera and the patent artifice of operatic productions. Perhaps with his admiration of the spontaneous and his profound seriousness in matters of love or sex in this mature period of his life Lawrence could no longer respond to the world of opera with other than very mixed feelings indeed. Cynthia Asquith's guess that "the only thing which seemed able temporarily to take Lawrence's mind off the war was opera" requires serious qualification as does Catherine Carswell's misleading conjecture that "opera, with its light formality and transparent artifice, was probably most to his taste."[30] No, during the years of the Great War and its aftermath, opera could never again be a simple or frivolous diversion for Lawrence. Yet, it is entirely typical of both his ambivalence and his transcendent genius that, while outraged like Josephine at the shoddy presentations of a poor production, Lawrence could also turn his ire to more satiric purposes as in the passages of brilliant social comedy cited above. He could even take pleasure in dressing Frieda up for the opera even though he lampooned the pretensions of the idle rich at Covent Garden. And yet at the same time, perhaps with more than a hint of inverse snobbery, Lawrence found it necessary to attack the folly of those privileged classes who were part of the older order, being destroyed, ironically by the same terrible war to which it had committed the nations of Europe.

Aaron's involvement with the opera world indicates to a certain extent his lack of purpose or self-awareness at this point in the novel, another example of the directionless nature of his new-found freedom. It is only later in Chapter 10 that he finally conceives a dislike for "regular work in the orchestra" of Covent Garden and resolves to disappear again, returning to the Midlands. Before Aaron arrives at the point at which he may reject entirely the falsity of his connection with the opera world and its frivolous patrons, his growing self-awareness must be tested by further encounters with the musical dilettantes of London society.

Feeling himself somewhat "at loose ends" at the conclusion of the opera season, Aaron is persuaded to join Cyril Scott (himself somewhat of a musician) and his wealthy friends "in a village by the sea":

> He accepted, and spent a pleasant month. It pleased the young men musically-inclined and bohemian by profession to patronise the flautist, whom they declared marvellous. Bohemians with well-to-do parents, they could already afford to squander a little spasmodic and self-gratifying patronage. And Aaron did not mind being patronised. He had nothing else to do. (143)

However, Aaron soon after recoils from the patronage of "indifferent young men younger than himself." The falseness of his position in the orchestra of Covent Garden brings about a "distaste for regular work in the orchestra" (143).

Another such circle is that of Lady Artemis Hooper, the famous hostess for whom Aaron plays, as she reclines in bed "after her famous escapade of falling through the window of her taxicab." Aaron is initially attracted to this rather eccentric socialite, like himself, a "modern, social freebooter." His fascination blinds him momentarily to the essential falsity of the dilettante's world. Lady Hooper's flirtatious, deliberately risqué banter is perfectly rendered by Lawrence:

> "Do you love playing?" she asked him. . . .
> "I don't think about it," he said.
> "I'm sure you don't. You wouldn't be so good if you did. You're awfully lucky, you know, to be able to pour yourself down your flute."
> "You think I go down easy?" he laughed. . . .
> "Do you find it a tight squeeze, then?" she said, turning to Aaron once more.
> "No, I can't say that," he answered. "What of me goes down goes down easy enough. It's what doesn't go down."
> "And how much is that?" she asked, eying him.
> "A good bit, maybe," he said.
> "Slops over, so to speak," she retorted sarcastically, "And which do you enjoy more, trickling down your flute or slopping over on to the lap of Mother Earth — of Miss, more probably!"
> "Depends," he said. (151–52)

Notice once again Aaron's reluctance to discuss or verbalize an art which is for him instinctive and inexpressible. As boring or as silly as such conversation, with its forced *double entendres,* might seem at a first reading, it becomes apparent that Lawrence is suggesting the very tedium of the socialite's milieu. The exchange harks back to the dreadfully boring pseudo-bohemians of the Bricknell set, engaged in their self-indulgent small-talk of love and revolution. At the same time Aaron's rather contemptuous exchange with Lady Artemis prepares us for similar skirmishes later in the same chapter with Lady Franks.

Aaron's brief stay at the home of Sir William Franks in Novara introduces Aaron to a fourth false, fashionable circle presided over, in this case, by a formidable *grande dame,* Lady Franks. Aaron's encounter with Lady Franks and her music is crucial to an understanding of the methods Lawrence has used to establish an antithesis throughout the novel of false and genuine forms of music. It is not simply that Lady Franks' professed love of music is a deliberate falsehood, or that she is even as much a trifler as Artemis Hooper or Francis Dekker. Her love is sincere in its own way. But Lady Franks is subtly condemned in her admiration for certain *false* kinds of musical composition, especially as her tastes directly oppose those of Aaron, and, as revealed later, those of the Marchesa. A detailed examination of this episode is in order.

Soon after his arrival at the Franks' estate Aaron becomes involved in a discussion of the previous opera season at Covent Garden:

> "And I hear you were playing in the orchestra at Covent Garden. We came back from London last week. I enjoyed Beecham's operas so much."
> "Which do you like best?" said Aaron.
> "Oh, the Russian I think, *Ivan*. It is such fine music."
> "I find *Ivan* artificial."
> "Do you? Oh, I don't think so. No, I don't think you can say that."
> Aaron wondered at her assurance. She seemed to put him just a tiny bit in his place, even in an opinion on music. Money gave her that right too. (159)

It seems typical that Lady Franks should be attracted to an opera which seems to Aaron quite artificial. The lines of battle have clearly been drawn. Aaron's ensuing wish for a return to "melody pure and simple" arouses a response in Lady Franks which defines perfectly for the reader her opposition to the more serious music of Aaron and his flute.

> "...but you can't mean that you would like all music to go back to melody pure and simple! Just a flute—just a pipe! Oh, Mr. Sisson, you are bigoted for your instrument. I just live in harmony—chords, chords!" She struck imaginary chords on the white damask, and her sapphires swam blue! (160)

Yet, within the symbolic framework of the novel, Lady Franks is a far more serious figure than the satiric tenor of such scenes above might seem to suggest. In the "very capable" hands of Lady Franks, music becomes symbolically connected with the destructive feminine will. In order to accomplish the fulfillment of her domestic and social purposes Lady Franks willfully contrives and manipulates people and circumstances. In still another debate with Aaron over the essential effects of music, Lady Franks professes her reverence for Bach and Beethoven and links the "great masters" to her unshakable faith in succeeding in all her undertakings:

> "...But I like big, deep music.... Oh, I love orchestra. But my instrument is the piano. I like the great masters, Bach, Beethoven. They have such faith. You were talking of faith—believing that things would work out well for you in the end. Beethoven inspires that in me, too."
> "He makes you feel that all will be well with you at last?"
> "Yes, he does. He makes me feel faith in my personal destiny. And I do feel that there is something in one's special fate. I feel that I myself have a special kind of fate, that will always look after me." (197)

The *reductio ad absurdum* is of course the association (a few lines later) by Lady Franks of Beethoven's music and the recovery of her misplaced fur stole! Lady Franks' will is later expressed through her own piano playing, as she summons Aaron and her dinner guests to the drawing room in order to avoid any excitement which might endanger Sir William's health. Aaron connects her willful music with his own childhood version of the popular hymn, "His Eye is on the Sparrow":

> His eye is on the spy-hole
> So I know he watches me.

> Which was just how it had all seemed to him, as a boy.
> Now, as ever, he felt the eye was on the spy-hole. There sat the woman playing music. But her inward eye was on the spy-hole of her vital affairs — her domestic arrangements, her control of her household, guests and husband included. The other eye was left for music, don't you know. (206)

It is not difficult to see the thematic connection in this chapter between Lady Franks and Lottie Sisson. Both women are presented as domestic tyrants presiding over their own petty matriarchy, each possessed of a "terrible, implacable, cunning" will which symbolically castrates the male. In order to preserve what Lilly speaks of as his "separate selfhood" Aaron must recoil from such deadly power in both women.

Two other "music lovers" in the novel are Francis Dekker and Angus Guest, who patronize Aaron in Milan and travel with him to Florence. These two are, indeed, much less sincere in their love of music than Lady Franks. The *fin de siècle* posturing, the self-conscious aestheticism of Francis immediately establish him as a typical figure of the post-war period. F. R. Leavis has noted perceptively that Francis is the "perfectly observed type of the artistic-intellectual nineteen-twenties in whom we recognize the Rico of *St. Mawr*."[31] The effeminate Francis and his strange companion respond in an implicitly homosexual manner to Aaron's blond attractiveness, of which his flute playing is merely an emblem. Lawrence's presentation of Francis's first approach to Aaron catches perfectly the superficial nature of Francis's musical interests, suggesting a thematic connection with other "dabblers" encountered earlier in the novel, for example, Cyril Scott's set of idle young men. Francis's conversational starting point is the disturbing "flag incident" witnessed by Aaron earlier. Francis is quite carried away by the excitement of the episode:

> "—But wasn't it perfectly marvellous! Oh, incredible, quite incredible! — And then your flute to finish it all! Oh! I felt it only wanted that. — I haven't got over it yet. But your playing was *marvellous,* really marvellous. Do you know, I can't forget it. You are a professional musician, of course."

"If you mean I play for a living," said Aaron. "I have played in orchestras in London."

"Of course! Of course! I knew you must be a professional. But don't you give private recitals, too?"

"No, I never have."

"Oh!" cried Francis, catching his breath. "I just can't believe it. But you play *marvellously!* Oh, I just loved it, it simply swept me away, after that scene in the street. It seemed to sum it all up, you know."

"Did it," said Aaron, rather grimly. (224–25)

To perceive the irony of Francis's remarks we have only to recall that for Aaron the playing of his flute was a deliberate escape from the alarming violence of the flag incident. Aaron may well grimace at Francis's programmatic interpretation of his flute playing, for the young aesthete has missed the point entirely. Once again, Lawrence has used a wrong-headed attitude to music to characterize insensitivity or inner weakness.

The close connection between Francis's superficial interest in music and his ruthless utilitarian approach to human relationships is made clear in another startling passage where he advises Aaron to take advantage of his supposed friends, the Florentine *cognoscenti*. Aaron's grudging acquiescence in this scheme is curious, for it suggests, once again, that Aaron is at this point unable to discern between true and false relationships. The reader and the narrator are both aware of the irony of Aaron's self-deception. Lawrence is suggesting that Aaron's quest for a social and personal awareness is very much a part of his search for musical self-expression in "melody pure and simple."

The sixth and final musical circle to which Aaron is introduced is that of the Marchese del Torre and his Saturday morning *musicales.* It is necessary to stress once again that here Lawrence is by no means asking the reader to condemn the Marchese and his acquaintances for musical insincerity. Yet, within the symbolic framework of the novel, Manfredi's music with its chords and polyphonic texture is explicitly opposed to the simpler music favored by Aaron and the Marchesa. The judgment levelled upon Manfredi and his music is complicated by the intense subjectivity of the Marchesa's point of view, her own perculiar neurosis at the time she meets Aaron Sisson. Since Manfredi's unconscious opposition to Aaron's music forms part of a discussion of the special music shared by Aaron and the Marchesa, I shall return to Manfredi's musical efforts later in this chapter.

I should like to discuss now some examples of a more positive, more symbolically powerful kind of musical expression in *Aaron's Rod.* This more vital type of music is naturally connected with the "melody pure and simple" of Aaron's flute. Before discussing the very important function which the flute performs in rejuvenating the Marchesa and confirming her sexual attraction to Aaron, I should like to review briefly the symbolic role which the more positive music of Aaron's flute has so far assumed in the novel.

In the early scenes of *Aaron's Rod,* as I mentioned earlier, the music of the flute provides an escape for Aaron from the sordid and unromantic triviality of his domestic life. The strains of Mozart restore a sense of order and serenity noticeably lacking in the conflicts of Aaron's home life and post-war environment. Similarly, after the flag incident, the music of the flute provides a relief from the ugly prospect of civil strife, as Aaron's soul once again "passes into his flute" (220). The regenerative powers of the flute are demonstrated even more explicitly in Chapter 10 where Aaron's recovery from a near fatal attack of influenza seems assured by his renewed urge to practice the flute. In a more symbolic sense, the music of the flute in this important scene marks a psychological turning point for Aaron, a recovery from the mental depression following his sexual encounter with Josephine Ford. As mentioned earlier, Lilly draws the reader's attention to the biblical imagery of the scene in which the miraculous budding of Aaron's staff signifies his pre-eminence as High Priest. In a musical sense the "budding"[32] of the flute signals a revitalization of the art which distinguishes Aaron Sisson. Aaron somehow recovers the independence and sense of self which he has previously lost in his brief but blighted affair with Josephine. The rejuvenation which Aaron experiences here is also a subtle forecast of the part his music will play later in the recovery of the Marchesa's own sexual power. Ironically Aaron's miraculous music here appears to initiate a wilful and sexually destructive relationship between himself and the Marchesa. A detailed examination of the symbolic values of music in this crucial episode will make this more clear.

The earliest suggestion that Aaron's flute might possibly promote a recovery of the Marchesa's voice comes from the owlish Algy Constable. At an afternoon tea party in his flat, Algy requests a song from the Marchesa, but is informed that "the bird has flown" (259). He turns to Aaron: "Perhaps, Mr. Sisson, your flute might call out the bird of song. As thrushes call each other into challenge, you know. Don't you think that is very probable?" (260). Later at the del Torre home the Marchesa expresses to Aaron her violent reactions to polyphonic music:

> "What I can't stand is chords, you know: harmonies. A number of sounds all sounding together. It just makes me ill. It makes me feel so sick."
>
> "What—do you want discords?—dissonances?"
>
> "No—they are nearly as bad. No, it's just when any number of musical notes, different notes, come together, harmonies or discords. Even a single chord struck on the piano. It makes me feel sick, I just feel as if I should retch. Isn't it strange?" (264)

Aaron himself concurs in the Marchesa's opinion:

> No—I was just wondering—I believe I feel something the same myself. I know orchestra makes me blind with hate or I don't know what. But I want to throw bombs. (264)

The Marchesa is quite explicit about the kind of music which unites her and Aaron:

> "But perhaps the flute is different. I have a feeling that it is. I can think of one single pipe-note—yes, I can think of it quite, quite calmly. And I can't even think of a piano, or of the violin with its tremolo, or of orchestra, or of a string quartette—or even a military band—I can't think of it without a shudder. I can only bear drum-and-fife. Isn't it crazy of me—but from the order, from what we call music proper, I've endured too much. But bring your flute one day. Bring it, will you? And let me hear it quite alone."
> ..."I've got it now in my overcoat pocket," he said, "if you like." (265)

Aaron's offer reveals that he has previously lied, that he actually did have his instrument with him at Algy's flat, but had refused to play.[33]

The bird imagery of the passage in which Aaron first plays for the Marchesa recalls the earlier reference to her voice as a bird that has "flown" and further suggests that the recovery of her voice will have explicit sexual overtones:

> And there, in the darkness of the big room, he put his flute to his lips, and began to play. It was a clear, sharp, lilted run-and-fall of notes, not a tune in any sense of the word, and yet a melody, a bright, quick sound of pure animation, a bright, quick animate noise, running and pausing. It was like a bird's singing, in that it had no human emotion or passion or intention or meaning—a ripple and poise of animate sound. But it was unlike a bird's singing, in that the notes followed clear and single one after the other, in their subtle gallop. A nightingale is rather like that—a wild sound. (266-67)

Yet in spite of the overtly sexual nature of this episode, with what taste and delicacy has Lawrence evoked the dual symbolism of the purest music and male potency! During the next visit of Aaron the insistent sounding of the flute, a symbolic call upon the Marchesa's femininity, prompts the rebirth of her voice. In "the lovely ease and lift of her own soul in its motion through the music" her voice soars like a bird or butterfly. The Marchesa exults in her newly rediscovered vocal powers "as if in a dream." The climax of the bird imagery in this episode is the elaborate simile in which the Marchesa is compared to a swan:

> And as in a dream the woman sat, feeling what a joy it was to float and move like a swan in the high air, flying upon the wings of her own spirit. She was as a swan which never before could get its wings quite open, and so which never could get up into the open, where alone it can sing. (300)

Later, Aaron returns to his room after the symbolic reawakening of the Marchesa and here reveals his awareness of the deeper sexual significance of the episode, addressing his flute as (the biblical) Aaron's blossoming rod. In some miraculous way Aaron too imagines himself to be sexually restored by the regenerative music of his flute. The male potency reasserts itself in images of thunder, lightning, and the power of the royal eagle.

A contrasting musical experience is Manfredi's Saturday morning musicale in Chapter 19. As suggested earlier, the emotional failures of her marriage to Manfredi are clearly reflected in the hatred and nausea which the Marchesa experiences at her husband's preferred type of music. Within a musical context, Manfredi is condemned for his love of chamber music and thick harmony. However we may wish to protest at such an arbitrary condemnation on Aaron's and the Marchesa's part, we must nevertheless accept it as consistent with the symbolic musical framework of the novel and accept this judgement as one of the premises of the attraction which the Marchesa feels for Aaron. Aaron's "bit of mediaeval phrasing written for the pipe and the viol" in its simplicity, apparently, has sounded the depths of the Marchesa's soul and makes "the piano seem a ponderous, nerve-wracking steam-roller of noise, and the violin, as we know it, a hateful, wire-drawn nerve-torturer" (267).

The criticism of Manfredi's music as antipathetic or harmful to the music of Aaron's flute is unmistakable here, and the reader is carried back to Aaron's earlier dispute with Lady Franks over the virtues of "melody pure and simple." Manfredi is further condemned in his unconscious opposition to the music of the Marchesa and Aaron when he proposes that Aaron "come to play one Saturday morning," adding, "with an accompaniment, you know. I should like so much to hear you with piano accompaniment" (297). Both Aaron and the Marchesa have avowed their hatred of accompaniments of any sort. It is perhaps significant that Lilly bolts from what he suspects to be the essential falsity of the Saturday morning music. One recalls that Lilly was not taken in by the sham *Aïda* at Covent Garden. Perhaps Lawrence is suggesting that Lilly's "speech music" transcends the superficial social element in which, to all appearances, and to Aaron's dismay, Nan del Torre is thriving. But why, one may still ask, does the love relationship of Aaron and the Marchesa fail? Why must their affair be considered deadly if it has been conceived in the life-restoring music of Aaron's miraculous flute?

The solution is not easily discovered within the *musical* symbolism of the novel. An answer might be easily posited at another level by glancing at Aaron's later reflections upon the destructive nature of the Marchesa's attraction to him. We might speak of destructive Lawrencean females, deadly wills, modern Cleopatras, and so on, much as the narrator does in

Chapter 9. But this probing still provides no easy answer to the question of destruction within a musical context. I would suggest that what Lawrence has attempted in his novel is a return to an earlier musical technique first learned and employed in his second novel, *The Trespasser,* that of *literary Wagnerism.* Before estimating Lawrence's special use of Wagnerian techniques to suggest the destructiveness of Aaron's affair, I should like to present a summary of Lawrence's acquaintance with the music of Wagner and his characteristic attitude to Wagner's music dramas.

Lawrence's familiarity with Wagnerian opera may be traced primarily to his friendship with Helen Corke, the Helena of *The Trespasser.* On 15 December 1908, Lawrence wrote a spirited letter to Blanche Jennings which reveals an early knowledge and interest in Wagnerian opera:

> As for a book on music—the way to learn about music is to listen to it and think about it afterwards... Surely you know Wagner's operas — *Tannhäuser* and *Lohengrin.* They will run a knowledge of music into your blood better than any criticisms. We are withering nowadays under the barren warmth of other people's opinions, and second-hand knowledge. It doesn't matter how little you *know,* so long as you are capable of feeling much, and giving discriminate sympathy.[34]

Note the emphasis on blood, feeling, and stimulation. Helen Corke's reminiscences of her friendship with Lawrence provide interesting insights into the extent of Lawrence's acquaintance with Wagner during the Croydon years. In one imaginary letter to her dead lover "H.B.M."—the Siegmund of *The Trespasser*—Helen Corke reveals that she will "try to do a little German with the help of D.H.L. so that I may gain more insight into Wagner's philosophy."[35]

Yet, Lawrence's correspondence with Louie Burrows reveals the development of a curious antipathy to the operas of Wagner which he was seeing at Covent Garden.[36] On 17 October, 1909, Lawrence reports attending *Tristan und Isolde* but being "very disappointed": "*Tristan* is long, feeble, a bit hysterical, without grip or force. I was frankly sick of it."[37] I have already quoted the lively letter written shortly after a vivid production of *Cavalleria Rusticana* and *Pagliacci* in which Lawrence rashly exclaims, "Damn Wagner, & his bellowings at Fate & death."[38] On 15 November, 1911, Lawrence writes of seeing *Siegfried* for the first time at Covent Garden, but proclaimed indifferently: "It was good, but it did not make any terrific impression on me."[39] One senses Lawrence's growing hostility even at this early stage towards the conventions of Wagnerian music drama, its stylization, its high-seriousness, and so on.

This impression is further strengthened by Lawrence's later references to Wagner's music,[40] particularly *Tristan* for which he seems to have conceived a special dislike. No doubt his later attitude had much to do with the idea of Isolde as a wilful and destructive female and with Tristan's submission to her power. Lawrence obviously objected to the extremity of sexual knowledge as an end in itself. In the famous essay "Pornography and Obscenity" (1929), we find Lawrence's harshest condemnation of Tristan:

> Boccaccio at his hottest seems to me less pornographical than *Pamela* or *Clarissa Harlowe* or even *Jane Eyre,* or a host of modern books or films which pass uncensored. At the same time Wagner's *Tristan and Isolde* seems to me very near to pornography, and so, even, do some quite popular christian hymns.[41]

Later, in the same essay he examines the psychology behind such "pornography":

> Wagner and Charlotte Bronte were both in the state where the strongest instincts have collapsed and sex has become slightly obscene to be wallowed in, but despised.[42]

In a letter dated 29 June 1912, Lawrence speaks of *Tristan* as a type of tragedy which is secondary to the tragedy of the marriage-battle:

> ...I don't think the *real* tragedy is in dying, or in the perversity of affairs, like the woman one loves being the wife of another man—like the last act of *Tristan.* I think the real tragedy is in the inner war which is waged between people who love each other, a war out of which comes knowledge...[43]

Perhaps, as this letter suggests, Lawrence had cast himself as Tristan in the strange Weekley-Frieda-D.H.L. triangle. In several letters he protests (in terms which echo the attacks on the pornography of *Tristan*), against "crawling under the mud," against the "subterfuge, lying, dirt, fear" involved in his adulterous affair with Frieda.[44]

Ironically, whatever his objections to the "pornography" of *Tristan,* Lawrence seems unable to conceal his partial admiration in the earlier essay "Love" for the "fierce, proud love of sensual fulfilment" in *Tristan,* the "lovely battle of sensual gratification, the beautiful but deadly counterposing of male against female.[45] Elsewhere Lawrence speaks of the "few isolated heroes of passionate and beautiful deaths: Tristan, Achilles, Napoleon. These are the royal lions and tigers of our life."[46] Lawrence's attitude to *Tristan und Isolde* is thus best described as ambivalent. Whatever similarity there might have been between the love-ethic of the young Lorenzo and that of Wagner,[47] as expressed in *Tristan,* by the end of his career Lawrence's hostility to the extremes of Wagnerian passion, to its supposed "prurience," was clearly established. With the abandoning of the notion of sexual fulfilment as a positive end in itself, the transition from the "love-urge" to the "power-mode" of the leadership novels, went the necessary rejection of Wagner's love-ethic.

The scarcity of Wagnerian allusion to *Aaron's Rod* suggests that Lawrence has made discerning use of only a *few* references to the music dramas of Wagner in order to focus our attention upon the destructiveness of the love affair of Aaron and the Marchesa. In Chapter 18 the strange effect of Aaron's music on the Marchesa is conveyed through a striking Wagnerian image:

> To her it was like a pure male voice — as a black-bird's when he calls: a pure male voice, not only calling, but telling her something, telling her something, and soothing her soul to sleep. It was like the fire-music putting Brunnhilde [sic] to sleep. (296–97)

The reference to the magic fire-music and Brünnhilde recalls the punishment levelled by Wotan upon his favorite half-mortal daughter in Act III of Wagner's *Die Walküre.* Brünnhilde is doomed to a deep sleep upon a rock, surrounded by a ring of fire impenetrable by all save "a fearless noble hero" ("ein furchtlos, freiester Held") who shall one day awaken her. In Act III of *Siegfried,* the young hero survives the ordeal of the magic fire, awakens her and ecstatically claims her as his own. The parallels in *Aaron's Rod* are obvious. Aaron Sisson is a modern version of the blond hero, Siegfried, the Marchesa a type of Brünnhilde, "in festem Schlaf," waiting to be revived by her young hero. This symbolism is borne out in the romance and fairy-tale analogues to the quest of Siegfried scattered throughout this chapter.[48] The Wagnerian analogy is of course ironic, for the anti-heroic Aaron Sisson and the phlegmatic Marchesa are really the antithesis of the Wagnerian demi-gods.

The mention of Brünnhilde suggests a further reference to the love affair of Siegfried and Brünnhilde which ends in betrayal, suffering, and death. In the final opera of Wagner's *Ring Cycle,* Siegfried deserts Brünnhilde for Gutrune and in turn suffers an ignominious death at the hands of the cowardly Hagen. Brünnhilde, heartbroken, immolates herself. I am not suggesting that Lawrence has carefully worked out a complex system of minute parallels to Wagner's *Ring Des Niebelungen* but that he has incorporated a few of the main aspects of the Brünnhilde-Siegfried affair into the narrative framework of *Aaron's Rod.* He is thus suggesting the deadly implication of Aaron's involvement with the Marchesa. With her drug-like effect upon Aaron, the Marchesa seems to become a false Gutrune who brings dishonor and ruin upon her Siegfried, Aaron Sisson.

An oblique reference in *Aaron's Rod* to the love glance motif of

Tristan und Isolde is provided by the recurring mention of the Marchesa's penetrating gaze turned constantly upon Aaron:

> And at last she turned her eyes to his, with a slow, dark smile, full of pain and fuller still of knowledge. A strange, dark, silent look of knowledge she gave him: from so far away, it seemed. And he felt all the bonds that held him melting away. His eyes remained fixed and gloomy, but with his mouth he smiled back at her. And he was terrified. He knew he was sinking towards her — sinking towards her. (294)

As in Tristan, the two "lovers" seem united in silent union by the love glance. The "wide incomprehensible glance" of the Marchesa, a modern Isolde, is another motif which signals to the reader the deadly sensuality of the feminine will as it entraps and endangers Aaron, her Tristan. One also recalls Lawrence's vivid comments on the lacerating tragedy of *Tristan und Isolde.* Aaron, somewhat like Tristan, has been wounded or bruised by his sexual experience. Here is Lawrence's description of the male orgasm in the uncensored typescript version:

> As his passion broke from him to her, he felt the long live hot fire thread drawn downwards through him, terribly down his legs and through his heels, leaving his heels feeling bruised, and himself feeling vacant. It was like a discharge of lightning, but longer, more terrible — And this night he slept with a deeper obliviousness than before. (TS445)

Throughout these episodes dealing with Aaron's nearly fatal attraction to the Marchesa, the emphasis upon drug-induced trances and similar hypnotic states unmistakably recalls the love-drug of *Tristan* and its euphoric effect upon the lovers.[49] The close connection in *Tristan* between love and death is suggested by Brangaene's substitution of the love philter for the lethal drug which Isolde has ordered for herself and Tristan. Surrendering to the drug-induced ecstasy of *liebestod,* Tristan and Isolde create for themselves a separate world of dark sensuality opposed to the ordinary world of day — "tückisher Tag." When Aaron first sees her the Marchesa sits "rather sad, remote-seeming" (257), much like Isolde in the first scene of *Tristan.* The Marchesa immediately suggests to Aaron "a modern Cleopatra brooding, Anthonyless [sic]" (257). The close connection between Isolde and Cleopatra in Lawrence's imagination is obvious: both are wilful temptresses who exert a deadly feminine power over their male consorts. Aaron notices that the Marchesa has "that peculiar heavy remote quality of preoccupation and neurosis" (261), and later hearkens to her "sing-song lapsing voice" resembling "one in a trance or a sleep-walker" (265). The flute music casts a spell not unlike the strange effect of the love potion in *Tristan.*

> Aaron retired to the other room, and waited awhile, to get back the spell which connected him with the woman, and gave the two of them this strange isolation, beyond the bounds of life, as it seemed. (266).

Returning for dinner a few days later, Aaron succumbs to the seductiveness of the Marchesa as if in a stupor: "He had never known a woman to exercise such power over him. It was a bare, occult force, something he could not cope with" (292). The Marchesa, hearing the flute on this occasion, seems momentarily roused from the "drug-like tension" which is upon her most of the time. Dazed, and silent "as if in a trance" after her magical recovery of her voice, the Marchesa sits opposite Aaron and the Marchese and gazes with "the glimmer of the open flower, the wonder-look" (300-301).

As their mutual attraction is sexually consummated, the Marchesa is described as a demonic priestess executing some magic rite upon her male consort. This may remind us that Isolde was herself a kind of sorceress whose knowledge of the black arts (inherited from her mother) provided her with special powers to heal or destroy Tristan, as he had first appeared to her, wounded in combat with her dead lover; and later, when he appeared before her on board the ship bearing her to Cornwall and King Mark.

In his essay "D. H. Lawrence and D'Annunzio, Wagner," William Blissett speaks of the sweep of Lawrence's grand Wagnerian passages:

> Like Wagner, Lawrence in his grand fortissimo passages uses thick harmony, full orchestration, oceanic feeling.[50]

In *The Trespasser,* Lawrence had experimented with such fortissimo passages in which the verbal rhythm approximates the flow of Wagner's music itself. It seems a pity, however, that so many passages of "Wagnerian" intensity in *The Trespasser* should be connected so closely with many rather precious love-scenes in which the diction descends to the level of mere novelese, "the second-hand poetry of the woman's magazine" as Graham Hough has called it.[51] Lawrence is clearly ill at ease in the difficult realm of erotic description. It took him much practice and several more novels to acquire the art of shaping the erotic "moment" in a style which might transcend any suggestion of the "purple" prose of the second-rate journalist. With artistic maturity came the ability to control such passages of rising emotional intensity and to use them with a fine discrimination for special effects.

In *Aaron's Rod* we find very few passages of Wagnerian intensity. As might be expected, these few are all connected with the love-affair of Aaron and the Marchesa. One such passage occurs when the Marchesa finds her voice again and feels her soul soar, regenerated supposedly by the music of the flute:

> She sang free, with the flute gliding along with her. And oh, how beautiful it was for her! How beautiful it was to sing the little song in the sweetness of her own spirit. How sweet it was to move pure and unhampered at last in the music! The lovely ease and lilt of her own soul in its motion through the music! She wasn't aware of the flute. She didn't know there was anything except for her own pure lovely song-drift.... For the first time! For the first time her soul drew its own deep breath. All her life, the breath had caught half-way. And now she breathed full, deep, to the deepest extent of her being. (299–300)

This splendid example of Lawrence's mature control of Wagnerian cadence is echoed later as Aaron's male potency reasserts itself, rising like the phoenix.

A later quite extraordinary passage suggests the destructive effect of Aaron's enthrallment by the Marchesa:

> She was absolutely gone, like a priestess utterly involved in her terrible rites. And he was part of the ritual only, God and victim in one. God and victim! All the time, God and victim. When his aloof soul realised, amid the welter of incantation, how he was being used, — not as himself but as something quite different — God and victim — then he dilated with intense surprise, and his remote soul stood up tall and knew itself alone. He didn't want it, not at all. He knew he was apart. (318)

The incantatory rhythm[52] of the crescendo suggests the weird ritual of the Marchesa, a priestess totally absorbed in the exercise of her demonic powers. This passage is of great significance, for it suggests that Lawrence's sparing use of Wagnerism in *Aaron's Rod* performs a special thematic function. The suggestion of the ultimate destructiveness of Aaron's love affair is fairly explicit here; but the symbolic implications of such Wagnerism are likely to escape us if we are not careful to place this musical device within the framework clearly established throughout the novel. In a novel in which the pure and simple melody of the flute is championed over the supposedly nauseating or superficial forms of grand orchestral and operatic works, might not Aaron's and the Marchesa's affair conceived musically, in Wagnerian terms, be considered a deplorable defection, a betrayal of their true selves?

Throughout the novel a decided superiority has been accorded medieval, baroque, and early classical music, all opposed in their purity and simplicity to the polyphonic complexities of the Romantic school, of which the music of Richard Wagner is an integral part. This streak of anti-Wagnerism is sustained by the harsh and cynical tone of the novel taken as a whole, by its decidedly anti-romantic texture. Through the prophetic message of Rawdon Lilly, the novel embodies a deliberate attempt to pull away from the cliceés of love and brotherhood. The great love urge is supposedly exhausted and corrupt. There is thus little place for Wagnerism—and the music which it suggests—in a novel as anti-romantic and grimly uncompromising as *Aaron's Rod*. When it does occur in the novel, i.e., in the love affair of Aaron and the Marchesa, we are being subtly alerted by Lawrence to the fact that this relationship can only end in revulsion or spiritual death like the relationship of Gerald Crich and Gudrun in *Women in Love*. This relationship has been based upon the wrong principles of possession by the destructive will, and the endless pursuit of sensual knowledge.

Through the affair with the Marchesa the music of Aaron's flute has symbolically been compromised, its regenerative powers perverted by the selfish will to possess or bully. Lawrence is by no means suggesting that the music of the flute *per se* is intrinsically destructive but that the music of the flute and the power which it conveys must be properly handled or directed towards more positive ends. These preclude sexual exploitation or selfish bullying. Because the music and the power it symbolizes are not properly controlled, the relationship of Aaron and the Marchesa which should have continued in the uninhibited condition in which it began is inevitably doomed. To convey the increasing destructiveness of the relationship Lawrence has made careful use of literary Wagnerism. Musically speaking, the Wagnerism of the sexual affair corrupts or overpowers the flute's "melody pure and simple." The "music" of the affair thus seems closer to the chords and clanging orchestral music associated with the Marchese and the dilettantes whom Aaron has encountered, the very type of music for which, ironically, Aaron and the Marchesa have previously expressed a loathing. In the hands of the spiritually inadequate or corrupt, Lawrence demonstrates once again, music may become simply an extension or an expression of that person's deadly will.

One final "coda" remains to this chapter on the music in *Aaron's Rod*. In an earlier chapter, I discussed the mysterious, seemingly magical properties of the flute in a biblical context, where Aaron Sisson's flute or rod was symbolically related to the miraculous staff of the high priest Aaron, brother of Moses. We have so far noticed also that Aaron Sisson's flute is virtually present and involved, most often through its rejuvenating powers, with each of the major turning points of the novel. Within the musical framework of allusion in the novel, Lawrence has provided the flute with added mythic significance in its unmistakable resemblance to other enchanted flutes. Lawrence is even suggesting, it seems, that Aaron's flute, like Tamino's enchanted flute in Mozart's *Die Zauberflöte* has special supernatural powers to control nature itself. Of course, Aaron's flute is an unmistakable echo of Pan's pipes, associated with the pastoral world of classical mythology about which I will say more in a later chapter. The breaking of Aaron's flute in the penultimate chapter might remind us that in Elizabethan pastoral romances such as *The Arcadia* or *The Shepherd's Calendar,* often the breaking of the flute or "shepherd's" pipe signalled the end of an old, self-defeating phase of life. Usually this former existence was centered upon a vain and enthralling homage paid to a proud and cruel mistress. The breaking of the flute often suggested the rejection of both unrequited love and the old "music" or poetry created to win the favor of the haughty mistress as well as a deliberate motion towards a new direction of endeavor. So too, Aaron has survived the ignominious surrender and enthrallment to false love and also to false music (at least, to corrupted music) symbolized in the later chapters of the novel by his subservience to the Marchesa's feminine will. However we take it, the shattering of Aaron's flute and its commitment to the Arno move Aaron towards a renewal of himself, towards a life based on different principles than before. Aaron must develop a new kind of inner music. In the final chapter, he reaches resignedly towards Lilly whose strange "speech music," having displaced for the time being the music of the flute, seems to be performing a call upon Aaron's soul. This soul-call is perhaps deeper than any Aaron has ever known; but for the time being it is nevertheless one which Aaron remains reluctant to acknowledge.

5

Poisonous Death: A Study of War and Its After-Effects in *Aaron's Rod*

> When people go mad, they understand only poisonous death,
> And they make war lustfully, even calling it peace.
>
> (D. H. Lawrence, *War*)

Although several recent critics of Lawrence's fiction, such as George Ford, have written persuasively of Lawrence's attitude to the Great War as reflected in the fiction of the period, particularly in *Women in Love,* few have given their attention to Lawrence's treatment of war in *Aaron's Rod.* His treatment of the disillusionment and unrest which war had fostered in the ensuing years of uneasy peace has virtually been ignored by Lawrence scholars.

In the first chapter of this study, I traced the conception of *Aaron's Rod* back to London, during the dark period of the final months of war with London still threatened by bombs and Zeppelin raids. The violence and rage coupled with a strange weariness which Lawrence felt during this period are manifested in his treatment in *Aaron's Rod* of war and its strange aftermath.

Although narrated from a perspective of civilian disenchantment rather than from the "front hell of war," *Aaron's Rod* is recognizably a "war novel" and a strange one at that. As Neil Myers has so admirably pointed out, the novel belongs with an important segment of Lawrence's fiction dealing with war, a distinct body which contains such titles as *Women in Love,* "The Nightmare" in *Kangaroo,* "England, My England," and so on.[1] At the same time, *Aaron's Rod* presents us with Lawrence's most expansive and eloquent treatment of the *malaise* which affected an entire post-war generation.

Through a succession of shell-shocked or battered figures—Herbertson and Angus Guest come easily to mind—the reader is kept constantly aware of the senseless violence of war as well as its shattering effect upon those who have survived it. Drifting in and out of the novel's many scenes is a constant parade of military figures. If we look closely enough, we may observe that Lawrence has deliberately planted uniformed figures in virtually every chapter, whose presence suggests both the proximity of the war as well as its threat to the peacetime activities of ordinary civilians. In Chapter 3, Robert Cunningham, wearing the khaki of an enlisted man, "a lieutenant, about to be demobilised" (33), interrogates the trespasser, Aaron, rather menacingly, obviously relishing his role as interrogating officer. Jim's command to "dry up the army touch" (43) seems quite appropriate.

Later, in Chapter 6 it is disclosed that Jim has been a "cavalry officer and fought in two wars" (68). In the tube at night, Tanny and Lilly witness the painful sight of men "still yelling like wild beasts" while soldiers sing (75). And so it continues—in each scene a military figure whose presence seems to threaten or unnerve: the war-blasted Herbertson; at the home of Sir William Franks in Novara, the robust Colonel in khaki and the more sinister Major, "tall, gaunt, erect, like a murdered Hamlet resurrected in khaki with the terrible black shutter over his eye" (203); the rapacious gangs of soldiers prowling the streets, who rob Aaron mercilessly; the uniformed Marchese del Torre who breaks in on the convivial atmosphere of Argyle's all-male tea-party. In the last instance the outraged protest of Argyle echoes Lawrence's attitude and suggests a thematic purpose in introducing such intrusive uniformed figures:

> "Look," said Lilly. "There's del Torre!"
> "Like some sort of midge, in that damned grey-and-yellow uniform. I can't stand it, I tell you. I can't stand the sight of any more of these uniforms. Like a blight on the human landscape. Like a blight. Like green-flies on rose-trees, smother-flies. Europe's got the smother-fly in these infernal shoddy militarists." (276)

The full horror of war is most vividly presented in Herbertson's feverish memories of the trenches in Chapter 10, "The War Again." The significant title of this chapter carries with it the suggestion of Herbertson's reliving of the war-experience, of an exorcism effected through this ghastly retelling of the sufferings of war. Like the very weapons of war which he has carried, Herbertson "rattle[s] away, rather spasmodic." Moving "by light transitions" to the trenches and the war, Herbertson rushes headlong from one terrifying tale to another, half-mesmerized, half-appalled, yet forever compelled, like Coleridge's Ancient Mariner, to relieve through compulsive reminiscence the horror and guilt which torture him. Herbertson's war-mania is most brilliantly evoked by Lawrence. Far from being a tedious digression the incident serves a specific thematic function and is one of the most dramatic scenes of the novel.

In his otherwise quite admirable treatment of *Women in Love* as a novel of the War, George Ford makes the following misleading statement in his comparison of *Women in Love* to *Aaron's Rod:*

> Shortly before her death Katherine Mansfield protested in a letter that some novels she had been reading had been written as if the war had not happened. "The novel can't just leave the war out," she said. Lawrence would have agreed, but he was aware that there are different ways of getting the war in. There was the direct way, as in his own *Aaron's Rod,* and there was the indirect way which we have been examining in *Women in Love.* In his *Foreword* he, himself, remarked that his novel "took its final shape in the midst of the period of war, through it does not concern the war itself."[2]

Ford obviously feels that the "indirect" treatment in *Women in Love* is superior, since he devotes almost sixty pages (two full chapters) to exploring *Women in Love* and testing his theories, but relegates *Aaron's Rod* to a position of relative unimportance. I would suggest however, that Lawrence's method is not as simple or "direct" as Ford seems to think. Nor does Lawrence's handling of such "war" episodes show evidence of the artistic naïveté which Ford's misleading distinction should seem to imply.

Lawrence has skillfully prepared us for Herbertson's neurotically compulsive recollections in earlier chapters of the novel. The dangerous atmosphere of post-war England has already been suggested in the "neurasthenic haste for excitement" in the Christmas Eve shoppers contending greedily for scarce or non-existent luxuries. In Chapter 7, Jim Bricknell's near-hysterical behavior suggests that, like Herbertson, he too has been spiritually maimed by war. Though doctors have supposedly examined him and pronounced him physically sound, he still staggers and stumbles in a state of nauseous relaxation "like a drunken man: or worse, like a man with locomotor ataxia: as if he had no power in his limbs" (94). His love-wish is actually a death-wish, as Lilly later points out.

Lilly himself anticipates Herbertson's war stories with his grisly tale of the mutilated victims in the Russo-Japanese war and of the terrible effect upon a Russian doctor of witnessing such an atrocity:

> I knew a Russian doctor who'd been through the Russo-Japanese war, and who had gone a bit cracked. He said he saw the Japs rush a trench. They threw everything away and flung themselves through the Russian fire and simply dropped in masses. But those that reached the trenches jumped in with bare hands on the Russians and tore their faces apart and bit their throats out — fairly ripped the faces off the bone. — It had sent the doctor a bit cracked. He said the wounded were awful, — their faces torn off and their throats mangled — and dead Japs with flesh between the teeth — God knows if it's

true. But that's the impression the Japanese had made on this man. — It had affected his mind really. (87–88)

Lilly's last statement applies equally to the society of post-war Europe, especially to Francis' friend, Angus Guest, a victim of war-induced neurosis who discredits the cheap glory of war once again in a later chapter.

It is important to observe that Herbertson's experience of war, while conveyed in direct speech, presumably for purposes of dramatic intensity, is actually an *indirect* reassessment of past experience. For from being presented directly, the events are narrated from a post-war perspective. Like all retrospective glances at past experience the narrative is subject to the limitations of the speaker and his particular point of view. Lawrence makes it clear that Herbertson's experience and his compulsion to relive it is symptomatic of an entire post-war generation:

> It was the same thing here in this officer as it was with the privates, and the same with this Englishman as with a Frenchman or a German or an Italian. Lilly had sat in a cowshed listening to a youth in the north country: he had sat on the corn-straw that the oxen had been treading out, in Calabria, under the moon: he had sat in a farm-kitchen with a German prisoner: and every time it was the same thing, the same hot, blind, anguished voice of a man who has seen too much, experienced too much, and doesn't know where to turn. None of the glamour of returned heroes, none of the romance of war: only a hot, blind, mesmerised voice, going on and on, mesmerised by a vision that the soul cannot bear. (133)

It is interesting to compare the anguish of Septimus Smith in Virginia Woolf's *Mrs. Dalloway,* published only three years after *Aaron's Rod,* or, within *Aaron's Rod* itself, the post-war shock of Angus Guest. Disenchanted and shattered Angus speaks of his involvement with war in images of swarming insects and putrefaction:

> The feelings all came on to me from the outside: like flies settling on meat. Before I knew where I was I was eaten up with a swarm of feelings, and I found myself in the trenches. God knows what for. And ever since then I've been trying to get out of my swarm of feelings, which buzz in and out of me and have nothing to do with me (227)

It is an indication of Lawrence's supreme powers of narration that Herbertson's illness is depicted in such a realistic and dramatic manner while the incident (occurring almost at the heart of the novel) gradually assumes a profound symbolic significance. The unhealing wounds of the medieval romance tradition are suggested by the psychological sores of these victims of war which also refuse to heal:

> In this officer, of course, there was a lightness and an appearance of bright diffidence and humour. But underneath it all was the same as in the common men of all the com-

batant nations: the hot, seared burn of unbearable experience, which did not heal nor cool, and whose irritation was not to be relieved. The experience gradually cooled on top: but only with a surface crust. The soul did not heal, did not recover. (133)

It is in this "dead land" of post-war civilization that Herbertson, Angus and Jim Bricknell as well as other anonymous "hollow men" assume their place. Of Herbertson's thematic role, Neil Myers has written perceptively:

Here is the essence of *Aaron's Rod* and of Lawrence's view of the war: the "decent" surface Victorianism, the empty ceremonies, the theaters, the Guards' tea party, and the fantastic pitiful agony beneath, the concentration camp below the Bredermyer, the meaningless destruction which is the full result of a society's denial of life.[3]

A closer examination of the Herbertson episode and the ensuing discussion between Lilly and Aaron also reveals that Lawrence has skilfully employed Herbertson's shell-shocked narrative as a catalyst for Lilly's heated attack on the foulness and unreality of the war. Lilly's condemnation of the love of death rather than of life which prompts such blind sacrifice to hollow ideals will be discussed in a later chapter.

One final aspect of Herbertson's visit is of particular interest: the unusual silence of Lilly throughout Herbertson's morally objectionable war anecdotes. Lilly's silent withdrawal suggests a compassion and sensitivity towards Herbertson's helpless condition not always noticeable in Lilly's violent denunciations of love and war during ensuing scenes of the novel. One such bitter harangue, occurring after Herbertson's visit divides Aaron and Lilly and threatens their growing friendship, when Aaron goadingly condones the use of poison gas and Lilly vents all his pent-up exasperation upon his guest. The two men split up and are not reunited until seven chapters later, in Florence.

In Chapter 14, the narrator interrupts his description of the "half litre of good old Chianti" which Aaron is consuming at Francis' table for an important aside — "the war was so near[,] but gone by."[4] This observation perfectly describes the sensation of the post-war period which Lawrence has created in *Aaron's Rod*. Like a great sphere enveloping the novel, war and its deadly conflict throw into relief those separate acts of civil or psychological violence somehow stemming from "the violence of the nightmare released into the atmosphere." Still, the war *is* over. *Aaron's Rod* is therefore much more a novel of the post-war world, of the difficult struggle towards sanity and wholeness of a society which war has burst apart.

In his illuminating study of *Aaron's Rod*, Keith Sagar has described the recurrent imagery of explosion and crashing which pervades the novel.[5] These images frequently echo similar images of bursting and universal destruction scattered throughout the letters of this period. The novel begins and ends with an explosion. In the first chapter the treasured blue ball breaks, a miniature symbol of the universe sundered by the holocaust of war, "coming to pieces bit by bit" as Lilly later phrases it. In the penultimate chapter an anarchist's bomb explodes; Aaron's flute is ripped apart by the impact, and Aaron himself seems psychologically shattered by his sudden loss. Although Professor Sagar is quite justified in his observation that "throughout *Aaron's Rod* things break, people separate, presenting a cumulative image of social disintegration,"[6] he fails to note that such a phenomenon is not so much a condition of wartime as of the post-war period. Even though the war is "so near, but gone by" and society seems threatened by collapse, the crashing and exploding gives way to the related sensations of numbness, shock, mindlessness and inertia. Scenes of civil disobedience or violence indicate that the conflict of the war goes on (in spite of the official declaration of peace) now reduced, in Yeats' phrase to "mere anarchy...loosed upon the world." Yet, at the same time Lawrence suggests that many persons, particularly the major characters of the novel, still remain dazed and uprooted, unable to summon the energy necessary for recovery. Several of the central figures of the novel thus resign themselves to another mood which invests the novel, that of spiritual and moral lethargy.

The two related, though irreconcilable, extremes of reaction to the extended conflict and misery of war manifest themselves quite clearly in Lawrence's letters during the final months of war and the uneasy first months of peace after the armistice. It is no secret that the war aroused in Lawrence outbursts of rage "unequalled," as Neil Meyers aptly observes, "in English Literature since the death of Swift."[7] Here is a more extreme outburst of misanthropy:

> I must say I hate mankind — talking of hatred, I have got a perfect androphobia. When I see people in the distance, walking along the path through the fields to Zennor, I want to crouch in the bushes and shoot them silently with the invisible arrows of death. I think truly the only righteousness is the destruction of mankind, as in Sodom. Fire and brimstone should fall down.[8]

In February of 1918 Lawrence felt his "androphobia" less pronounced; but he was still waiting desperately for the final smash-up which he had forecasted or hoped for all along:

> Still I wait for the day when this foul tension of war and pot-bellied world will break, when we can meet in something like freedom and enjoy each other's company in something like decency. Nowadays one can do nothing but glance behind to see who now is creeping up to do something horrible to the back of one's neck.[9]

A few days later he informed Koteliansky of his hatred of "world builders" like "Bertrand Russell and Lansbury," whom he despised as "negators of life": "I want their world smashed up, not set up—all the world smashed up."[10] In yet another violent letter, the tone of which resembles the extravagant "bolshing" of the Bricknell set in Chapter 6 of *Aaron's Rod,* Lawrence speaks of revolution as a means of destroying the decadent old world:

> About the world I feel that nothing but a quite bloody, merciless, almost anarchistic revolution will be any good for this country; a fearful chaos of smashing up. And I think it will come sooner or later: and I wish it would come soon. And yet, somehow, I don't want to be in it. I know it *should* come, and must come: yet I would like to go away, not to see it.[11]

Lawrence's final qualification is important, for it indicates an ultimate reluctance to commit himself to the same mob-violence which he abhors in the war-machine. A distinct disenchantment even with the activity of smashing and collapsing is noticeable.

It is no simple coincidence that *Aaron's Rod* was being written during this period of artistic restlessness, when Lawrence himself seemed torn between the extremes of violent or frenetic activity and the inevitable inertia of post-war depression. Running counterpoint to the reiterated wish for violence and "smash-up," we find in Lawrence an unmistakable longing for England's past, a nostalgia for the old world which the war had destroyed. This touching letter written by Mary Cannan on 14 June 1918 suggests perfectly the sense of loss which accompanies Lawrence's more violent longing for an apocalyptic holocaust:

> I can't tell you with what pain I think of that autumn at Cholesbury...and our cottage was hot and full of the smell of sage and onions—then the times we came to you, and had your wine—those pretty wine-glasses on your long table. Sometimes inside one weeps and won't be comforted.... [T]here was *something* in those still days, before the war had gone into us, which was beautiful and generous...[12]

Though he wrote the "Nightmare" chapter of *Kangaroo* years later, in the summer of 1922, Lawrence's description of the collapse in 1915 remains his most eloquent eulogy for a vanishing era.[13]

Compounded with such feelings of nostalgia were Lawrence's feelings of suffocation and imprisonment in a country whose ideals had become unbearable to him. In the early stages of the war, he had spoken hopefully to Lady Cynthia Asquith of fighting "another kind of fight: the fight of that which is to come, not the fight of that which is passing away," affirming his faith in the reality of peace which lay within the heart of the people:

> We should say "enough of war" while yet we are alive. We should say enough of war, because the desire of something else is strong and most living in us. It is foolish to drop down at last in inertia, and let the war end so — in inertia while we have the vitality to create, we ought to stop fighting — otherwise, when the end comes, we are spiritually bankrupt: which is final disaster.[14]

Lawrence's worst fears seemed realized as the war dragged on and the armistice brought only a "false" peace. This strange inertia affected even Lawrence's spirits. In the first chapter of this study, I stressed that *Aaron's Rod* was conceived and written during these long months of artistic inactivity and restlessness. The letters of this period are a study themselves in end-of-the-war disillusionment and frustration. The numbed shock of Lawrence as he faced the terrible blank of the months lying before him is expressed in this typical letter written to Koteliansky:

> No, I haven't any news.... I have finished up all the things I am writing at present — have a complete blank in front of me — feel very desperate, and ready for anything good or bad. I think something critical will happen this month... If it doesn't I shall bust.[15]

Unable to work and unable to secure the passports necessary to escape England, Lawrence speaks of his "after-the-war ideal" of becoming a gypsy, able to "move on forever, and never have a neighbour" utterly forswearing all personal contacts, craving only "some sort of free, lawless, life ...where one can move about and take no notice of anything."[16] Yet, once free of his English cage Lawrence found himself immersed in the restless society of post-war Italy, mysteriously surrendering to his own artistic lethargy.

I have entered into considerable detail in describing Lawrence's emotional outlook at the end-of-the-war period in order to suggest the strange *mélange* of violent *misanthropy* combined with *nostalgia* and inescapable *inertia* which has passed into *Aaron's Rod* to give the novel its peculiar restless yet static quality. I should like to examine these extremes of reaction to the prolonged conflict of war and the upheaval of the post-war era as they are presented in *Aaron's Rod.*

I mentioned earlier that the excess of violence of the war, "so near, but gone by" provides a thematic background for the novel, the requisite tension for a number of scenes of conflict. The brilliantly evocative opening chapter of the novel suggests two types of conflict which underlie most of the action of the novel: the public and the private (or sexual) conflict: each in its own way related to the "foul tension" of war; each the inevitable and tragic result of the "love-urge" which afflicts society. The first paragraph quickly sketches the environment of the post-war period:

There was a large, brilliant evening star in the early twilight, and underfoot the earth was half frozen. It was Christmas Eve. Also the War was over, and there was a sense of relief that was almost a new menace. A man felt the violence of the nightmare released now into the general air. Also there had been another wrangle among the men on the pit bank that evening. (7)

The bright presence of a nativity star is grimly ironic, for it foretells no rebirth for humanity. The absence of any real "peace on earth" is emphasized by the disgruntled wrangling of the miners; in the "vocal violence" later of the half-hearted carollers; and most obviously, in the "frictional, . . . neurasthenic haste for excitement" which possesses the villagers:

There seemed to have been some violent but quiet contest, a subdued fight, going on all the afternoon and evening: people struggling to buy things, to get things. . . . There was a wild grumbling, but a deep satisfaction in the fight, the struggle. The same fight and the same satisfaction in the fight was witnessed whenever a tram-car stopped, or when it heaved its way into sight. Then the struggle to mount on board became desperate and savage, but stimulating. Souls surcharged with hostility found now some outlet for their feelings. (18–19)

The final sentence of the paragraph looks ahead to later scenes of violence in the streets of Italy. Later, it is revealed that the war has "killed the little market of the town," (20) the first of a series of losses or deprivations to be registered throughout the novel: the paucity of sweets and customary Christmas luxuries; the unavailability of port — even to wealthy Sir William Franks; the decline of traditional courtesy in trains and restaurants, where "sir" is dropped as being "too old fashioned now, since the war" (221).

The novel is punctuated by a series of political or public conflicts each arising out of the electrical tension which charges the post-war atmosphere. Though the scene shifts from England to Italy, the desperate climate of the *dopoguerra* remains essentially the same. The narrator even draws our attention to the "horrible sameness" that is spreading "like a disease over Italy from England and the north" (179). Gangs of soldiers roam the streets restlessly, robbing civilians; street fights erupt; corpses are surreptitiously borne off; gun-fire rings out to be passed off later as shots fired at a stray dog; bombs explode amid unsuspecting café patrons — and so on. The war-maddened atmosphere is splendidly recreated.

The most extended scene of anarchistic unrest is of course the flag incident in Chapter 14, "XX Settembre" in which Lawrence depicts a street clash between a socialist mob and the royalist *carabinieri*. Lawrence himself must have witnessed a similar scene of civil unrest so typical of post-war Italy torn by the partisan rivalry of Nationalists, Catholics,

Arditi, Socialists and, most important, the ascendant *fascisti*. The title of this chapter calls for some clarification.

As any history of the Italian unification reveals, 20 September 1870 marks the date of the liberation of Rome by Victor Emmanuel's Bersaglieri, the ultimate stage in the unification of Italy:

> The result of the first battles in the Franco-Prussian war caused the withdrawal of the French garrison from Rome, and September 20, 1870, less than three weeks after Sedan, Victor Emmanuel's Bersaglieri entered by the breach near the Porta Pia.... So fell the Temporal Power, which Mazzini and Garibaldi had defied on the Janiculum twenty-one years before. Italy had her capital, and the *risorgimento* epoch came to an end.[17]

As a national holiday commemorating the victory of a great king, XX Settembre would obviously be an appropriate excuse for a street riot by the socialists or "bolshevists." With their red flag fluttering, the angry crowd attempts to pull down all national tricolors in its path and so terrorize any who refuse submission to the rule of the mob. The violent clash between the official police and the revolutionary communists is entirely typical of the times. Italy during the *dopoguerra* was afflicted to an unprecedented degree by civil unrest, strikes, partisan violence. It was such internal strife which led, unfortunately, to the rise of the fascists and their colorful *duce,* Benito Mussolini.

In 1920 September 20 had an added significance. The date marked the climax of a series of seizures by the revolutionary proletariat of factories throughout Italy. In *The Fruits of Fascism,* Herbert Matthews describes the abortive take-over of the factories by the workers:

> The occupation began in Aug. 30, 1920, and reached its peak on Sept. 20. In Milan 200 factories were immediately occupied by the workers, and 200 more had been taken over by Sept 9. Similar events occurred in Rome, Naples and many other places. In Turin, thanks to the strength of the Communists, there were very grave disorders, but, generally speaking, the occupation was as peaceful as were the sit-down strikes in France years later.... It was a month of waste, financial panic and some disorder.... For the most part, the workers had their chance to run the factories—and three weeks were enough to show them that they could not do it without expert supervision and capital. There was a preliminary accord with the employers on Sept. 20, and the next day the evacuation of the factories began, slowly at first and with opposition, but the battle was lost.... The worst thing the workers had done, as time showed, was to play into the hands of the Fascists who had also sat back and who then profited by the reaction.[18]

Herman Finer, in his study *Mussolini's Italy* explains the political consequences of this "bolshevik scare":

> The episode had some very important moral effects. Any fear of a real Bolshevik menace was shown to be false. This was the time for the Revolution, if ever; but talk

had merely been talk. Yet the agitation and the occupation had been sufficiently frightening, and caused the rich and the middle classes to look to *any* saviour. The weakness of the Governments which had allowed the country to arrive at such a threat, the actual terrorisation of the countryside, the continual strikes, all made the middle classes determine to take permanent and forcible counter-measures against the risen tide of Socialism.... While hitherto the belief had existed that a constituted authority stood between the propertied and the propertyless, between order and the "subversives," the people now saw that the Government could not be relied on.[19]

It was at this point that Mussolini "still in the position of a revolutionary but patriotic socialist" but leader of the powerful Milanese *fascisti* emerged as a self-styled "saviour." In his notorious speech of 20 September, 1920, Mussolini signalled his approval of the seizure of the factories:

Everything must be changed in the modern city...It is possible to destroy in order to create anew in a form more beautiful and great, for destruction must never be carried out in the method of a savage, who breaks open a machine in order to see what is inside.... No social transformation which is necessary is repugnant to me. Hence I accept the famous workers' supervision of the factories and also their co-operative social management: I only ask that there shall be a clear conscience and technical capacity, and that there shall be increased production. If this is guaranteed by the workmen's unions, instead of by the employers, I have no hesitation in saying that the former have the right to take the place of the latter.[20]

When criticized for his new, turncoat allegiance to the proletariat, Mussolini claimed that he had changed sides to "save Italy from Bolshevism." By October the fascist takeover of Northern Italy was virtually complete with seizure of prefectures, and police headquarters and the "guarding" of railroads and telegraph offices.

All of this contemporary Italian history is particularly relevant to *Aaron's Rod.* In September 1920 Lawrence was staying near Florence in an "explosion shattered" villa belonging to Rosalind Baynes.[21] He must have witnessed an actual street demonstration similar to others going on all over Italy on this particular holiday, a decisive turning point in Italy's destiny. Lawrence's use of the doubly significant date for the title of the fourteenth chapter of *Aaron's Rod* is in no way accidental. The collapse of socialist aspirations, the futility of anarchistic activity such as described in the flag incident of *Aaron's Rod,* no doubt lie behind Lilly's bitter attack upon the bullying of the mob and its striving after the "common good." Though the name of Mussolini never comes to the surface of *Aaron's Rod,* it is entirely possible that Lilly, or at least Lawrence, has in mind a specific leader of men in the final chapter of the novel. In any case it may be argued that Lilly has at least a clearer notion than might be suspected of the nature of the "heroic soul in a greater man" to whom he mysteriously urges a "deep, fathomless submission." The identification of September XX thus enriches our reading of the flag incident considerably. The strong impression which the rise of fascism (and its aristocratic-elitist ideals) must have made upon Lawrence is unmistakable, especially at a time when he found himself half way through *Aaron's Rod.*

In *Aaron's Rod,* Lawrence suggests that the violence of the war is sustained in the post-war period in a series of marital or sexual conflicts leaving both partners "dazed, horrified, and mortified." Naturally, the destructive relationship of Aaron and Lottie is most expansively treated. The moral implications of Aaron's desertion of Lottie are not the concern of this present chapter, but will be discussed later in a reply to Eliseo Vivas' charges against the morality of the novel. The sexual relationship of Aaron and Lottie is an exhausting and deadly battle of wills which sets the pattern for a series of similar sexual battles and abortive human relationships pervading the novel.

Aaron's rejection of the landlady's advances is similarly connected to a determined opposition to the feminine will: "He disliked her at her tricks. Her and all women. Bah! the love game!" (27). The violation of selfhood and infringements upon personal liberty which various facile social measures during the war and its aftermath inflict are associated in *Aaron's Rod* with the modern love-urge:

> Fair, wise, even benevolent words: always the human good speaking, and always underneath, something hateful, something detestable and murderous. Wise speech and good intentions — they were invariably maggoty with these secret inclinations to destroy the man in the man. Whenever he heard anyone holding forth: the landlady, this doctor, the spokesman on the pit bank: or when he read the all-righteous newspaper, his soul curdled with revulsion as from something foul. Even the infernal love and good-will of his wife. To hell with good-will! It was more hateful than ill-will. Self-righteous bullying, like poison gas! (29)

Aaron's opposition to the self-important landlady is thus more than a simple resistance to her sexual wiles. The suggestion of poison gas recalls the earlier imagery of the violence of war released into the atmosphere and also anticipates Lilly's quarrel with Aaron in Chapter 10 over the atrocity of using poison gas in the trenches.

The deadly sexual conflict between the masculine and feminine will continues through the novel as Aaron later encounters Josephine Ford, Lady Franks and her music, and finally, the Marchesa del Torre, conceived of as a modern Cleopatra symbolically destroying her victims. The curious dissonance of the novel is further sustained by other abrasive or unsatisfactory relationships each one paralleling thematically that of Aaron and Lottie. Josephine Ford's engagement to Jim Bricknell ends in bitter hostility and we are told that Jim has previously been unsuccessful in his marriage to "a French wife." The discontentment of Julia and Robert's marriage is similar, as is the barren and frustrating relationship of the Marchese del Torre and his wife. Argyle also speaks of his stormy marriage, a "hell" which has driven him to renounce "marriage and woman." Even Lilly and Tanny seem deadlocked at times in the battle of wills and Lilly speaks repeatedly of Tanny resisting his authority. All such sexual conflicts are typical of the social unrest and *ennui* of the post-war period which pervades the novel.[22]

Yet in spite of the wilful conflicts of various couples which seem to permeate the novel, one is struck by the curiously static quality of the novel even in such scenes as Aaron's bitter encounter with Lottie in Chapter 11, "More Pillar of Salt." The characters, even the self-pitying Lottie seem curiously detached from their conflicts, often repressing their urge for physical violence. Impotent rage, such as that of Jim Bricknell glowering and threatening at Covent Garden, or that of Aaron—seething with icy fury in the "Royal Oak" or wanting to throw bombs or cause physical damage at the sound of orchestral harmony—seems to have replaced the frequent and more intensely realized, physical violence of the earlier novels. The characters in *Aaron's Rod* are instantly frustrated in their attempts to find an outlet for the violent physical energies which the war seems to have stimulated in them.

In his study of conflict in Lawrence's fiction, Yudhishtar draws our attention to the thematic connections between *Women in Love* and *Aaron's Rod:*

> *Aaron's Rod,* in fact, continues Lawrence's "life and thought adventure" at the point where *Women in Love* had left it, and further explores the theme of man-woman relationship, bringing out its limitations and inadequacies, and defining at length man's need for coming into possession of his own soul, for "his isolate self-responsibility."[23]

Though no one would seriously dispute Yudhishtar's important observations, it should be pointed out as well that Lawrence's treatment of the physical and psychological violence of the sexual struggle has altered significantly in *Aaron's Rod.* I would argue that the change has been effected by the odd depression and inertia of Lawrence's end-of-the-war outlook as outlined above. In *Aaron's Rod* Lawrence was attempting to portray the *malaise* of the post-war generation. His exploration of the conflict of the man-woman relationship naturally shifted its emphasis to the dissatisfaction of frustrated violent energy. A glance at the abundance of violent conflicts with which *Women in Love* pulsates suggests to us that Lawrence was attempting something altogether different in *Women in Love* than in the later *Aaron's Rod.* In his "Foreword" to *Women in Love*

Lawrence himself suggests that the "bitterness of the war may be taken for granted in the characters." I would suggest that similarly in *Aaron's Rod* the maddening impotence and inertia of the post-war era must be assumed in the major characters. The change of emphasis and effect is quite apparent if we compare two thematically similar scenes, the "lapis lazuli" scene (Chapter 8) of *Women in Love* with the scene of Aaron's return to Beldover and his bitter encounter with Lottie.

In the famous lapis lazuli scene in *Women in Love* Rupert Birkin goads Hermione into an outburst of destructive energy. The sexual implications of Hermione's assault are quite obvious; her wounded vanity and frustrated sexual energy drive her to a sadistic consummation, a voluptuous gratification. The attack itself is conveyed in a torrent of muscular prose, filled with the desperate tension which the violence of the episode demands.[24] A strange ritual of cleansing in the surrounding woods follows, as Birkin energetically strives to remove the taint of Hermione's murderous feminine will.

It is instructive to compare this violent scene with that of Aaron's homecoming in "More Pillar of Salt." The hideous physical violence of the lapis lazuli scene has been replaced entirely by vituperation and recrimination. The terrible blows to Birkin's head and shoulders are replaced by verbal rather than physical attacks as Lottie vilifies Aaron's manhood. The closest Lottie comes to an actual physical manifestation of her fury is to clutch violently at Aaron's collar, half choking him. Aaron's silent, almost mindless reaction to Lottie's single attempt at a violent act contrasts strikingly with Birkin's more prolonged and decisive release from Hermione's deadly violence. Unlike Hermione who assumes a perverted "almost religious expression" of near-triumph, Lottie weakly succumbs to her defeat, swearing silently never to yield: "She was frantic with weariness and would be glad to get to bed and sleep" (150).

I present this comparison of these two scenes, not to demonstrate the superiority of the scene from *Women in Love* — clearly one of Lawrence's finest achievements — but to stress once again the difference in tone and intent between such scenes in *Women in Love,* a novel of the mid-war, and *Aaron's Rod,* a novel of the end-of-the-war period. Physical violence as an expression of uncontrollable fury or hatred has been almost entirely sublimated in *Aaron's Rod*. The realistically presented sexual battles of *Women in Love* have been replaced in *Aaron's Rod* by sexual debates or silent resistance, most often by recollections of emotional conflict, as characters like Aaron, del Torre, and Argyle look back at bitter past experiences. The physical manifestations of *Blutbrüderschaft* — embodied in *Women in Love* by the purgative violence of the wrestling match — have been supplanted by a more mysterious incantatory anointing. In a trance-like state Lilly massages the passive, stricken Aaron, attempting to draw him from the state of inertia which amounts to a denial of life.

It is also interesting that the characters who speak freely of, or approach physical violence seem to recoil immediately, repelled by their own violent energy. Jim Bricknell punches Lilly in the solar plexus but sheepishly relents. His blows seem merely to harm Lilly's dignity rather than to jeopardize his physical or spiritual state. In any case, Lawrence soon disposes of Jim Bricknell who is mentioned later, significantly, by Herbertson, but is never actually seen again. Likewise the "bolshy" enthusiasm of the pseudo-bohemians for a "bloody revolution" or smash up in Chapter 6 remains mere talk (as the appropriate title of the chapter suggests) and is soon forgotten.

I am by no means suggesting that Lawrence advocates more physical violence as an easy means of surviving the intolerable *ennui* of the post-war years. By Aaron's own admission, in Chapter 12, physical violence — the cruel beatings which he inflicts upon Lottie — is no solution to the sexual deadlock. I would suggest, however, that Lawrence is affirming, not simply the need for a healthier release from tension and hatred, but that the energy of destruction which has gone into creating the war machine (and has thus brought about the collapse of the old world) must be used to build a "new and freer world." As Lawrence informed Lady Asquith in the illuminating letter cited earlier, this new world must be dedicated to the principles of life rather than death.

In the meantime, the major characters of the novel, particularly Aaron, drift about or simply resign themselves to the inertia and emptiness which has seized post-war Europe. The global conflict of war seems reduced to a series of petty skirmishes, which are the inevitable result of post-war ferment. Though there are scenes of dangerous anarchy, such as the flag incident, the main characters are noticeably uncommitted to such expressions of energy. They seem content to watch disaffectedly, like Francis, from balconies or, like Levison, to recount the violence of such scenes in the relative comfort of cafés or salons. Even the enigmatic Lilly, the only major figure possessing any degree of energy of decisiveness, seems afflicted at times by the same unproductive restlessness of which he seeks to cure Aaron. As his new "disciple" points out with painful accuracy in Chapter 10, Lilly is often plagued with self-doubt. Yet Lilly does offer a cure for the strange end of the war illness. His concept of the poisonous love-urge being replaced by a fresh commitment to the deeper power-urge will be discussed later, at the conclusion of this chapter and in the final chapter of my study.

The noticeable change in tone and emphasis in *Aaron's Rod* must be seen as a reflection of the change in Lawrence's outlook which I have previously described. The active hatred or misanthropy which attended the writing of *Women in Love* has subsided into the numbness and listlessness with which *Aaron's Rod* is imbued. As part of his attempt to place the general malaise of the post-war era Lawrence populates the novel with characters who are either mesmerized or psychologically paralyzed. Even the instigators of civil unrest appear stunned in the midst of their anarchistic acts. The youthful climber in the flag incident stands high up on the housefront as if in a trance, weakly allowing himself later to be led away by the *carabinieri*. The groups of hangdog men who remain to grumble and await the next outbreak of violence seem typical of the futility and impotence of the restless *dopoguerra*.

Among the major figures of the novel, as in Joyce's fiction, talk has replaced action. The social debate or symposium increases in thematic importance as the novel moves along. Neither the subjects of each of these debates nor the particular unity which they impose upon the novel lie within the scope of this present chapter, but will be discussed in a later chapter. The abundance of verbal clashes or exchanges of opinion, some quite heated, is entirely consistent with the picture Lawrence is presenting of a restless post-war period which has mysteriously been deprived of its ability to act decisively. The bewildered members of such a society anxiously probe the causes of this illness yet fall back upon talk for talk's sake, dazed or frustrated. Frequently their exchanges of opinion end only in an ideological stalemate rather than illumination.

The nostalgia for a civilization which has been swallowed up in the holocaust of war is suggested in *Aaron's Rod* by several aging figures. Their presence in a post-war society seems strangely anachronistic. At Algy's flat Aaron encounters an "old Italian elegant" who "studie[s] his formalities with a delightful Mid-Victorian dash" (257). The elaborate social conduct of the old *beau* can only seem grotesquely out of place in the shattered social milieu of the *dopoguerra*.

At the home of the Marchesa Aaron is similarly amused by the aging authoress, Corinna Wade, who sums up a vanished pre-war civilization:

> All the old culture and choice ideas seemed like blowing bubbles. And dear old Corinna Wade, she seemed to be blowing bubbles still, as she sat there so charming in her soft white dress, and talked with her bright animation about the influence of woman in Parliament and the influence of woman in the Periclean day. Aaron listened spell-bound, watching the bubbles float round his head, and almost hearing them go pop. (314)

The imagery of bubbles bursting no doubt reminds the reader of other explosions or crashes in the novel (such as the symbolic shattering of the blue ball), each one echoing the cataclysm of global conflict which has shattered Miss Wade's comfortable world. Another such figure also present in this scene is an elderly littérateur, Mr. French, "more proud of his not-very-important social standing than of his literature...one of those English snobs of the old order, living abroad" (314). The flirtation of this quaint pair makes Aaron, an alienated figure of the *dopoguerra,* feel "very much out of it."

I mentioned earlier that Lawrence also introduces us to a number of "shell-shocked" figures in order to illustrate the devastating effect of war upon the survivors of the disaster. One other such character, although a civilian, is the Marchesa, who deserves a special place in any discussion of Lawrence's treatment of the tragic aftermath of war. The strange suffering and heavy languor of the Marchesa seem to symbolize the malady which paralyzes the entire "lost generation" of the post-war period. In an earlier chapter, I discussed the "drug-like tension" which afflicts the Marchesa, her "peculiar heavy remote quality of preoccupation and neurosis" (261). The themes of love and music and war all come together in Aaron's brief relationship with the Marchesa. In Chapter 16 the Marchesa reveals to Algy that the sad loss of her singing voice must be attributed to the war. Algy replies, significantly, "Oh, but don't let the war deprive us of this, as of everything else" (259), later adding: "But this is really another disaster added to the war list" (260). The Marchese later confides to Aaron, "The war seemed to take her life away" (263).

Earlier I suggested that the loss of the Marchesa's voice was intimately connected to deeper psycho-sexual causes. Like Herbertson's psychological wound, the Marchesa's sexual wound refused to heal. Her abortive love affair with Aaron simply duplicates the sterility of sexual deadlock which has blighted her marriage to Manfredi.

The strange numbness of inertia which envelops the society of post-war Europe is further suggested in *Aaron's Rod* by Lawrence's ingenious use of recurring images of the abyss: emptiness, hollowness, darkness. The first five chapters of the novel take place in symbolic post-war darkness. The "hollow, dark" countryside "re-echoe[s] like a shell with shouts and calls" (18). Aaron's opposition to the deadly will of the landlady and her muddled altruism is defined as a "hard opposing core" sitting in his breast like an "invisible black dog" (26). Aaron deliberately resists the "melting... into oneness with the dark" (29) which the forced conviviality of the pub produces.

Images of darkness and emptiness continue throughout the novel. The interior of Covent Garden is viewed as a "hollow shell," an appropriate metaphor for the superficiality of the patrons of the opera. In Chapter 7, entitled, significantly, "The Dark Square Garden," Aaron and Josephine sit together "on a dark blowy night," and the dark square gradually assumes symbolic overtones of a terrible psychological hollowness or darkness at the center of war-torn London; a darkness which negates the life-force:

> It seemed dark and deserted, dark like a savage wilderness in the heart of London. The wind was roaring in the great bare trees of the centre, as if it were some wild dark grove deep in a forgotten land. (81)

In Chapter 8, the emptiness and sterility of Jim Bricknell is suggested metaphorically by his huge appetite and his strange need to consume chunks of bread during the night. When questioned about his curious compulsion Jim replies "I've got to feed up. I've been starved during this war." Jim's faith in the therapeutic value of bread suggests that a symbolic hollowness within him must be filled up (89).

A similar hollowness is suggested by Aaron's spiritual condition during his attack of influenza. The influenza attack brings him to the brink of a psychological abyss and is used by Lawrence as another emblem of the sickness of the post-war world. Similarly, after his encounter with the vituperative Lottie in Chapter 11, Aaron escapes back into the darkness of the post-war countryside, "swallowed in a black unconsciousness" (149).

In post-war Italy, the atmosphere of emptiness and inertia continues. "It was too soon after the war for life to be flowing very fast. The feeling of emptiness, of neglect, of lack of supplies was evident everywhere" (178). In Milan Aaron witnesses the disquieting flag-incident by early evening light, observes the black garbed crowd's seething like "boiling pitch" (216). Later, the insidious sexual power of the Marchesa causes Aaron dark nightmares, "violent dreams of strange black strife, something like the street riot in Milan, but more terrible" (302). Perhaps the most striking image of the nightmarish darkness of the post-war abyss occurs in Chapter 20 with the bomb outrage:

> There intervened one awful minute of pure shock, when the soul was in darkness.
> Out of this shock Aaron felt himself issuing amid a mass of terrible sensations: the fearful blow of the explosion, the noise of glass, the hoarse howl of people, the rushing of men, the sudden gulf, the awful gulfing whirlpool of horror in the social life.
> He stood in agony and semi-blindness amid a chaos. (329)

Yet another type of darkness also occupies the center of the novel, the fertile darkness of gestation or incubation most noticeably connected with Lilly's special influences and doctrine. At the same time Lawrence is using the recurrent imagery of hollowness and darkness to suggest the terrible gulf which has opened at the center of post-war society, he is also suggesting, through images of a more *fecund* darkness, that there is a way out of such chaos for those who will commit themselves to the life-urge. It is no accident this commitment should be connected with Rawdon Lilly or that Lilly himself is described many times as the "dark little man." His eyes and coloring are part of the subtle power exerted by him upon his listeners.

An analagous use of such seemingly ambivalent darkness may be discovered in Shaw's *Heartbreak House* (1919), a drama which also grew out of the impact of war upon the artistic conscience. Towards the conclusion of *Heartbreak House,* Hector speaks prophetically of two directions which may be taken out of the surrounding darkness:

> I tell you, one of two things must happen. Either out of that darkness some new creation will come to supplant us . . . or the heavens will fall in thunder and destroy us.[25]

It is precisely this new creation for the individual which Lilly seeks and the imagery of a fertile or brooding darkness conveys.

In Chapter 9, the dark Lilly sits in his Covent Garden lodging "motionless and inscrutable" as Aaron's questions fall "into the twilight like a drop of water falling down a deep shaft into a well" (122). The suggestion of the anticipation of a secular pentecost (or perhaps an epiphany) in the pregnant-seeming darkness is unmistakable:

> It was not yet seven o'clock, but the sky was dark. Aaron sat in the firelight. . . . Darkness, silence, the firelight in the upper room, and the two men together. (121)

Lilly, it is later revealed, is himself strongly attracted to darkness and the river "flowing blackly towards the sea." (130) The ambivalent nature of darkness is apparent here. We cannot completely ascertain the significance of the darkness at this point in the novel. Is it the negative darkness of the bleak post-war milieu or the darkness of a period of gestation? After Lilly enters the novel, darkness seems to acquire more positive associations, increasingly suggesting a period of expectation which surrounds the rebirth of a society based on entirely new principles. The same strangely ambivalent darkness surrounds Aaron's playing of his flute in the darkened *salotta* of the del Torre home and his subsequent affair with the Marchesa.

The suggestions of a more positive darkness recur in Chapter 15 when Aaron flees the "cozy brightness" of his room for the brooding darkness of the Piazza Vecchio. The "dark, strong inviolate square" here contrasts with the windy square of Bloomsbury (Chapter 7) with its suggestions of spiritual desolation. In spite of the decline of the post-war years, the Piazza's ambivalent yet ancient darkness seems through such qualities to suggest the former grandeur of Florence, and, in its statuary, a once superior race of Tuscan men.

It is, of course, significant that in a city such as this Aaron and Lilly should be reunited. Aaron at this point seems to move closer to the dark little Lilly, who leads his potential follower from the dark chaos of the café explosion and subsequently rouses Aaron from the spiritual torpor which follows the shattering of his flute. Surrendering, at least for the moment, to his "mind's hero" (337), Aaron listens to Lilly's new doctrine of power and submission while Lilly's face remains dark and remote-seeming.

Lilly's fervent "speech-music" in the final chapter of the novel at last makes clear to the reader his stand against war and the shabby fervor of the post-war period. According to Lilly the pursuit of the decadent "love-urge" has brought unprecedented hatred and war upon Europe and has resulted in the submission of lost souls to leaders, like Lloyd George, "mere instrument[s] for their use" (347). The love-urge has transformed Europe into a cage for Lilly who (like Lawrence himself) feels "riveted" down by the outworn ideals of "religion, God, and love." Lilly clarifies the direct connection between the bullying love-urge and the violence which it inevitably fosters.

Europe in its love-whooshing, according to Lilly, has destroyed itself, committed itself to the death urge, actually the recoil of the love-urge. Shaw clearly summed up the nature of the commitment of the lovesick denizens of *Heartbreak House* ("cultured, leisured Europe before the war") to the paths of war and death:

> Heartbreak House was far too lazy and shallow to extricate itself from this palace of evil enchantment. It rhapsodized about love; but it believed in cruelty. It was afraid of the cruel people; and it saw that cruelty was at least effective. Cruelty did things that made money.... Heartbreak House, in short, did not know how to live, at which point all that was left to it was the boast that at least it knew how to die: a melancholy accomplishment which the outbreak of war presently gave it practically unlimited opportunities of displaying. Thus were the firstborn of Heartbreak House smitten; and the young, the innocent, the hopeful expiated the folly and worthlessness of their elders.[26]

The reference to the biblical slaughter of the firstborn seems particularly relevant to *Aaron's Rod*. Shaw's entire *Preface to Heartbreak House* must be considered an indispensible gloss upon many of the issues examined by Lawrence in *Aaron's Rod* and other works of this period.

If we examine Lilly's "harangue" in the final chapter of the novel and return to his denunciation of war in Chapter 10 we can begin to understand the condemnation of Herbertson and the heroes of the war in *Aaron's Rod*. The love which binds Herbertson to his fallen comrades represents for Lilly a manifestation of a love of death rather than life. His celebrated "courage" seems simply the capacity to *die* rather than *live*. Yet Lilly is not as merciless or unfeeling as might be assumed upon a first exposure to his harsh indictment of those who have fought and fallen. His violent hatred of the "love-whoosh" and its deadly effect prompts his outburst against the unsuspecting Herbertson.

Another extreme figure, a type of civilian Herbertson, condemned for his part in the glorification of war, is the *nouveau riche* Sir William Franks. Trusting to "providence plus a bank account," the old knight has obviously used war as an excuse for profiteering and indulging in supposedly humanitarian activities. The scene in the library of the Franks estate in which the old knight is presented, resplendent in his decorations, his own trophies of war, is a piece of consummate irony. At the same time, it forms an integral part of the novel's bitter attack upon the false love-urge, actually a lust for death, which threatens civilization. Like the corrupt leaders of the war era Lady Franks grotesquely assumes that a man's dignity or worth may be measured by public recognition and the presentation of medals. Even the Major, who has himself sacrificed an eye to the heroic ideals of war, refers to his decoration as "a reassuring sign that a nation knows how to distinguish her valuable men" (163). The inflated grandeur of the ritual is savagely undercut a few lines later when Aaron examines more closely Sir William's orders and sees them as "just metal playthings." (165)

Along with Alfred Bricknell, the mines-boss, Sir William Franks embodies the lust for power and possession of a modern industrial force which has corrupted civilization and brought it to the disaster of war. In his study "Lawrence and the War," Keith Myers sums up Lawrence's condemnation of the industrial consciousness:

> Yet before and after the war, Lawrence's conception of evil remains fundamentally the same. . . . It lies in the general will of a monolithic, industrial, technocratic power which automatizes society into a "ghastly mob sleep," and leaves only lust for total possession, of whatever is "loved." It is blind to the "otherness" of things outside its ego. . . . It hates what it cannot absorb, and since things are either independent and "quick" or they die, it ends in hating and destroying itself. The war is simply its tremendous symbol, paralyzing in the extent of its horror but familiar in its essential nature.[27]

Later, through the recurrent imagery of masks and play-acting Lady Franks and Sir William are placed as doomed inhabitants of a collapsing world:

> Lady Franks, Sir William, . . . they talked and manoeuvered with their visible personalities, manipulating the masks of themselves. And underneath there was something invisible and dying — something fading, wilting: the essential plasm of themselves: their invisible being. (192)

In a similar way Lady Franks' dream of an attack by Novarese anarchists, terrifying in its suddenness, suggests an imaginative foreshadowing by Lawrence of the fall of corrupt authority.

Sir William's philanthropic projects are exposed as rather paltry, certainly, ineffectual when they are actually described by Lady Franks herself (183). Such charitable efforts, Lawrence seems to be saying, are associated with a guilty conscience. The spurious magnanimity of the corrupt love-urge here recoils upon the giver. At the same time the stupidity of Italian officialdom is exposed. The false love of humility of Sir William Franks is akin to that of misguided contemporary politicians like Woodrow Wilson, as Lilly demonstrates in the last chapter of the novel. A similar misguided faith in the efficacy of sacrifice and a philanthropic love-urge has weakened Jim Bricknell to the point of psychosomatic paralysis which Lilly terms the "sloppy relaxation" of the will. His "love-whooshing" leads him to spend his time "wavering about, going to various meetings, philandering and weeping (87)."

In the final chapter of the novel, Lilly condemns war and deplores its bleak aftermath, maintaining that the power-mode must supplant the love-mode. Yet he never suggests exactly how his theories might work for the many, i.e., at a practical social level. Perhaps it may be argued that in the café debate of Chapter 20, Lilly claims to speak only for himself and asserts that perhaps his solutions will work only for himself. However, it seems quite evident that Lilly himself presumes to speak for humanity's needs in the final chapter of the novel. At least, his diagnosis of the world's sickness certainly extends beyond himself and Aaron to deal with society as a whole. Lilly seems anxious to offer a kind of solution or "way out" of the chaos of the post-war period.

Having attacked war and the present upheaval of society which war has produced, Lilly seems able to offer little more than a proposal which *may* work, but only, it seems, at an intensely personal level and only for a chosen few. Although he speaks confidently of the new devotion to the power-urge Lawrence illustrates dramatically that Lilly remains uncertain about the practical applications of his power theories.

Perhaps Lilly is himself trapped, as George Ford suggests Lawrence was himself, in the dilemma of being neither an anarchist nor a pacifist.[28] Lilly's fear of the mob and the swarming millions makes him a strangely elitist "savior" — a role which, we are told, he fancies for himself. Aaron's suspicion of Lilly's new doctrine seems at a first reading to be justified by the contradictions of Lilly's position. Is not Lilly's solution (as he develops his theories before Aaron in the final chapter) simply another "Morrison's Pill," as Carlyle would have described it — a quick cure-all for society's ills? In any case, no matter which way we read the exhortation of Lilly at the conclusion of the novel, *Aaron's Rod* taken as a whole remains Lawrence's most powerful indictment of the machinery of war and a superb recreation of the restless period following the Great War.

6

Profile of an Anti-hero: A Reconsideration of Aaron Sisson

In an earlier chapter, I described in detail the gradual evolution of Aaron Sisson's anti-heroic nature as reflected in the numerous alterations which Lawrence made to his typescript version of the novel.[1] These significant revisions demonstrate clearly that Lawrence's initial concept of Aaron became radically altered as his new novel progressed and the character of Aaron took its final form in his mind. Whereas the *earlier* Aaron had been characterized as fundamentally naïve and impressionable, especially in the presence of the Bricknell set, the Aaron of Lawrence's *final* version has been deliberately rendered more anti-heroic and anti-social. Indifference and aloofness, bordering often on insolence, have replaced wonder and impressionability. The resulting characterization of the unusual protagonist is more complex with its suggestion of inscrutability and silent power. In this chapter, I shall examine at greater length the character of Aaron Sisson as developed through various stages of the novel, suggesting at the same time the devices employed by Lawrence to distance Aaron from both his surroundings and the reader. Finally I shall investigate briefly the peculiar double relationship of Aaron and Lilly.

It should be stated at the outset that, placed against the vast array of characters created by Lawrence, Aaron Sisson stands out as unique, and, indeed, as somewhat of an anomaly. Yet this emphatically does *not* imply that the character of Aaron owes nothing to the earlier fiction nor that he is unrelated to other protagonists created by Lawrence during the remaining years of his career. I shall have more to say of the relation of Aaron to other Lawrencean protagonists later, but would suggest at this point that Lawrence's presentation of the alienated, taciturn Aaron as well as the crucial role to which he assigns this inarticulate protagonist marks a radical departure from his usual strategy.

Most readers of Lawrence have been struck (with varying degrees of annoyance) by the fact that in much of the fiction the chief interest or development seems often to be centered upon a Lawrencean *persona*—at times unabashedly autobiographical, as in the case of Somers in *Kangaroo*. Often this dark, irascible hero seems inevitably committed to an exploration of Lawrence's private theories at whatever time in his career the novel happened to be written.[2] In *Aaron's Rod*, however, we have one of those rarer instances in the novels of the focus shifting subtly (though by no means totally) away from the dark, bearded and vigorously assertive Lawrence-figure to a blond, sexually attractive, yet silent anti-hero who opposes the doctrine advanced by the Lawrencean *persona*, Rawdon Lilly. However often critics may object to Aaron's mysterious inarticulateness, suggesting that Lilly is by far a more vital or plausible character, it cannot be denied that Aaron Sisson's developing awareness lies at the heart of the novel. Accordingly, most of the novel's chapters are built around a crucially formative experience of Aaron, even those chapters in which Lilly appears as the fervent would-be mentor of his reluctant disciple.[3] As highly developed and utterly indispensable as Lilly undoubtedly is, his principal role in the novel depends upon his participation in Aaron's personal development.

It is fascinating to re-explore Lawrence's earlier works in order to estimate the extent to which Lawrence has drawn on previous characterizations for the creation of Aaron Sisson. In a previous chapter discussing music in *Aaron's Rod*, I compared Siegmund (of *The Trespasser*) and Aaron Sisson as "musician-heroes." Without a repetition of the entire argument of that chapter, it may be stated unequivocally that *Aaron's Rod* owes much to *The Trespasser*. Aaron Sisson is artistically a superior creation, at least a more successful musician-hero. As I suggested earlier, Aaron's inarticulateness itself accounts for his dependence upon his flute as a mode of self-expression. Even his innermost thoughts are transcribed by the wry narrator in Chapter 13 as "speech music." The descriptions of Aaron *en famille* and his decision to free himself from the soul-destroying world of Lottie and the mining countryside recall somewhat Siegmund's earlier imprisonment by the tedium of his family life as well as Siegmund's pitiable attempts to escape the hostility of his shrewish wife Beatrice.

Perhaps Aaron's stubborn aloofness owes something to Lawrence's earlier depictions of the ill-fated Siegmund's brooding introspection. Yet the character of the earlier fiction who most directly resembles and in a sense anticipates Aaron is in fact Tom Brangwen. Aaron's physical robustness and colouring (blond hair, blue eyes) recall Tom Brangwen's; like Tom he is sexually attractive. His educational background also recalls Tom's. Mrs. Brangwen has "roused herself to determination" to send her favorite son "forcibly away to grammar school in Derby."[4] She attempts to cultivate a gentleman-scholar in the family with the hope that he will surely rise above his humble origins. Tom of course fails miserably to "her mortification and chagrin." Aaron too has been encouraged in school by a zealous mother, as we discover in a brief reminiscence in Chapter 7:

> His father had been a shaft-sinker, earning good money, but had been killed by a fall down the shaft when Aaron was only four years old. The widow had opened a shop: Aaron was her only child. She had done well in her shop. She had wanted Aaron to be a schoolteacher. He had served three years apprenticeship, then suddenly thrown it up and gone to the pit. (76)

The bourgeois desire to transcend lower class origins may remind us also of Gertrude Morel's similar aspirations for her sons in *Sons and Lovers*. Aaron has failed like Tom, though more out of rebellion than for lack of intelligence.

The psychological makeup of Aaron is also reminiscent of the strange mixture in Tom of "brutality and delicacy."[5] There is more of a suggestion of humility in Tom Brangwen's character, and much of his silence may simply be interpreted as mere self-absorption or reticence. The popular esteem in which Aaron is held among the frequenters of the "Royal Oak" pub (in spite of his frequent ill-humour) recalls somewhat Lawrence's descriptions of Tom in the early scenes of *The Rainbow:*

> He got a special corner for himself at the "Red Lion" at Cossethay, and became a usual figure by the fire, a fresh, fair young fellow with heavy limbs and head held back, mostly silent, though alert and attentive, very hearty in his greeting of everybody he knew, shy of strangers.[6]

Tom also remains silently withdrawn from his neighbors: "He liked people, so long as they remained in the background."[7] Aaron is certainly less "hearty" or affable than Tom, much more enigmatic, but like Tom he often chooses not to obey social custom: "He never went with the stream, but made a side current of his own. His wife said he was contrary" (17). In Aaron Sisson, Tom's simple withdrawal is transformed into a misanthropic denial of social connections and the compulsion to constant flight.

Aaron's mysterious attraction to the exotic yet remote Marchesa del Torre in Florence may owe something to the earlier treatment of Tom's fascination with the "foreignness" and "remoteness" of Lydia Lensky. At Algy's teaparty in Chapter 16 of *Aaron's Rod*, in which he encounters the Marchesa del Torre for the first time, Aaron is immediately struck by the Marchesa's curious remoteness and silence as she sits smoking continuously, "sad" and "remote-seeming....a modern Cleopatra brooding, Anthony-less" (257). She remains "abstracted, a sort of cloud on her level dark brows" and later speaks with "a certain heavy languor" as "one in trance—or a sleep-walker" (265). Of course, Tom's fascination with Lydia's remoteness signals the beginning of a healthy and productive union which contrasts with the destructive, wilful relationship of Aaron and the Marchesa, the danger of which is hinted at in the reference to Cleopatra and Anthony. It must be noted also that Aaron's stormy domestic life with Lottie bears a more striking resemblance to that of Will and Anna Brangwen. Like Will, Aaron also escapes the harsh reality of his domestic life in art. Will's fascination lies first in the plastic arts and, later, in arranging and performing church music. Aaron's escape lies in the abstractions of his flute playing.

The inscrutable silence of both Tom and Aaron naturally imposes severe demands upon Lawwrence's artistic powers. How may the silent "hero" be rendered dramatically plausible, how may his growing self-awareness be best conveyed to the reader? How and when must the hero give voice to his innermost thoughts? In the celebrated wedding-dinner scene in *The Rainbow* (Chapter 5), Lawrence contrives to render Tom Brangwen semi-intoxicated before he is able to rise and relate his parable of the angels. The unusual "talkativeness" of Tom and gentle charm of his important speech are ironically juxtaposed by Lawrence with the derisive banter of the wedding guests, most notably that of Tom's brothers Alfred and Ted.

In the first half of *Aaron's Rod*, Aaron must also be inebriated (or else semi-delirious in the throes of influenza) before he can become communicative at all. On one notable occasion in a later chapter, during a discussion of love and marriage, Aaron is suddenly roused to articulateness. His newly-found speech is used by Lawrence as an indication that Aaron is falling more under the influence of Lilly at this point and also as a sign of Aaron's growing understanding of his futile position. As the conclusion of this chapter reveals, Aaron now feels compelled to reassess the importance to his own life of Lilly and his doctrines. With renewed feelings of both fascination and revulsion toward Lilly he begins to seek a more intimate relationship with this curious individual.

Elsewhere in the novel most other crucial revelations of Aaron's innermost thoughts are conveyed to the reader through a variety of devices. Sometimes Lawrence as narrator translates Aaron's inarticulate "speech music" into the intelligible speech of ordinary communication. At one point Aaron's savage inner hostility toward human relationships is conveyed to the reader as the substance of a letter to William Franks.[9] Lawrence constantly draws our attention to the difficulties of presenting convincingly a silent protagonist. At most times Aaron is aloofly withdrawn and non-communicative, much like his fictional predecessor Tom Brangwen, yet without the gentle acquiescence of that earlier character. The characterization of Aaron as first conceived by Lawrence in the early stages of writing the novel must certainly have been more reminiscent of Tom than in the final published version of the novel. In fact, the robustly handsome stranger who sits silently in the drawing room in Shottle House in Chapter 3 with "faint wondering" (TS147) could easily pass for Tom Brangwen himself.

The more negative or anti-social aspect of Aaron's silences derives from Lawrence's powerful characterization of Gerald Crich. Aaron's wilful abstraction owes something to that of Gerald, and carries with it some of the same implications of brutal mechanical will, and his near surrender to despair and death during his influenza might recall the suicidal impulse to which Gerald eventually succumbs. Aaron displays the same tendency as Gerald toward self-destructiveness as he engages in a series of soul-blasting sexual relationships throughout the novel: the result (in Lilly's view) of giving in to the moribund love-urge. Aaron's blondness is similar to that of Gerald but is not made to bear the same weight of symbolic suggestiveness as Gerald's Nordic colouring, with its connotations of "ice-destructiveness."

Aaron's and Lilly's relationship of course recalls to a large extent Birkin's abortive attempts at a deeper intimacy with Gerald Crich. *Aaron's Rod* might even be seen in this sense as a sequel to Lawrence's exploration of *Blutbrüderschaft* as an extension of the modern marriage.

After Aaron, Lawrence never again attempted such a silent anti-hero.[10] Yet it should be noted that Somers' silent witholding of himself both from Harriet and Kangaroo owes something to Aaron's frequently annoying aloofness. Likewise the inscrutability of Cipriano in *The Plumed Serpent*, especially his treatment of Kate Leslie. In *Lady Chatterley's Lover*, Lawrence re-used elements of Aaron Sisson in his characterization of Mellors. Both are in a sense escaped members of the proletariat who nevertheless reject the supposed falsity of intellectualism. Aaron has thrown over a career as school teacher to enter the pit just as Mellors has left a commission in the cavalry to be an "overhead blacksmith" at the mine, and eventually, gamekeeper to Sir Clifford. Both men especially favor the use of vernacular in defiance of society. Both Aaron and Mellors seek a withdrawal from a destructive marriage to one of Lawrence's typical viragoes, "castrators" of the "proud male." Both men overstep the boundaries of class in a semi-taboo relationship with an upper-class woman. Of course the union of Aaron and the Marchesa in its willful destructiveness contrasts sharply with the creative "tenderness" of Mellors' liberating relationsip with Constance Chatterley.

Throughout the novel the character of Aaron is deliberately presented to the reader as somewhat ambiguous or elusive. A device which may be best described as *distancing* has been employed by Lawrence in order to separate Aaron slightly from the reader's struggling apprehension of his inner self as well as to suggest Aaron's successive withdrawal from those experiences which surround or affect him. The narrator also plays an important part in this distancing scheme, for his observations act as a screen held carefully between the reader's knowledge of Aaron and the intuitions of Aaron himself.

The alienation and withdrawal of Aaron are suggested at a simpler physical level by the series of removed or elevated *loci* from which the detached and silent anti-hero observes life about him. At a deeper psychological level, this constant placing of Aaron outside the fringes of social activity is paralleled by Aaron's self-imposed distance, as he moves farther and farther away from human intimacy or commitment.

Instances of physical distancing abound. Returning home for the first time, Aaron stands mutely at the bottom of his garden surveying "the whole row of houses" from the distance as if "through the wrong end of a telescope" (46). Observed from afar, the "contiguous stretch of back premises" is revolting to Aaron. In Chapter 5, "At the Opera," Aaron, seemingly sharing the narrator's sardonic sense of detachment from this milieu of social pretense, looks down with Josephine Ford at the "dishevelled theatre," and comments drily, "You get all the view" (64). A few chapters later, Aaron lies recuperating in Lilly's tiny flat perched over Covent Garden. The episode is rich in realistic descriptions of the market setting with its carters, its intrigues and frequent assignations: all observed from above. At once connected yet removed from its surroundings, Lilly's flat provides the background from the fierce denial by both men of the cult of the *magna mater*. Aaron and Lilly seem at times to withdraw into a separate world where mutual reassessment of life alone seems possible. Having brought Aaron and Lilly alone together for the first time, Lawrence may now expose Aaron to Lilly's doctrines, particularly after Aaron has been revived by the determined ministrations of Lilly.

Similarly, the home of Sir William Franks is remotely situated on a hill overlooking Novara. During his brief stay here we find Aaron constantly detached or withdrawn, observing the scene about him. He watches the servants frolicking but is physically (and psychologically) remote. (175) A few pages later he gazes with mixed feelings of involvement and alienation at an Italian street scene:

> Men and women were moving about, and he noticed for the first time the littleness and the momentaneousness of the Italians in the street. Perhaps it was the wideness of the bridge and the subsequent big, open boulevard. But there it was: the people seemed little, upright brisk figures moving in a certain isolation, like tiny figures on a big stage.

And he felt himself moving in the space between. All the northern cosiness gone. He was set down with a space round him. (178)

The stage imagery contributes to the effect of curious detachment yet vicarious participation of Aaron's part in the scene before him. Like Fitzgerald's Nick Carraway, Aaron is both "within and without, simultaneously enchanted and repelled by the inexhaustible variety of life"[11] about him, both in this scene and throughout the novel.

Aaron's removed position on a balcony during the flag incident in Milan provides an opportunity for Lawrence to sound the characteristic note of political discord which pervades the post-war atmosphere of Europe. At the same time, he is able to register the disturbing effect of the political climate upon the developing consciousness of Aaron himself. In Florence also, the physical remoteness of the various settings in which Aaron has been placed are linked to the psychological movement of the anti-hero away from the world about him. With its view of the busy piazza below, Argyle's tower flat (in "High Up Over The Cathedral Square") recalls Lilly's Covent Garden flat. Passersby seem ironically dwarfed and insignificant as they are observed from above by Argyle, Lilly and Aaron, with both fascination and detachment. The remote tower is established as a perfect setting for the serious colloquium which follows. A sense of withdrawal is once more provided which is necessary to a reconsideration of the position and importance of the love-urge, or as Argyle poignantly phrases it, the lifelong "search for a friend."

In Florence also Aaron observes from the wings, as it were, scenes of clandestine political activity, the most memorable of which is the nocturnal removal of a corpse through the dark narrow streets of Florence. From his "big bleak room" in the pension Nardini, Aaron looks down in his solitude at the river Arno. Escaping the ornate drawing room of the *pensione*, as well as the suggestive glances of the "foreign women" (245), Aaron returns to his "far-off regions, lonely and cheerless, away above" relishing the "remoteness of the big old Florentine house" (245). Ensconced in his room, he feels a satisfaction "as if he were in a castle with the draw-bridge drawn up" (247). Still later, after the sudden bomb explosion in the café, Aaron stands with Lilly on Ponte San Trinità looking down at the Arno and surrenders the remnants of his flute to the muddy flood. The physical distance between Aaron and his broken flute is at this point the symbolic measure of the widening gap between his old life of restless wandering and his new life under the influence of Lilly.

All such physical distancing reinforces Aaron's psychological withdrawal throughout the novel. Early examples of this psychological distancing of Aaron from his surroundings include Aaron's voluntary oblivion as he practises the flute amid the tensions of domestic life and his subsequent resistance to the landlady's skillful wiles. His silent withdrawal is here presented in the vivid image of an invisible black dog which constantly besets him.[12]

These actions of psychological withdrawal underlie Aaron's constant rejection of his surroundings and his increasing "urge to disappear" through restless wandering. The sense of wilful alienation or psychological distance permeates all of Aaron's sexual relationships in the novel. Throughout his married life with Lottie, as we discover in Chapter 13, Aaron has kept himself distant, withholding himself even in those moments which for Lottie are full of "heaven rending passion." (188) The manner in which Aaron is able to withhold "the very centre of himself" is strikingly demonstrated during his final confrontation with Lottie. Aaron sits silently enduring the flood of Lottie's recriminations, yet all the time quite removed, psychologically, from the scene. (149)

The same withdrawal characterizes Aaron's relationship with Josephine Ford. Dining in a Soho restaurant with him, Josephine notices Aaron's indifference to his surroundings (76). She is forced to recognize "the curious cold distance" which Aaron constantly imposes between himself and others. (77)

Much later the Marchesa registers her own fear of this aloofness (297). Aaron's final rejection of the Marchesa and her supposedly fatal will also manifests itself in images of psychological distance. As he makes love to the Marchesa for the last time he feels his "aloof soul" standing "far off, like Moses' sister Miriam." (318)

Yet Aaron's self-imposed psychological distance must not be construed as healthy or positive. Though the anti-heroic Aaron has early in the novel foresworn marriage, he still continues to vacillate between the extremes of sexual intimacy and revulsion in a series of unfortunate love affairs. As might be expected, it is Lilly alone who possesses a more positive theory of singleness:

> "Can't one be alone—quite alone?" said Lilly.
> "But no—it is absurd. Like Saint Simeon Stylites on a pillar. But it is absurd!" cried the Italian.
> "I don't mean like Simeon Stylites. I mean can't one live with one's wife, and be fond of her: and with one's friends, and enjoy their company: and with the world and everything, pleasantly: and yet *know* that one is alone? Essentially, at the very core of me, alone. Eternally alone. And choosing to be alone. Not sentimental or *lonely*. Alone, choosing to be alone, because by one's own nature one is alone. The being with another person is secondary," said Lilly. (289)

Lilly's withdrawal into singleness is thus more creative. It emphatically does not exclude intimacy yet still preserves the integrity of the individual soul. But Aaron is a great distance yet from being able to understand or accept Lilly's doctrine of aloneness. The progress which Aaron makes towards the proper acknowledgement of the validity of Lilly's doctrine is another phase in the continuing drama of self-discovery which shapes the novel and supposedly will lead Aaron to ask his soul the "overwhelming question."

Aaron's search for a true self-awareness involving the singleness of self-possession preached by Lilly determines the unique structure of *Aaron's Rod*. In a penetrating examination of the novel, F. R. Leavis has observed the uncommon "spirit of unabashed tentativeness" which informs *Aaron's Rod*. No one could argue seriously with Leavis' judgement as a description of the unique texture or total effect of the novel. Yet it seems to me that Leavis' description must be extended beyond its immediate relevance to the state of Lawrence's mind during the writing of *Aaron's Rod*. In a wider sense, the description must be applied to a very deliberately calculated effect in *Aaron's Rod*, a highly unified and skillfully integrated work of art. The "unabashed tentativeness" applies (far more readily than Leavis seems willing to consider) to the developing awareness of Aaron as well as to the peculiar form of the novel. As a kind of "drama" of self-discovery, the novel has been conceived partially as a traditional novel of development with picaresque elements incorporated into it. The growth from youth to maturity or "consciousness" of the traditional *bildungsroman* is conceived in Lawrencean terms as the struggle of one man to escape the fetters of a life both meaningless and destructive. In so doing, the protagonist is seen as obeying what Lawrence called the "promptings of desire and aspiration" which the "creative spontaneous soul sends forth."[13] The structure of the novel as it develops according to the successive stages of Aaron's fitful quest towards self-discovery suggests that the work is itself a mimesis of such an experience. It conveys to us in its very form the immense difficulty of such a quest, forcing the reader into a vicarious participation—even towards a sense of sympathy for the painful groping of the protagonist towards a true freedom and understanding of himself.

One recollection of Lawrence while he was writing *Aaron's Rod* (preserved by Achsah Brewster) provides us with a clearer insight into what he was attempting in the figure of Aaron and in what way Aaron's evolving fate determined the form of the novel. In Capri, Mrs. Brewster recalled that

in the afternoon Lawrence came swinging up the garden path. We were alone, and he told us that he was writing *Aaron's Rod*, and began outlining the story. It seemed more beautiful as he narrated it in his low sonorous voice with the quiet gesture of his hands, than it ever could written in a book. Suddenly he stopped, after Aaron had left his wife

and home and broken with his past, gravely asking what he should do with him now.
We ventured that only two possible courses were left to a men in his straits—either to go to Monte Cassino and repent, or else to go through the whole cycle of experience.
He gave a quiet chuckle of surprise and added that those were the very possibilities he had seen, that first he had intended sending him to Monte Cassino, but found instead that Aaron had to go to destruction to find his way through from the lowest depths.[14]

The mention of the imperative "whole cycle of experience" suggests a Dantesque pattern of moral degeneration, suffering and ultimately, spiritual regeneration. This insight into Lawrence's intentions is fascinating, for it indicates that the novel was conceived half as a kind of romance, half as a *bildungsroman*. Its structure was to be determined by the moral quest of a strange anti-hero compelled, like so many of Conrad's characters, to immerse himself in the entire destructive experience in order eventually to achieve a higher form of self-knowledge.

The central action of *Aaron's Rod* properly begins with Aaron's fateful decision not to return to his family on Christmas Eve. Leaving the "Royal Oak" he chooses instead another direction which takes him far from the home path in search of himself (30). The moment is highly portentous, and Lawrence places upon this moment the symbolic suggestiveness of the famous opening lines of the *Divina Commedia*. The incident also recalls Paul Morel's momentous decision at the conclusion of *Sons and Lovers*—an ambivalent decision for some readers—to turn from the abyss to the "faintly, glowing, humming town."

Another major turning point in Aaron's fate (hense in the structure of the novel) occurs in Chapter 11, "More Pillar of Salt," immediately after his second return to Lottie and her domestic world. Escaping Lottie's violent recriminations he makes the important decision never to return to Lottie, nor to surrender to her will:

> Love was a battle in which each party strove for the mastery of the other's soul. So far, man had yielded the mastery to woman. Now he was fighting for it back again. And too late, for the woman would never yield.
> But whether woman yielded or not, he would keep the mastery of his own soul and conscience and actions. He would never yield himself up to her judgment again. He would hold himself forever beyond her jurisdiction....
> As for future unions, too soon to think about it. Let there be clean and pure division first, perfected singleness. That is the only way to final, living unison: through sheer, finished singleness. (150)

In this early example of indirect interior monologue Lawrence has subtly suggested that Aaron has as yet little understanding of the nature of love. He conceives of it simply as a process of the willful domination of one individual by another. Indeed, his coarse and imperfect concept of the marital relationship is almost an ironic parody of Lilly's mysterious theories of marriage outlined in the final pages of the novel. His hazy notions are at this point at the farthest reach from the Lawrencean theory of the perfect sexual relationship, specifically imaged in *Aaron's Rod* by a paraphrase of Whitman's "Dalliance of Eagles":

> Two eagles in mid-air, grappling, whirling, coming to the intensification of love-oneness there in mid-air. In mid-air the love consummation. But all the time each lifted on its own wings: each bearing itself up on its own wings at every moment of the mid-air consummation. That is the splendid love-way. (196)

Aaron's position is more ambiguous than might be first surmised. Nevertheless, his decision to keep "the mastery of his soul" suggests a more positive aspect of his renunciation of Lottie here. Lawrence further suggests the larger symbolic overtones of Aaron's decision in the seeming assent of the natural universe, particularly that of the stars, each shining in its isolation. In terms of the novel's structure, this episode is a major turning-point, for it provides a fitting climax to what Lawrence, according to Achsah Brewster, considered to be the culmination of the first phase in Aaron's personal development.

An important phase of Aaron's development takes place in Novara and is highlighted by the extended indirect monologue in Chapter 13, "Wie es Ihnen Gefaellt." This recognition scene, one of the most difficult and abstract portions of the novel, illuminates for the reader the inner agony of Aaron's struggle as well as the considerable tentativeness of his position at this point. For the first time in the novel, Aaron is compelled to face the terrible failure of his marriage and is forced to assess truthfully his present dilemma.

The reader is skillfully prepared for this extraordinary recognition scene by the change noted in Aaron himself as he makes the physical and mental transition from England to Italy. In his new Italian setting with its distant view of the Alps, Aaron has previously "felt himself changing inside his skin," the metaphor suggesting the process of renewal as invertebrates shed their old skin and begin a new cycle. Earlier in the same chapter, Aaron has been driven to choose sides with Lilly for the first time in the novel. He defends his desertion of Lottie and his subsequent wandering before Sir William's probing inquiry. At the same time, he is indirectly defending Lilly's insistent doctrine of proud singleness, and the responsibility of the individual to obey the promptings of his soul. Finally, in Chapter 13, Aaron is forced "to open his darkest eyes and wake up to a new responsibility":

> Wake up and enter on the responsibility of a new self in himself. Ach, the horror of responsibility! He had all his life slept and shelved the burden. And he wanted to go on

sleeping. It was so hateful to have to get a new grip on his own bowels, a new hard reck-lessness into his heart, a new and responsible consciousness into his mind and soul. He felt some finger prodding, prodding, prodding him awake out of the sleep of pathos and tragedy and spasmodic passion, and he wriggled, unwilling, oh, most unwilling to undertake the new business. (177)

The actual recognition scene begins as a deceptively realistic fireside reverie, with Aaron's recollection of the tediously familiar domestic scene he has abandoned:

He thought of his wife and children at home: of the church-bells ringing so loudly across the field beyond his garden end: of the dark-clad people trailing unevenly across the two paths, one to the left, one to the right, forking their way towards the houses of the town, to church or to chapel: mostly to chapel. At this hour he himself would be dressed in his best clothes, tying his bow, ready to go out to the public house. And his wife would be resenting his holiday departure, whilst she was left fastened to the chil-dren. (185)

Aaron's "musing" falls roughly into three rather heterogeneous sections held together loosely by the inquiring consciousness of the protagonist. The first and most coherent portion of this indirect monologue reveals the nature of the deadly clash of wills of Aaron and Lottie and traces the deep-er sources of that deadlock, presenting us with an indirect flash-back to the early married life of the Sissons and a prolonged diatribe against the female will, as "flat and inflexible as a sheet of iron." The flash-back suggests both guilt and resentment on Aaron's part. Lottie with her impla-cable will may have mistakenly asserted that "she as a woman, was the cen-tre of creation, the man was but an adjunct"; but Aaron still admits that he always "withheld the very centre of himself" from his wife. He also "made play with her tremendous passional soul":

Yes, in those supreme and sacred times which for her were the whole culmination life and being, the ecstasy of unspeakable passional conjunction, he was not really hers. He was withheld. Hé withheld the central core of himself, like the devil and hell-fiend he was. He cheated and made play with her tremendous passional soul, her sacred sex passion, most sacred of all things for a woman. All the time, some central part of him stood apart from her, aside, looking on. (188)

Aaron's subsequent assessment of his share in the breakdown of his mar-riage seems admirable in its candor, while his recollections of his brutality in the sexual deadlock suggest that he has been more profoundly affected by the destructive struggle with Lottie than has so far been revealed, cer-tainly more emotionally bruised than might be suspected from his earlier evasive or apparently callous replies to Josephine's or Lady Franks' med-dlesome inquiries. Nevertheless, Aaron rationalizes, his escape was inevi-table, "as a broken spring flies from its hold." (190)

The second part of this recognition scene deals more with Aaron's assessment of his present situation. The confusion of Aaron's mind is skillfully evoked as the image of the broken spring is pursued even further:

> Not that he was broken. He would not do her even that credit. He had only flown loose from the old centre-fixture. His will was still entire and unabated. Only he did not know: he did not understand. He swung wildly about from place to place, as if he were broken. (190)

Aaron holds up his constant vacillation and aimless freedom to rigorous scrutiny. The chief focus of this section is Aaron's reaffirmation that salvation alone lies in the preservation of his intrinsic and central aloneness:

> Then suddenly, on this Sunday evening in the strange country, he realised something about himself. He realised that he had never intended to yield himself fully to her or to anything: that he did not intend ever to yield himself up entirely to her or to anything: that his very being pivoted on the fact of his isolate self-responsibility, aloneness. His intrinsic and central aloneness was the very centre of his being. Break it, and he broke his being. Break this central aloneness, and he broke everything. It was the great temptation, to yield himself: and it was the final sacrilege. Anyhow, it was something which, from his profoundest soul, he did not intend to do. By the innermost isolation and singleness of his own soul he would abide though the skies fell on top of one another, and seven heavens collapsed. (191)

The extravagance of the hyperbole here suggests ironically that Aaron is not yet as free from the temptation to yield himself as he assumes. During the course of the novel he will succumb momentarily to the dangerous wiles of the Marchesa which, like Lottie's willful manipulations, threaten to rob him of his sacred selfhood.

This second section of Aaron's recognition scene is remarkable for its repeated reference to Wells' *The Invisible Man*[15] in connection with Aaron's self-revelation:

> His mask, his idea of himself dropped and was broken to bits. There he sat now maskless and invisible. That was how he strictly felt: invisible and undefined, rather like Wells' *Invisible Man*. He no longer had a mask to present to people... (192)

The agony of Aaron's changing awareness is conveyed in a further reference to *The Invisible Man*: "The old Aaron Sisson was as if transmuted, as the Invisible Man when he underwent his transmutations." (192)

Lawrence is attempting to convey through his imagery of invisibility the sudden stripping away of all social pretension as Aaron rejects his former dependence upon superficial charm and physical beauty. Perhaps Lawrence expects us to recall Lilly's earlier condemnation of Aaron's relying upon the the illusions of personal charm. In this crucial scene, Aaron moves a step beyond the limitations of "social passports," approaching a realization of the greater freedom of "intrinsic and central aloneness." At the same time, the scattered allusions to *The Invisible Man* hint ominously at the perils of a life of the selfish ego, the possible monomania of a life which, like that of Griffin, remains isolated and without reference whatsoever to the world outside the self. Lawrence is thus pointing out again that Aaron's confession to himself is but a crucial turning point in his development rather than an end *per se*. Aaron has but scarcely begun to comprehend his strange position; his future course of action lies dimly before him.

Aaron's vulnerability (as well as his potential self-renewal) is further suggested at this point by a favorite Lawrencean image:

> Having in some curious manner tumbled from the tree of modern knowledge, and cracked and rolled out from the shell of the preconceived idea of himself like some dark, night-lustrous chestnut from the green ostensibility of the burr, he lay as it were exposed, but invisible on the floor knowing,...but having no idea. (192)

In the third and final portion of the recognition scene, the emphasis shifts somewhat from Aaron *per se* to the varied commentary of the narrator. In a prolonged address to the "gentle reader" the narrator defends the method of an indirect presentation of Aaron's thoughts by explaining his intermediary function:

> He was a musician. And hence even his deepest *ideas* were not word-ideas, his very thoughts were not composed of words and ideal concepts. They too, his thoughts and his ideas, were dark and invisible, as electric vibrations are invisible no matter how many words they may purport. If I, as a word-user, must translate his deep conscious vibrations into finite words, that is my own business. I do but make a translation of the man. He would speak in music. I speak with words. His mind was music.
>
> The inaudible music of his conscious soul conveyed his meaning in him quite as clearly. But in his own mode only: and it was in his own mode only he realised what I must put into words. These words are my own affair. His mind was music.
>
> Don't grumble at me then, gentle reader, and swear at me that this damned fellow wasn't half clever enough to think all these smart things, and realise all these finedrawn-out subtleties. You are quite right, he wasn't, yet it all resolved itself in him as I say, and it is for you to prove that it didn't. (193)

Lawrence in the guise of his omniscient narrator might well feel defensive; the entire episode has been severely criticized largely because of the device of an intrusive narrator. In any case, the third section of this recognition scene certainly moves considerably beyond the limits of Aaron's private conscience and must be considered as more properly concerned with the larger moral or philosophical questions of the novel as a whole. This third section can be seen as the legitimate extension of Aaron's foregoing self-revelation and as crucial to his development. Lawrence is simply attempting, as he so often does in his novels, to enlarge in a more discursive manner upon the essential significance of his central character's experience. Thus he extends for his imagined audience Aaron's meditations upon the female obsession with domination, at the same time placing the strife of Aaron and Lottie within the larger frame of the universal struggle peculiar to Christian society:

> The *idée fixe* of today is that every individual shall not only give himself, but shall achieve the last glory of giving himself away. And since this takes two—you can't even make a present of yourself unless you've got somebody to receive the present; since this last extra-divine act takes two people to perform it, you've got to take into count not only your giver but your receiver. Who is going to be the giver and who the receiver.
> Why of course, in our long-drawn-out Christian day, man is giver and woman is recipient. Man is the gift, woman the receiver. This is the sacrament we live by; the holy Communion we live for. That man gives himself to woman in an utter and sacred abandon, all, all, all himself given, and taken. Woman, eternal woman, she is the communicant. She receives the sacramental body and spirit of the man. And when she's got it, according to her passionate and all-too-sacred desire, completely, when she possesses her man at last finally and ultimately, without blemish or reservation in the perfection of the sacrament: then, also, poor woman, the blood and the body of which she has partaken become insipid or nauseous to her, she is driven mad by the endless meal of the marriage sacrament, poisoned by the sacred communion which was her goal and her soul's ambition. (194)

This third and somewhat unorthodox section of the recognition scene further defines Aaron's predicament, in more general or abstract terms, and hints strongly at Aaron's closer relationship with Lilly in future. In a sense, the self-reliance and creative independence embodies in Lilly's "aloneness" will become a goal for Aaron. All of this is indirectly and very subtly suggested by the crucial explanation of the thematic significance of Lilly's unusual name. Recalling Christ's exhortation, in the Sermon on the Mount, to "consider the lilies,"[16] Lawrence describes how Aaron's acceptance of his singleness is a condition of his ultimate fulfillment:

> So Aaron, crossing a certain border-line and finding himself alone completely, accepted his loneliness or singleness as a fulfilment, a state of fulfilment. The long fight with Lottie had driven him at last to himself, so that he was quiet as a thing which has its root deep in life, and has lost its anxiety. (195)

The lily is superior because unlike modern man it is unfettered by the *idée fixe* of modern civilization, the false ideal of self-sacrifice:

> As for considering the lily, it is not a matter of consideration. The lily toils and spins hard enough, in her own way. But without that strain and that anxiety with which we try to weave ourselves a life. The lily is life-rooted, life-central. She *cannot* worry. She is life itself, a little, delicate fountain playing creatively, for as long or as short a time as may be, and unable to be anxious. She may be sad or sorry, if the north wind blows.

But even then, anxious she cannot be. Whether her fountain play or cease to play, from out of the cold, damp earth, she cannot be anxious. She may only be glad or sorry, and continue her way. She is perfectly herself, whatever befall! even if frosts cut her off. Happy lilly, never to be saddled with an *idée fixe*, never to be in the grip of a mono-mania for happiness or love or fulfilment. It is not *laisser aller*. It is life-rootedness. It is being by oneself, life-living, like the much-mooted lily. (195)

This passage is essential to our understanding of Lilly's "aloneness" and of his special role in the novel. Lawrence makes it very clear here that Lilly's doctrine of intrinsic self-aloneness is closer to the strength of self-reliance than to the terrible weakness of monomania or solipsism. Some-how Lilly must bring the wandering, often erring Aaron closer to his doc-trine of creative and vital selfhood. He must teach Aaron to free himself from his compulsive enslavement to the destructive love-urge.

In view of this, the conclusion of this final section of the recognition scene with its elaborate "Dalliance of Eagles" simile requires further ex-planation. The image of the coupling eagles makes it abundantly clear that love and sexuality are not be excluded from the fulfilment of the indivi-dual.[17] However, the love-urge must never be allowed to rule the individual completely. It must be held in balance with the urge to power and there must be no surrender or compromise of the intrinsic self. The image of the eagles no doubt recalls Rupert Birkin's theory of star-equilibrium advanced in *Women in Love*. Yet at this stage of the novel—the major turning point of Aaron's destiny—our understanding of what Lawrence is striving to communicate in a spirit of "unabashed tentativeness" may be as uncertain as Aaron's own floundering attempts to understand himself. It is only when we have reached the conclusion of the novel that we begin to under-stand the full import of the simile and the true meaning of Lilly's concepts of self-aloneness. Having passed at this point with Aaron through his second ordeal of consciousness, we require, along with Aaron, the guiding hand of Lilly who alone is able to illuminate what seem to be some puzzling contradictions in the philosophical *cadre* of the novel. Further, the dependence of both reader and protagonist on the spokesman of vital selfhood is cleverly contrived to arouse our expectations and carry us with Aaron forward to his fateful reunion with Lilly in Florence, the "lily-town."

It is appropriate that Lilly should renew his attempts to instill in Aaron the spirit of true selfhood in the city of Florence, the lily-town. In Chapter 17, Lilly speaks of Florence as a lily, not a rose:

"I love it," said Lilly. "I love this place. I love the cathedral and the tower. I love its pinkness and its paleness. The Gothic souls find fault with it, and say it is gimcrack and tawdry and cheap. But I love it, it is delicate and rosy, and the dark stripes are as they should be, like the tiger marks on a pink lily. It's a lily, not a rose; a pinky white lily with dark tigery marks. And heavy, too, in its own substance: earth-substance, risen from earth into the air: and never forgetting the dark, black-fierce earth—I reckon here men for a moment were themselves, as a plant in flower is for the moment completely itself. Then it goes off. As Florence has gone off. No flowers now. But it *has* flowered. And I don't see why a race should be like an aloe tree, flower once and die. Why should it? Why not flower again? Why not?" (273)

Like modern man, Lilly seems to say, Florence has lost some of its proud and fierce singleness. To Lilly's concluding rhetorical questions (reaffirming his faith that one day Florence will recover its former pride) Aaron replies rather argumentatively, "If it's going to, it will[.]... Our deciding about it won't alter it." Lilly's reply to Aaron's typical objections suggests that the spirit of selfhood connected with a true and creative relation to the "circumambient universe" must be awakened once more, not by democracy or the masses, but only through the individual's responsibility to himself and his soul: "The decision is part of the business" (273).

Lilly's speech here takes us back to Aaron's earlier discovery of the statuary in the Piazza della Signoria and particularly to Lawrence's description of Michaelangelo's David. The deep effect upon Aaron's imagination of the sight of the piazza and its statuary is quite striking:

> Aaron looked and looked at the three great naked men. David so much white, and standing forward, self-conscious: then at the great splendid front of the Palazzo Vecchio: and at the fountain splashing water upon its wet, wet figures; and the distant equestrian statue; and the stone-flagged space of the grim square. And he felt that here he was in one of the world's living centres, here, in the Piazza della Signoria. The sense of having arrived—of having reached a perfect centre of the human world: this he had. ...The physical, self-conscious adolescent, Michelangelo's David, shrinking and exposing himself, with his white, slack limbs! Florence, passionate, fearless Florence had spoken herself out. — Aaron was fascinated by the Piazza della Signoria. He never went into the town, nor returned from it to his lodging, without contriving to pass through the square. And he never passed through it without satisfaction. Here men had been at their intensest, most naked pitch, here, at the end of the old world and the beginning of the new. Since then, always rather puling and apologetic. (248–49)

The close connection here between Aaron, hesitant and newly tumbled out of the chestnut burr of his former self, and Michaelangelo's David, shrinking and exposed, is obvious. The essay "David," most likely inspired around the same time as the descriptive commentary which was to appear in *Aaron's Rod*,[18] makes this connection even more explicit. David as he stands now in the Piazza, the young lily arrested in adolescence, is a grim reminder of all the "pride of life," a "perfect soul erect, holding the eternal elements consummate in itself," which was *once* the embodiment of Florence, but now seems lost or buried in the rubble of modern decadence. The essay ends with a characteristic Lawrencean expression of hope that David will some day be reborn:

> One day David finishes his adolescence. One day he reaps his mates. It is a throbbing through the centuries of unquenchable fire, that will still leap out to consummation. The pride of life, the pride of the fulfilled self. The bud is not nipped; it awaits its maturity. Not the frail lily. Not even the clinging purple vine. But the full tree of life in blossom.[19]

The rebirth of David and the true spirit of Dionysus will be akin to the blossoming of the "full tree of life," transcending even the frail lily.

Returning to *Aaron's Rod* we may now perceive that Aaron is clearly intended to be identified with the incomplete David who must some day be reborn and flourish in "the pride of life." It is of considerable importance that in Florence Aaron has already begun to feel "a new self, a new life-urge rising inside himself. Florence seemed to start a new man in him" (249). These early sensations of renewal are to be nurtured by Lilly, whose name itself is associated with his firm belief in himself and his sacred selfhood. Under the guidance of Lilly, Lawrence is implying the spirit of proud selfhood, (identifiable with the spirit of Dionysus-Pan) must flourish again in Aaron, as it must one day in David and the race of Florentines now weakened and "rather puling." Rather than bringing forth the red Florentine lilies of modern love and sexuality (as it did during the destructive affair with the Marchesa) Aaron's rod of selfhood must shoot forth the almond blossoms of the inviolate soul. Lilly himself speaks later of the way in which Aaron's tree of life within must blossom:

> You are your own Tree of Life, roots and limbs and trunk. Somewhere within the wholeness of the tree lies the very self, the quick: its own innate Holy Ghost. And this Holy Ghost puts forth new buds, and pushes past old limits, and shakes off a whole body of dying leaves. And the old limits hate being empassed, and the old leaves, hate to fall. But they must, if the tree-soul says so.... (344)

It is interesting that Aaron should be reunited by an accidental meeting with Lilly in the Via Nazionale. Mysteriously, Lilly is not at all surprised. He speaks of the coincidence as coming "naturally" enough — a significant echo of Aaron's description earlier of the desertion of his family:

> "It happened to me: as a birth happened to me once — and death will happen. It was a sort of death, too: or a sort of birth. But as undeniable as either....
> "A natural event," said Sir William.
> "A natural event," said Aaron. (171)

The ensuing symposium at Argyle's flat on love and the eternal search for a friend continues for several pages and is a crucial part of Aaron's development. His sudden articulateness is revealed as the direct result of his renewed friendship with Lilly. He seems almost to have absorbed some of Lilly's remarkable vitality as he moves closer to the dark, little man. Aaron's comments contain the further suggestion of growing self-criticism:

> You can be alone just in that minute when you've broken free, and you feel heart thankful to be alone, because the other thing wasn't to be borne. But you can't keep on being alone. No matter how many times you've broken free, and feel, thank God to be alone...it wears off every time, and you begin to look again—and you begin to roam around. And even if you don't admit it to yourself, still you are seeking—seeking. (282-83)

Up to this point, Aaron seems to have been fairly content to remain aloof, even misanthropic. His aloneness has amounted simply to the severing of "old connections" and, during his self-imposed exile, performing impersonal acts of lust. With the renewal of his association with Lilly will come a greater understanding of true aloneness, perhaps of the "fathomless submission" to a greater soul. Aaron is exposed in this chapter to Lilly's concept of a new kind of aloneness far removed from his own narrow understanding of the term. From now to the end of the novel Aaron must move closer to Lilly and his positive doctrine of isolate selfhood as he is exposed more and more to Lilly's subtle power. The chapter concludes with a minute of revelation. Aaron's heart stands still momentarily as he listens with his sensitive ears to Lilly's voice, "so like a simple, deliberate amiability." Though he realizes for the first time that Lilly's words come "out of his isolation," at this point Aaron is still not ready to accept either Lilly's personal force or the truth of his doctrine of intrinsic selfhood, much less Lilly's bitter condemnation of the decadent love-urge, especially as it applies to Aaron's own case. Aaron is nevertheless even more fascinated by the curious Lilly:

> Aaron felt that Lilly was *there*, existing in life, yet neither asking for connection nor preventing any connection. He was present, he was the real centre of the group. And yet...Lilly would receive no gift of friendship in equality. Neither would he violently refuse it. He let it lie unmarked. And yet at the same time Aaron knew that he could depend on the other man for help, almost for life itself—so long as it entailed no breaking of the intrinsic isolation of Lilly's soul. But this condition was also hateful. And there was also a great fascination in it. (290)

The most violent turning point in Aaron's personal fate occurs in Chapter 20, appropriately entitled "The Broken Rod." Shattered as suddenly and hopelessly as the precious blue ball in Chapter 1, Aaron's flute is committed to the waters of the Arno. The gesture is part of a ritual both of completion and initiation. Aaron himself recognizes that the destruction of his flute symbolizes the end of his futile former existence:

> "Throw it in the river," repeated Lilly. "It's an end." Aaron nervelessly dropped the flute into the stream....
>
> Aaron was quite dumbfounded by the night's event: the loss of his flute. Here was a blow he had not expected. And the loss was for him symbolistic. It chimed with something in his soul: the bomb, the smashed flute, the end. (331)

Characteristically, Lilly enlarges the symbolic meaning of the incident in his replies to Aaron:

> "There goes Aaron's Rod, then," he said to Lilly.
> "It'll grow again. It's a reed, a water-plant — you can't kill it." said Lilly, unheeding.
> "And me?"
> "You'll have to live without a rod, meanwhile." (331)

As in *The Waste Land* (published the same year as *Aaron's Rod*) Aaron's symbolic "death by water," as his flute disappears in the Arno, signals both the destruction of the old self as well as the beginning of a new cycle of human experience. Lawrence uses this crucial "peripeteia" to deliver the unwilling disciple once more to the ministrations of the prophet Lilly, who will enlarge Aaron's awareness. As I suggested in an earlier chapter on music in *Aaron's Rod*, Aaron can no longer rely upon his flute or his personal charm to sustain the egotistical and false independence which he has so far enjoyed throughout the novel. His new self must take root afresh, attuned somehow more intimately to the strange "speech music" of Lilly.

Aaron's disturbing dream-visions occuring in Chapter 21 are an integral part of his development and therefore require considerably more critical attentional than they have so far received.[20] The immediate cause of Aaron's dream is obviously the bomb-explosion and the shattering of his flute. Yet the dream sequence symbolically encompasses in surrealistic terms Aaron's entire life so far: both his family life and his ensuing existence as a restless exile, and, like the earlier recognition scene in Novara, consists of three distinct divisions. The dream takes place in a strange underworld, which, while recalling *visually* the country of the Morlocks in H.G. Wells' *The Time Machine*,[21] seems more thematically related to Dante's landscape of Hell or Purgatory. The mining countryside of the Midlands reappears in Aaron's dream as "a country" of "tin miners," who, like Wells' underworld creatures, are also cannibals:

> He wandered from vast apartment to apartment, down narrow corridors like the roads in a mine. In one of the great square rooms, the men were going to eat. And it seemed to him that what they were going to eat was a man, naked man. But his second self knew that what appeared to his eyes as a man was really a man's skin stuffed tight with prepared meat, as the skin of a Bologna sausage. This did not prevent his seeing the naked man who was to be eaten walk slowly and stiffly across the gangway and down

the corridor. He saw him from behind. It was a big handsome man in the prime of life, quite naked and perhaps stupid. But of course he was only a skin stuffed with meat, whom the grey tin-miners were going to eat. (332)

The "big, handsome man" undoubtedly represents Aaron in his earlier life as miner and checkweighman, symbolically devoured—i.e., exploited and wasted—publicly, by the mines and wrangling miners; privately, by the terrible will of Lottie. The demonic, devouring power of the Marchesa, linked by her cunning will to the destructive Lottie, is also implied in the symbolic cannibalism. Once again stirred by guilty feelings towards his deserted children, Aaron is haunted next by images of white-gowned children:

> Aaron...turned another way and...came into one room where there were many children, all in white gowns. And they were all busily putting themselves to bed, in the many beds scattered about the room at haphazard. And each child went to bed with a wreath of flowers on its head, white flowers and pink, so it seemed. So there they all lay, in their flower-crowns in the vast space of the rooms. And Aaron went away. (332–33)

It should be remembered that previously Aaron has returned home twice, both times at bed-time. A few days after Christmas Aaron has also seen Millicent emerge from the house "her white pinafore fluttering," discovering later as he stood outside the bedroom window the alarming illness of Marjory. The dream symbol of the children lying in their flower-crowns is a funeral image of Aaron's children now "dead" to their father and perhaps even recalls the earlier talk of "sacred children and sacred motherhood" (116–17). The final short sentence concluding this first part of Aaron's dream-sequence duplicates exactly Aaron's abrupt departure, early in the novel, from his children and wife.

The second portion of Aaron's dream, a similar vision of grey domestic apartments filled with women, "all greyish in their clothes and appearance," suggests both Aaron's tedious former life with Lottie as well as the naturalistic presentation in the earlier chapters of the novel of life in the English Midlands, particularly in the town of Beldover. This brief passage, a transition to the third and most extended portion of the sequence, also suggests symbolically the *ennui* of London society (as encountered by Aaron) with its pseudo-bohemians, its lionising hostesses and their fatuous gatherings.

The third phase of Aaron's dream-vision is more complex: more profoundly disturbing in its nightmarish presentation of self-destruction. Aaron has now split into a palpable self being ferried in a small boat across a "great lake in the underworld," and a conscious self hovering "before the prow of the bow of the boat, seeing and knowing, but unseen" (333). It requires no feat of imagination to realize that the boat as it moves across the lake is a tangible representation of Aaron's uncertain search for true self-hood through the vast unconscious, through the unknown waters of life itself.[22] The invisible Aaron watching the fishes "suspended in the clear, beautiful dark-blue water" (333), recalls Lawrence's response to the independence of the sea-creatures in his interesting poem "Fish":

> Admitted, they swarm in companies,
> Fishes.
> They drive in shoals.
> But soundless, and out of contact.
> They exchange no word, no spasm,
>   not even anger.
> Not one touch.
> Many suspended together, forever apart,
> Each one alone with the waters,
>   upon one wave with the rest.[23]

The three stakes against which Aaron strikes his elbow painfully are quite obviously intended to refer to the three most destructive relationships in which Aaron has involved himself: his strife torn marriage to Lottie; the abortive encounter with Josephine Ford; his nearly "fatal" relationship with the Marchesa. Yet this rather easy interpretation of the three violent blows seems to me unsatisfactory—or at best, incomplete. Although the three stakes most certainly could be associated with the *femmes fatals* of Aaron's past life, I would suggest that the stakes are more directly associated with Aaron's stubborn, self-damaging resistance to Lilly's influence. Aaron's refusal of Lilly's deeper friendship continually drives him in the wrong direction to other unsatisfactory relationships, including a superficial acquaintance with Francis and Angus (which ends in bitter chagrin) and several ominously destructive sexual affairs. It is no coincidence that before Aaron's dream, a decisive turning point in his relation to Lilly, Lilly has made three symbolic calls upon Aaron's soul.

Lilly's first call comes shortly after his ritualistic massaging and anointing of Aaron in Chapter 9. Though mysteriously healed by Lilly, Aaron obstinately refuses to commit himself, as the conclusion of Chapter 10 clearly points out:

Aaron did not find his friend at home when he called. He took it rather as a slap in the face. But he knew quite well that Lilly had made a certain call on his, Aaron's soul: a call which he, Aaron did not intend to obey. If in return the soul-caller chose to shut his street door in the face of the world friend—well let it be quits. He was not sure whether he felt superior to his unworldly enemy or not. He rather thought he did. (142)

At this point Aaron's notions of his true nature and future relation to Lilly are so imperfectly formed as to obstruct his acceptance of Lilly as friend or mentor. He has been unable to comprehend Lilly's theory of friendship. In the following chapter we are not surprised to find Aaron restlessly whiling away his time with dilettantes or turning homewards to the tedium of Beldover and the vindictive Lottie.

Lilly later makes a second, "telepathic" call upon Aaron's soul in Chapter 14 as Aaron, feeling irresistibly drawn towards Lilly, prepares to set out through Italy. Yet he does not accept unequivocally Lilly's silent call. Lilly's offer meets this time with a different, less tangible kind of resistance: moral inertia. Though he has earlier defended Lilly's position of independence against the formidable materialistic ethics of Sir William, Aaron still finds himself vacillating between commitment and lethargy, now "paralyzed fascinated, overcome" by the wealth of the Franks, now denying all direction or commitment whatsoever. Before leaving Novara Aaron also denies once more the influence of Lilly. He realizes that "ultimately he wanted to join Lilly," but maintains that this was hardly more than a sop, and excuse for his own irrational behavior (209). He confesses to himself that though he has "perhaps a faint sense of Lilly ahead of him," still this feeling may simply be "impulse" or "merely an illusion":

> But our hero roused himself with a wrench. The very act of lifting himself from the pillow was like a fight this morning. Why? He recognised his own wrench, the pain with which he struggled under the necessity to move. Why shouldn't he want to move?... True, he said that ultimately he wanted to join Lilly. But this was hardly more than a sop, an excuse for his own irrational behaviour. He was breaking loose from one connection after another; and what for? Why break every tie? Snap, snap, snap went the bonds and ligatures which bound him to the life that had formed him, the people he had loved or liked. He found all his affections snapping off, all the ties which united him with his own people coming asunder. And why? In God's name, why? What was there instead?
>
> There was nothingness. There was just himself, and blank nothingness. He had perhaps a faint sense of Lilly ahead of him; an impulse in that direction, or else merely an illusion. He could not persuade himself that he was seeking for love, for any kind of unison or communion. He knew well enough that the thought of any loving, any sort of real coming together between himself and anybody or anything, was just objectionable to him. No—he was not moving *towards* anything: he was moving almost violently away from everything. And that was what he wanted. Only that. Only let him *not* run into any sort of embrace with anything or anybody—this was what he asked. Let no new connection be made between himself and anything on earth. Let all old connections break. This was his craving. (209–10)

Aaron's present misanthropy thus extends even to Lilly. For a second time, Aaron refuses a commitment to Lilly, choosing instead world-weariness and the self-delusion that he is somehow "fulfilling his own inward destiny" (210), *without* Lilly's guidance.

Lilly's third and most significant overture to Aaron of friendship or guidance—the two are virtually synonymous—occurs at the symposium on love and marriage at Argyle's flat. Typically, Aaron first refuses to acknowledge the validity of Lilly's claims. With del Torre he plays "devil's advocate" interjecting with leading questions as "Aren't you yourself seeking?" (283), or "And what's your way out?" (287). Aaron, however, clearly begins to change in his attitude to Lilly as his eyes meet the "quiet, half-amused, yet frightening eyes" of Lilly. Though deeply affected by Lilly and palpably convinced by his arguments, Aaron still resists his peculiar kind of powerful friendship, at once fascinating and rather hateful.

The interesting, open-ended quality of the chapter suggests that Aaron might soon capitulate to Lilly's power but also that Aaron is at this stage of the novel still hesitating, unsure of what is involved in a relationship with Lilly. Significantly, in the next episode of the novel he succumbs to the harmful attractions of the Marchesa, a near-fatal love affair which is the direct reflex of his third denial of Lilly.[24] Once again he must recoil from a sterile sexual relationship in pain and amazement. The concluding third blow on the elbow of Aaron's dream is related also, in a larger sense, to the sudden blow of the bomb outrage which destroys his flute and directs him towards Lilly, while the conclusion itself of Aaron's dream is a prophecy of his renewed motion towards Lilly, as the *conscious* self replaces the old palpable self, hitherto unresponsive and insensitive to the warning cries of the truer "conscious self." Heeding for the first time the call of his inner soul, Aaron therefore reverses his dream position in the boat. In one decisive gesture the direction of his life is symbolically altered. The reversal of Aaron's dream position carries us forward without pause to his awakening and his decision to follow the "thread of destiny" attaching him to Lilly. Forced to choose not between life and death, but between the world and the uncertain, assertive Lilly, Aaron decides that he would rather "give in to the little Lilly than to the beastly people of the world" (336). Aaron admits to himself for the first time at this crucial turning point that in Lilly "there was something incomprehensible, which had dominion over him, if he chose to allow it" (336). For the first time in the novel Aaron seems ready both to accept the fact that his previous wanderings have been fruitless and self-annihilating and that he must make a crucial decision to change the direction of his life. For the first time also, Aaron finds "a peculiar delight in giving his soul to his mind's hero":

> As he lay pondering this over, escaping from the *cul de sac* in which he had been running for so long, by yielding to one of his pursuers: yielding to the peculiar mastery of

one man's nature rather than to the quicksands of woman or the stinking bogs of society: yielding, since yield he must, in some direction or other: yielding in a new direction now, to one strange and incalculable little individual: as Aaron lay so relaxing, finding a peculiar delight in giving his soul to his mind's hero, the self-same hero tapped and entered. (336-337)

The final movement of the novel thus begins and Aaron seems for the moment to be ready to surrender himself to Lilly's "speech music."

This brings us to a discussion of the strange dual relationship of Aaron and Lilly, and Lawrence's experiements in *Aaron's Rod* with the device of the literary double. An extensive survey of the pervasive use of this popular device by nineteenth century novelists—Stevenson, Dickens, Dostoevsky, to name but a few—lies beyond the scope of this study. It should be observed that Lawrence had been no doubt familiar with the device since his early years.[25] Falling heir to the *Doppelgänger* tradition, he knew exactly how to adapt the device to the demands of his own fiction, in this case employing the device of the double to convey to us that curious repulsion and attraction of Aaron and Lilly which fundamentally determines the tension and rhythm of most of the novel.

A clear-cut definition of the double is extremely difficult, especially in view of the variety of ways in which the device has been used in such diverse works as Dostoevsky's *The Double* or Stevenson's *Dr. Jekyll and Mr. Hyde.* In the preface to his useful anthology *Stories of the Double* — an indispensable starting point for any study of the nature and use of the device —Albert Guerard points to the difficulty of summing up the nature and uses of the double:

The word *double* is embarrassingly vague, as used in literary criticism. It need not imply autoscopic hallucination or even close physical resemblance. Freud, citing Stekels, observes that two dramatized human beings may constitute a single personality. The fear that stirs in Macbeth develops not in him but in Lady Macbeth; in this sense they are doubles. Characters who seem occultly connected in the author's imagination (and such connection may take many forms) may reenact a major character's traumatic experience, if only because the author could not leave the trauma alone. A strong feeling of sympathetic identification may lead to a sense of doubleness, an immobilizing recognition of the self one might have been. To the degree that Brierly sees himself in Lord Jim —or Lord Jim sees himself in Gentleman Brown—Jim and Brown function as doubles and elicit unexpected allegiances.[26]

The double may be either generated from within as in *The Double* in which Golyadkin's double is largely the product of autoscopic hallucination or else two seemingly different characters (such as Lord Jim and Gentleman Brown) may be singled out in a peculiar relationship or duality based upon both on attraction *and* opposition. The duel relationship of Aaron and

Lilly is more in this latter vein. As in so many stories of the double, there is both a recognition and a willful rejection of this strange duality. Guerard observes that in any case the "experience of encountering a double is indeed uncanny: a response not merely to strangeness but to familiarity."[27] Sometimes the recognition is slow to come as in Melville's *Bartleby*. The narrator and Bartleby are doubles, but for a long time the narrator simply feels uneasy with Bartleby, "...There was something about Bartleby that not only strangely disarmed me, but in a wonderful manner touched and disconcerted me."[28]

In *Aaron's Rod*, this response to the encounter with the double is expressed in Lilly's and Aaron's "uncanny understanding" of each other. There are moments of surprising intimacy but they are short-lived, followed most often by outbursts of hostility or rejection. Each man acts as a kind of mirror to the other and each seems in turn to be violently repelled by what is revealed to him through the "mirror" of his double. Aaron and Lilly are thus presented by Lawrence as two similar yet diverse, often conflicting personalities. While their fundamental similarities seem to draw them more closely together, at times their ideological differences drive them apart, especially at the conclusion of "The War Again."

It must be stated, however, that the use of this device has provoked as much critical confusion as fascination since the novel's publication. One of the first critics to notice the strange dual relationship of Aaron and Lilly was (as might be expected) Middleton Murry. Recognising also the extent to which he was himself implicated in what he conceived to be Lawrence's pathetic "life-long search for a friend," Murry described the part which Aaron played in that search:

> In the unimpeded freedom of the imagination, Lawrence is trying, in *Aaron's Rod*, to solve his personal problem. ...He needs a man, and he needs a man of realisation like his own. He creates the man—Aaron Sisson. Sisson is a dream-Lawrence: Lawrence without his physical weakness, but with his spiritual sensibility—Lawrence metamorphosed into "the hardy indomitable male" and yet still Lawrence. ...Aaron Sisson is an astonishing creation. He is Lawrence's dream friend and he embodies much of Lawrence's ultimate knowledge about himself. Aaron's suspicion of Lilly is Lawrence's suspicion of himself, Aaron's foreknowledge of Lilly is Lawrence's foreknowledge of himself.[29]

Examining Chapters 9 and 10 he also found praise for the "self-mastery displayed by Lawrence in this lucid interrogation himself."[30] Murry may be sound in his approval of Lawrence's artistic integrity in refusing to subordinate the submission of the dream-friend to his private needs; but his equation of either Lilly or Aaron simply as a fictional embodiment of Lawrence is a misunderstanding of the novel. There were of course personal reasons for Murry to assume that Lilly was the Lawrence which he, Murry, felt he knew — "in spirit...the friend and lover of all men, in life, ...the friend and lover of none."[31] The sickroom scenes in *Aaron's Rod* after all had been inspired by Lawrence's nursing of Murry during an attack of the *grippe* in 1915.[32] Yet Aaron is much more than a fictional version of Lawrence or a portrait of Middleton Murry in his curious relation to Lawrence, either as reluctant blood-brother or disciple *manqué*.

F. R. Leavis further confuses the issue by treating Aaron and Lilly solely as extensions of opposite facets of Lawrence's nature. Noting the "curious dual presence of Lawrence"[33] Leavis examines the novel as mere fictionalized autobiography, observing that the Lawrencean presence shifts erratically from Lilly to Aaron throughout the novel, but seems confined to Lilly in the final chapters. Leavis comments illuminatingly upon the effect of Aaron's presence as an "ironical *alter ego*," but instead of following up the more interesting implications of his perception, proceeds rather to judge the novel a failure:

> We might conclude at this point that Lawrence's intention bore some relation to Henry James's in *The Lesson of the Master*, and that Aaron, figuring what Lawrence might very well have been if he had married in his own class and things had gone more ordinarily, represented a special imaginative effort on Lawrence's part to transcend the peculiarities of his actual situation. And it would seem that some such intention must, in some measure, have entered into the tentative conception with which Lawrence started on *Aaron's Rod*. If, however, we make this note, it must be to observe when we have read the book through that actually it fails to give full imaginative realization to Aaron's case as one different from Lawrence's own. And 'fails' seems the right word: that is, we are faced with an inadvertence, a default of imagination, which is very significant.[34]

In his anxiety to account for what only *seems* to be a failure of imagination Leavis thus reduces the novel to a thinly disguised autobiography which must be foredoomed on account of the disturbing failures of Lawrence's own life.

More recent critics have also gone astray (though for apparently different reasons) in their investigation of the double in *Aaron's Rod*. Kate Millett, as might be expected, uses the "dual" relationship of Lilly and Aaron to air her contempt for what she conceives to be the "narcissistic character of homosexuality"[35] in Lawrence, convinced wrongheadedly that Lilly and Aaron cannot exist independent of their creator. Another critic, Sandra Berry, though not willfully distorting Lawrence, misguidedly attempts to vindicate what she considers a "dead" novel by suggesting that Aaron and Lilly only "live" for the reader when they are seen as one character. Berry argues further that Aaron and Lilly are personifications of the Lawrencean dichotomy of Law and Love. "Lilly is the Female in the male and Aaron is the Male in the male!"[36] Her study fails largely because she confuses and over-complicates what is after all the conscious use by Lawrence of a novelistic device in his characterization of two very individual and separate characters.

Because of such prevailing critical misunderstanding concerning Lawrence's artistic intentions it is necessary to make several points about Lawrence's use of the double in *Aaron's Rod*. First, Aaron and Lilly are two successful and separate creations and are emphatically not "flat" personifications of Lawrencean abstracts. Forster's oft-misused terms (never quite satisfactory to begin with) simply do not apply here anyway. Second, the double relationship of Aaron and Lilly must be seen as far more than a simple extension of dual aspects of Lawrence's personality. The use of the double must be seen rather as an aspect of style, as a *device* which the novelist had ready at his disposal to suit his artistic purposes, particularly in a novel as replete with literary device and allusion as *Aaron's Rod*.

A closer look at Chapter 10 reveals more exactly the manner in which the double is presented. Lawrence takes pains to establish for the reader the idea that Aaron and Lilly are doubles, similar in background and education (even if Aaron has thrown his over):

> The two men had an almost uncanny understanding of one another—like brothers. They came from the same district, from the same class. Each might have been born into the other's circumstances. Like brothers, there was a profound hostility between them. But hostility is not antipathy. (123)

The characters may be somehow linked but they are kept strictly separate in the reader's mind through their physical presence and appearance in the episode:

> Aaron sat in the low arm-chair at table. So his face was below, in the full light. Lilly sat high on a small chair, so that his face was in the green shadow. Aaron was handsome, and always had that peculiar well-dressed look of his type. Lilly was indifferent to his own appearance, and his collar was a rag. (124)

The two men are driven constantly apart in this chapter by the inevitable hostility of their close relation to each other. In one bitter exchange, Lilly inadvertently draws attention to the close resemblance of his quarrelsome relationship with Aaron to his stormy marital relationship with Tanny. Perhaps there is even a parallel being drawn (at such times of extreme antagonism) to the marital deadlock of Aaron and Lottie, as at one point when Lilly speaks of "possessing one's own soul—and the being together with someone else in silence, beyond speech":

"I've got a *bit* of the real quietness inside me."

"So has a dog on a mat."

"So I believe, too."

"Or a man in a pub."

"Which I don't believe."

"You prefer the dog?"

"Maybe."

There was silence for a few moments.

"And I'm the man in the pub," said Aaron.

"You aren't the dog on the mat, anyhow."

"And you're the idol on the mountain top, worshipping yourself."

"You talk to me like a woman, Aaron."

"How do you talk to *me*, do you think?"

"How do I?"

"Are the potatoes done?"

Lilly turned quickly aside, and switched on the electric light. Everything changed. Aaron sat still before the fire, irritated. Lilly went about preparing the supper. (123)

The rapid exchanges of the dialogue between the two recalls Hemingway's use of the device in such fiction as "A Clean, Well-Lighted Place" to dissolve the barriers or distinctions between the speakers in their respective identities. Lawrence suggests that the roles are interchangeable and the conversation acquires also something of the quality of *dialogue intérieur*.

Lawrence is, however, quite careful not to merge completely the two: "brothers" in soul, perhaps, but quite separate and opposed in circumstance and ideology. Lilly resentfully draws attention to the advantages Aaron has always enjoyed with his charm and easier upbringing:

I was a dirty-nosed boy when you were a clean-nosed little boy. And I always had more patches on my breeches than you: neat patches too, my poor mother! So what's the good of talking about advantages? You had the start. At this very moment you could buy me up, lock, stock, and barrel. So don't feel hard done by. It's a lie. (127-28)

Later Lilly sarcastically refers to the ironic similarity of his and Aaron's position:

My dear Aaron, I agree with you perfectly. There is no difference between us, save for the fictitious advantage given to me by my job. Save for my job—which is to write lies —Aaron and I are two identical little men in one and the same little boat. (128)

Lawrence is suggesting that there exists between the physically slight, yet powerful Lilly and the robust, handsome, yet uncertain Aaron a strange "Cain-Abel" brother-relationship, one of attraction and hostility in which the roles are constantly interchanged. The double relationship is supported by the substructure of biblical symbolism and allusion (particularly

the relationship of the two brothers, Moses and Aaron) discussed in an earlier chapter. There I suggested ways in which roles were frequently reversed
for ironic effect.

During his convalescence, Aaron seems clearly antagonistic to Lilly's
demands upon him, mistrusting Lilly's motives. An interesting exchange
occurs as Aaron is preparing to retire:

> "What is the difference then between you and me, Lilly?" he said.
> "Haven't we shaken hands on it—a difference of jobs."
> "You don't believe that, though, do you?"
> "Nay, now I reckon you're trespassing."
> "Why am I? I know you don't believe it."
> "What do I believe then?" said Lilly.
> "You believe you know something better than me—and that you are something better
> than me. Don't you?"
> "Do *you* believe it?"
> "What?"
> "That I *am* something better than you, and that I *know* something better?"
> "No, because I don't see it," said Aaron.
> "Then if you don't see it, it isn't there. So go to bed and sleep the sleep of the just and
> the convalescent. I am not to be badgered any more."
> "Am I badgering you?" said Aaron.
> "Indeed you are."
> "So I'm in the wrong again?"
> "Once more, my dear."
> "You're a God-Almighty in your way, you know."
> "So long as I'm not in anybody else's way—" (129–30)

Once again, the curious overlap of dialogue, the suggestion of a marital
disagreement, and, in Aaron's vituperative final replay, an unmistakable
echo of the forthright Tanny herself. The chapter ends as the two men,
split even further apart by their mutual hostility and their incompatible
views on poison-gas warfare, are left alone for several chapters, each to
pursue his individual fate.

As we read further, it becomes increasingly evident that Lawrence is
employing the device of the double not simply as a formidable exercise in
self-criticism—if we accept the premise that several of Lilly's concepts are
derived from Lawrence's present preoccupations—but as a means of deep-
ening our appreciation of the fluctuating relationship of the two central
characters. Not only does the device add an undeniable fascination to the
novel, but from an aesthetic point of view it unifies the novel, drawing together disparate strands as our understanding of the profound and subtle
power of Lilly over Aaron increases.

Finally, in a modern romance of the post-war era involving the troubled search of man for wholeness and illumination, the double device

serves to establish an object for this quest. The object lies seemingly outside the selfish ego yet supposedly must be nourished by the strange promptings of the soul itself. It might even be said that symbolically Aaron's goal lies to a certain extent within Lilly and Lilly's within Aaron. Both men are kept distinct yet deeply attached one to the other. The double device reinforces the need for retaining a sense of separate selfhood while at the same time raising the mystery of Aaron's ultimate submission to some "heroic soul" beyond the self. The thematic use of the double stresses the paradoxical nature of Lilly's belief that there must be union as well as the perfect singleness of the unviolated individual soul.

One final word must be said, concerning Lawrence's use of the Pan-Christ myth in his characterization of Aaron and Lilly. In her extensive study of the pervasive influence of the Pan myth upon western literature, Patricia Merivale states that as "both critic and exponent of the Pan tradition, [Lawrence] has no serious competitors in modern literature."[37] Pan for Lawrence is directly linked to the mysterious urgings of blood-consciousness or the dark centers of the self: the cult of Pan is diametrically opposed to the cult of repressed or intellectualized sex associated by Lawrence with the mechanized societies of the late Christian era. In "Pan in America" Lawrence associates Pan with a vital and elemental force of which the present "mechanical conquered universe of modern humanity" has been robbed and which must be one day reawakened in man.[38] In *The Man Who Died*, Lawrence employed a Christ-Pan dichotomy to explore the possibilities of a Christ being reborn "into a more Pan-like way of life" in which there is "desire and fulfilment in and of the flesh."[39]

Aaron is clearly meant by Lawrence to be associated with the mythical Pan, in several ways. Aaron's flute, the source of his independence and (sexual) fascination to others is a variation on Pan's pipes, used frequently to entertan the nymphs in classical mythology, while his virility and sexual attractiveness are to be associated with the sexual aspects of the Pan mythology. Yet, ironically, even though there is violent sexual consummation in Aaron's various relationships with women, there is still little sense of fulfilment. Aaron's desultory "love" affairs seem rather remote from the salutary and liberating vitality of Pan as Lawrence conceives of him.

If we look closer at the novel, and Lilly's special function in it, we may observe that Lawrence has strengthened the bond between Lilly and Aaron through their mutual connection with the Pan myth. It is Lilly after all who seems more in touch with the hidden or dark places of intrinsic selfhood, with those vital forces of renewal embodied in the figure of Pan. With his dark complexion and slightly sinister physiogomy, Lilly is closer to the goatish Pan than Aaron.[40] Lilly's pan-pipes are not a musical instrument but rather his eloquent speech-music, employed with considerable fervor to persuade Aaron of the vital need to awaken within himself a force related to the true Pan.

In the light of this Aaron must be seen at times as a false or ironic Pan — the mistaken proponent of the modern "love-whoosh" which denies and destroys both the individual and the spirit of the true, vital Pan. In *Aaron's Rod*, however, the spurious cult of modern love is most clearly associated with the outworn ideals of Christian love or brotherhood. We may see that, working with the Pan-Christ dichotomy, Lawrence has created an ironic Pan figure in Aaron whose failures and misconceptions seem to connect him more with Lawrence's concept of Christ in *Aaron's Rod*. Like Christ (at the time of his death), Aaron is thirty-three years old (a favorite Lawrencean age, it would seem) and also performs miracles of regeneration, as in the Marchesa's case. In his later sexual relations with the Marchesa Aaron is clearly intended as a potential dying-god victim, a type of Christ who must eventually be "crucified" by the fatal will of the female.

Yet Lilly is capable of performing miracles too, most notable in his ritualistic anointing and reviving of Aaron. In fact, Lilly seems in retrospect perhaps even more closely connected than Aaron with the figure of Christ. According to Tanny he is an ironic "little Jesus" who bullies, meddles and invites betrayal. In a harangue directed at Jim Bricknell Lilly viciously attacks the "foul" Judas-Christ "combination" for ushering in a civilization based upon the unnatural premise of love and sacrifice to an abstract ideal. Although the narrator has informed us that Lilly "had a certain belief in himself as a saviour" Lilly nevertheless seems reluctant in this chapter to accept the fact that he is guilty (in Tanny's eyes) of the same obscene bullying of Christianity: "You shouldn't play at little Jesus, coming so near people, wanting to help them" (99).

Yet in the next chapter, we have Lilly speculating on the extent of Aaron's ingratitude. In somewhat of a reversal of his earlier position, he now willingly assumes the role of man of sorrows but curses his own savior complex. He specifically links Aaron and Jim Bricknell in their capacity as Judases for betraying him, their Christ-savior. With insight, he seems ready to accept a certain amount of the blame for inviting "betrayal":

> Well if one will be a Jesus he must expect his Judas. That's why Abraham Lincoln gets shot. A Jesus makes a Judas inevitable. A man should remain himself, not try to spread himself over humanity. He should pivot himself on his own pride. I suppose really I ought to have packed this Aaron off to the hospital. Instead of which here am I rubbing him with oil to rub the life into him. And I *know* he'll bite me, like a warmed snake, the moment he recovers. And Tanny will say "Quite right, too," I shouldn't have been so intimate. . . . Last time I break my bread for anybody, this is. So get better my flautist, so that I can go away. (113–14)

The strain of evident self-pity detracts significantly from the admirable candor of Lilly's observations; but the indictment still holds. Lilly thus accepts yet condemns his role as saver of souls, a latter day Christ who seems compelled at times to urge or bully as he is forced more and more to justify the apparent weaknesses of his *credo* against the skeptical attacks of Aaron and others.

Lilly is thus both Pan and Christ to the same extent that Aaron is also implicated in this Lawrencean dichotomy. Lawrence skillfully contrives to reaffirm the double relationship of Aaron and Lilly through their mutual association with the dualistic Pan-Christ symbolism, playing off one aspect of each against another to create ironic effects and a unique tension.

One further reverberation struck by Lawrence's use of Pan symbolism concerns his presentation of Lilly as an ironic Pan-figure. In "Pan in America," Lawrence sums up the essential inexpressibility of the Pan force:

> [The Indian] is careful never to utter one word of the mystery. Speech is the death of Pan, who can but laugh and sound the reed-flute.[41]

This, of course, places a great deal of Aaron's strange silences within the larger framework of the Pan myth as interpreted by Lawrence. Yet the essay states clearly what is only implied in the concluding "Words" of *Aaron's Rod* and is expressed most strongly in Aaron's stubborn resistance to Lilly's doctrines. Lawrence is suggesting as he was earlier that Lilly is once more "too earnest, and vehement" (139). Perhaps his credo is, as Aaron earlier suspected, "a lot of words and a bit of wriggling out of a hole" (139). In any case, Lilly seems defeated by his own "words" as he struggles to verbalize what is in essence inexpressible.

In an earlier chapter, I spoke of the thematic effect of "words" throughout the novel as the symbolic equivalent of the curious restlessness and inertia of the post-war period. Lilly's abundant "words," particularly the perverse doctrines with which he toys (in Chapter 20) involving slavery and racism, "disappear into silence" and unmistakably become part of the disaffected talk which has replaced creative activity during the *dopoguerra*. Yet in the final chapter of the novel, Lilly attempts to verbalize and theorize what can after all only be an inner call or an inarticulate urging of the soul. Lawrence has skillfully—and rather courageously—presented in dramatic terms one disciple or spokesman of Pan who, while possessing certain keys to the problem of renewal and fulfilment, must first learn the true meaning of possessing one's "soul in patience." Lilly must follow the strict discipline which he preaches, eschewing the very bullying—actually a misuse of power—which he condemns in Christianity. I would not suggest that Aaron's position is made to seem enviable or more justifiable, at

Lilly's expense. Nor should Aaron's earlier accusation, "what have you got more than me or Jim Bricknell! Only a bigger choice of words, it seems to me" (121), be construed as a final verdict on Lilly's "words." Lilly's dilemma is presented in dramatic terms as he vacillates between the extremes of separate selfhood and a conviction that he must be a priest of personal salvation, converting the unwilling Aaron to a new realization of himself. Lilly's theories are contradictory and tentative, certainly problematic. He must learn that the doctrine of selfhood and the spirit can never be conveyed into words without somehow being corrupted or distorted. Together with Aaron's repeated opposition and interjections of disapproval, Lilly's failure to qualify or justify his equivocal position is part of the dramatic form of the final chapter of *Aaron's Rod*. Lilly's poignant failure to convince Aaron (and perhaps himself) carries us forward as to the renewed attempts in Lawrence's two other "leadership" novels to resolve the apparent incongruities and paradoxes of Lilly's arguments. At the same time the problematic attempts on Lilly's part to initiate a *true* friendship based on pure selfhood, not upon love or sacrifice, carry us another step beyond Rupert Birkin's gestures of proposal to Gerald Crich in *Women in Love*. Lilly's attempts also anticipate the even more misguided efforts of Kangaroo to win over Lovat Somers. In a larger sense, the failure of Lilly represents but another stage in Lawrence's continuing search for the means of reviving the elemental Pan force, now stifled in the ruins of the "mechanical conquered universe of modern humanity."[42]

In the Thick of the Scrimmage:
Aaron's Rod and the Critics

In my introduction to this study, I indicated that for years *Aaron's Rod* has suffered both from critical neglect and abuse. The final chapter of this study, therefore, devotes itself to four problematic aspects of form or substance involved in a critical re-reading of *Aaron's Rod*: 1) the morality of Aaron's desertion; 2) the question of "realism" in the novel; 3) the so-called "formlessness" of *Aaron's Rod*; and 4) the conspicuously large amount of "talk" throughout the novel. At the same time, however, this chapter builds upon the preceding chapters of my study, in which several larger, unifying themes or aspects of the novel were examined in considerable detail. In many cases the argument of this final chapter consists of a re-examination of prevailing critical judgements (frequently misrepresentations) of *Aaron's Rod*. Any harshness or impatience on my part in this chapter with what seem to me to be willful misreadings should be construed not as arrogance but rather as part of a sincere attempt to re-examine carefully *Aaron's Rod,* attempting to clarify perennial confusion surrounding the novel.

One outstanding source of critical confusion has been Lawrence's presentation of the marital deadlock between Aaron and Lottie and Aaron's subsequent "desertion" of his family. The most sustained attack upon the morality of the novel comes from Eliseo Vivas, who, in his curious study of Lawrence (entitled, significantly, *The Failure and Triumph of Art*), insists upon the radical incoherence of *Aaron's Rod*:

> But the worst defect of the book is its radical incoherence. This defect shows itself in two closely connected senses: in its utter lack of form and in its failure to elucidate an important point in which the reader is legitimately interested, the grounds on which Aaron leaves his wife and children.[1]

Vivas' attack upon the supposed "incoherence of form" will be taken up later in a discussion of structural problems in *Aaron's Rod*. At present we must examine more closely his dissatisfactions with the novel's morality, obviously a great source of pique to him and probably the original stimulus for his narrow examination of the novel.[2]

To Eliseo Vivas, Aaron's desertion of Lottie is an unmitigatedly caddish act. He seems anxious to point out that he is seeking no moral justification for such villainy but rather as a critic, an "aesthetic justification; a rendering, in whatever way the author chooses to give it, of that which gives Aaron's action its intelligibility in the story."[3] It is soon apparent that Vivas would in fact allow Lawrence an extremely limited range of choice in presenting the desertion of Aaron or justifying it to his own offended sensibility. He even suggests at one point that Lawrence has merely presented the reader with a "puzzling ethical problem" and that the serious reader is morally bound to ask "whether men are justified in acting as Aaron did."[4] The tone of moral indignation seems to increase throughout as Vivas relentlessly attacks Lawrence's presentation of the marital deadlock and Aaron's desertion:

> The unexplained caddishness of Aaron forces on us a suspicion that some values are being presented in, and some are being withheld from, the novel, in which we have a serious moral interest.... No ground is offered, we saw, for Aaron's desertion of his family. For if we accept as adequate ground his expressed desire, reiterated in various occasions, "to keep the mastery of his soul and conscience and actions," we have to ask exactly what is the meaning of this conviction of his and what is its validity for him. If we say the intense desire to be free is enough to justify his leaving his wife and children, we are saying that *a man who does not feel any obligations does not have any....* We do not know in what sense Aaron's wife, Lottie, was an impossible person. But even if she was, and Aaron was justified in leaving her, the manner in which he chose to do it heaped on her humiliation and injury, and the conclusion must be that Aaron is no less contemptible than the Bricknells and their set. To the serious reader, endowed with moral responsibility, what *Aaron's Rod* signifies is the widening area of infection which is poisoning our society.[5]

This passage is important for its revelation of the fundamental "wrong-headedness" of Vivas' approach. I would question the notion that we *do* have a serious moral interest in the novel at least of the nature or to the extent that we should feel free to impose our own moral biases or aesthetic demands upon the novelist. A novel may obviously have serious moral implications or overtones without the reader being required to choose sides or to submit every aspect of the narrative to his own moral biases, however they may seem to be at odds with what the ethical responses of the reader. This passage also reveals to us Vivas' apparent unwillingness to acknowledge properly the considerable dramatic evidence which Lawrence *does* present to us, indicating the nature and causes of the marital strife between Aaron and Lottie. This dramatic portrayal of the marital deadlock will be discussed presently. Finally, we might note that Vivas' last statement concerning the social "infection" which the novel conveys to us contains a certain amount of truth — an ironic touch of which he was no doubt unconscious in this utter condemnation of the novel. This is precisely the point that Lawrence is making both in *Aaron's Rod* and throughout his subsequent works.

As a novelist of great insight and objectivity, Lawrence never feels obliged to champion every action which his characters perform. He is by no means endorsing Aaron's behaviour at every step of the way. On the contrary, as I pointed out earlier, Lawrence clearly presents in negative terms Aaron's misanthropic denial of human contacts, his egocentric withdrawal from the world about him. Like his wandering biblical namesake, Aaron Sisson is prone to error, and the dubious freedom which he seeks or exercises is more than often a movement in the wrong direction, towards self-destruction. Further, Aaron's moral vacillation is clearly presented by Lawrence as part of the post-war malaise which paralyzes or poisons the atmosphere of post-war Europe. In no sense then is Lawrence heartily condoning Aaron's constant weakness and flight throughout the novel. But, of course, Vivas is offering such tendentious criticism as part of his reply to Leavis, whose general admiration for Lawrence and whose critical interest in the novel are well known.

Leavis' account of the Sissons' strife still remains one of the most perceptive and indispensable treatments of this difficult aspect of the novel:

> It is a familiar situation, a familiar kind of life-frustrating deadlock. The presenting of it transcends ordinary moral judgments; to judge Aaron selfish and irresponsible for leaving his wife in the lurch with the children on her hands (though he provides for her financially), or to say that, whatever the total account of rights and wrongs might be, plainly the domineering, demanding, complaining woman was at fault, and had made his life intolerable, wouldn't, we know, be to the point. The presenting sensibility and the inquiring intelligence engaged are, of course, profoundly and essentially moral; the moral concern goes far deeper than the level of those judgments. What is wrong here? What laws of life have been ignored that there should be *this* situation, this dreadful deadlock, between a man and a woman? These questions give the informing preoccupation.[6]

Leavis' rejection of any facile solutions or moral formulae in discussing Aaron's mental failure and desertion is admirable and much to the point. What Vivas seems to be objecting to, however, throughout his study is that the reader has not been provided by Lawrence with any easy system of explanations or obvious symbols which might clarify the complexities of the situation. His fundamental quarrel with Lawrence's presentation — aside from what he deplores as the immorality of the act of desertion *per se* — seems to be that Aaron has been characterized as inarticulate or incapable of formulating the *precise* causes of marital dissatisfaction and failure. "What the reader must object to is that Lawrence is not able to tell him what Aaron had against Lottie—except in the most general and abstract terms."[7] At another point Vivas suggests that the novel provides us with no dramatic evidence at all of "what revulsions and what inspirations led Aaron to abandon his family":

> But one is not given even an inkling, in terms of specific acts, of the soul's outrage or humiliation or enslavement, which would enable the reader to understand his revolt. We are told Aaron was outraged. But no *dramatic* evidence is provided. How does a woman get a man under herself? And when a woman gets a man under, exactly what does he lose, what does she gain? In a novel, which is not a philosophical essay, we expect more than abstractions and generalizations.[8]

The perception that the novel is very different from the "philosophical essay" is ironically quite true. Yet, we could reply that the novel is also emphatically *not* a sociological case-history or exposé, a particular kind of realistic acount which Vivas seems to favor in his insistence upon documentary evidence.[9] I would argue that Lawrence's refusal to formulate or explain away the failures of Aaron's marriage to Lottie must also be attributed to the novelist's attempt to suggest once again, as he had in previous novels, that the roots of sexual or marital discord run deeper than the superficialities of fact or mere appearance. The relationship of the sexes is extremely complex, at times utterly enigmatic. Also, Lawrence's refusal to explain in literal terms the breakdown of Aaron's marriage is consistent with his characterization of Aaron throughout the novel. The silence of Aaron conveys both a typical mistrust of words and carries the suggestion that at this early stage of his development Aaron is motivated merely by vague and inarticulate yearnings for the freedom necessary to self-discovery. In this state, he is at times both vulnerable and directionless. Yet in spite of his refusal to formulate or list precisely the deep causes of Aaron's and Lottie's strife, Lawrence has presented us with several scenes of considerable dramatic impact, in which Lottie's indomitable feminine will and the threat which it provides to Aaron's selfhood are clearly portrayed. Yet it seems that Vivas has failed to take sufficient account of the "naturalistic" opening scenes of the novel in which the unbearable tedium of Aaron's home life as well as the tensions of marital dissatisfaction are presented,[10] *dramatically,* through Lottie's shrewish rebukes and Aaron's silent yet firm resistance; and *symbolically,* through the incident in which the blue ball is shattered.[11] Other similar scenes provide us with all the dramatic evidence required to comprehend Aaron's desertion. Lottie's embittered denunciation of Aaron's character and her marriage to him is presented in Chapter 4 as a conversation between Lottie and the local doctor, overheard by Aaron himself as he stands motionless and unseen outside his home:

> "What makes me so mad is that he should go off like that — never a word — coolly takes his hook. I could kill him for it."
>
> "Were you ever happy together?"
>
> "We were all right at first. I know I was fond of *him*. But he'd kill anything. — He kept himself back, always kept himself back, couldn't give himself—"
>
> "Ah well," sighed the doctor. "Marriage is a mystery. I'm glad I'm not entangled in it."
>
> "Yes, to make some woman's life a misery. — I'm sure it was death to live with him, he seemed to kill everything off inside you. He was a man you couldn't quarrel with, and get it over. Quiet — quiet in his tempers, and selfish through and through. I've lived with him twelve years — I know what it is. Killing! You don't know what he was—" (51)

Aaron's unsuspected presence during Lottie's tirade adds a certain amount of dramatic irony, as it were, to the scene and prepares us for both his later final encounter with Lottie and his own private assessment in "Wie es Ihnen Gefaellt" of his own marital dissatisfactions. It is also significant that it is *Aaron* (not Lottie) who is so deeply affected by such disclosed rancor as he stands outside (characteristically withdrawn yet involved in the scene before him) that he is transformed like Lot's wife into a pillar of salt, an appropriate metaphor for his inner turmoil and revulsion. It is important also that Aaron (and the reader) should witness Lottie's denunciation of his behavior *before* the important interior monologue of "Wie es Ihnen Gefaellt," in which the marital deadlock is reviewed primarily through the medium of Aaron's own consciousness. The conventional acquiescence of the Indian doctor who merely nods and weeps sympathetically with Lottie, quite overpowered by this forceful statement of *her* position, seems to suggest an ironic parallel to Aaron's own anguished yet firm resistance at this point. The incident further suggests Lottie's tendency to indulge in displays of histrionic self-pity and similar acts of petulance which conceal for the unsuspecting her aggressiveness.

There is also the superbly rendered scene of Aaron's second homecoming in which Lottie's frustrated yet unyielding feminine will is manifested in her tears, violent recriminations and physical abuse. We must also not overlook the far-reaching implications of the male symposium in Chapter 17 in which the failure of the del Torres' marriage and sexual relationship is vividly and dramatically presented in the confession of del Torre and related further to the relationship of Aaron and Lottie, even to Lilly and Tanny. The dissatisfaction of the marriage must be traced to deeper sources than simple disagreement, rather to the deadly pressure of the feminine will which the Marchese terms the "Eve" principle.

There is also the unifying theme of "bullying" presented, not merely in the conflict of Aaron and Lottie, but all through the novel, most notably in Aaron's sexual affair with the Marchesa. What of the succession of willful or destructive women presented *dramatically* in almost every episode—the sensual landlady, Josephine Ford and Julia Cunningham, Lady Franks, Lady Artemis Hooper, to name a few? Even Tanny is to some degree implicated in the charge of wilfulness directed to the feminine psyche during the course of the novel. Lottie's treatment of Aaron and Aaron's rejection of his wife are part of a larger thematic scheme of which Vivas was apparently unaware. He has failed to grasp the very close connection between Aaron's marital and sexual failures and Lilly's warnings throughout concerning the destructiveness of the love-urge and the grief to which it has brought the world.

These scenes all complement the crucial interior monologue of Chapter 13, "Wie es Ihnen Gefaellt," in which the primal causes of Aaron's marital failure are examined at considerable length, the deadlock of wills described in detail:

> She sometimes wished he would kill her: or that she would kill him. Neither event happened.
> And neither of them understood what was happening. How should they? They were both dazed, horrified, and mortified. He took to leaving her alone as much as was possible. (189)

We are indeed presented explicitly with a great deal of Lottie's side of the terrible deadlock, with her sense of feminine outrage, frustration and deadly hatred. Through the medium of the narrator who supposedly translates Aaron's "music-thoughts" into ordinary language, we learn that Aaron is to be blamed for much of the failure of his marriage. He confesses to himself that he has always remained essentially withheld or aloof in his marriage to Lottie, much to her "chagrin and agony" and that he has behaved brutally and insensitively to her, beating her, coldly ignoring her, and even worse, cheating on her in a succession of village affairs. All of this is revealed with great frankness from Aaron's own point of view;[12] and there seems to be little here of the smug self-satisfaction or cold indifference of which Aaron has been accused both by other characters in the novel itself and by various critics alike. Lawrence has cleverly manipulated the point of view during this crucial indirect monologue, in order to take in both sides of the marital problem. At one moment we are presented with Aaron's view of Lottie's implacable female will, coiled like a serpent ready to strike and destroy. At the next we have Lottie's view of Aaron's brutality or unfaithfulness conveyed to us by means of indirect interior monologue. At other times, the narrator interjects with his own omniscient comments upon the deadlock, summing up both sides or relating the strife of Aaron and Lottie to the larger context of Christian marriage which has degenerated into such a terrifying sexual deadlock in Western society.

We may perhaps object quite rightly that the point of view at times shifts erratically and awkwardly from Aaron to Lottie to the narrator, but this complexity is clearly a part of Lawrence's intentions, his refusal to explain in simplified terms what is after all a very subtle and intricate matter. The monologue thus serves Lawrence's artistic purposes well as well as indicating both to the reader and to Aaron a turning point in his private destiny in such a moment of heightened self-awareness. Rather than "floating above the character" as Vivas suggests,[13] the monologue is firmly anchored to Aaron's increasing awareness of his unfolding destiny. Through its shifting point of view the monologue corroborates further our suspicions up to this point of Lottie's suffocating willfulness, her urge to possess and destroy. Far from being an abstract discourse of "irritating obscurity"[14] the monologue clearly places before us in more *philosophical* or *psychological* terms what we have already observed dramatically in the opening scenes of the novel and in both of Aaron's brief homecomings — namely, that Lottie and Aaron are quite incompatible and must exist apart in order that each may regain and preserve his individual indentity.

It may, of course, be objected that the monologue comes strangely late in the novel and that it does not alter the reader's reaction to the earlier chapters. This argument may be partially plausible for the casual or indiscriminate first reader, but is quite untenable for the critic. Before passing judgement upon a work of art, especially one as ostensibly problematic as *Aaron's Rod,* the critic must surely be expected to be in full possession of the entire work. He must have read and carefully studied the work at greater length than the casual reader, at least before making pronouncements concerning that work's relative artistic success or failure! Finally, although the form of *Aaron's Rod* and the accusation that it is formless will be taken up later in this chapter, I would observe that, in retrospect, the monologue has been placed strategically by Lawrence, virtually at the center of the novel, and that its thematic substance is both anticipated and followed by other crucial scenes of marital strife and sexual bullying.

Vivas' account of the novel raises the very significant problem of realism in *Aaron's Rod,* particularly in the characterization and presentation of Aaron himself. It must be confessed that at times even Leavis confuses art with life in his insistence upon a "real Aaron" and the splitting of Lawrence into Lilly and Aaron. Nevertheless Leavis' perceptive comments on the nature of the marital deadlock suggest that, unlike Vivas, he *does* understand at least that Lawrence is writing neither a socio-moralistic treatise, nor a work of naturalistic fiction. Though he quotes freely from Lawrence's essay "The Novel," particularly Lawrence's famous statement that the beauty of the novel lies in the fact that "everything is true in its own relationship," Vivas obviously cannot accept the concept of Lawrence's novel creating a "self contained universe." Any critic who employs such terminology as "cads," "villains," "stinkers" or speaks of a character in "the grip of lust" as being "close to a mere animal"[15] may be judged to be little interested in investigating with sufficient detachment the very unusual kind of novel which Lawrence is choosing to write or the aesthetically imitative world which Lawrence creates for us. I shall have more to say later of this unusual and, for Lawrence, quite new kind of novel which *Aaron's Rod* represents. At this point, it might be recalled that in *Aaron's Rod* Lawrence was deliberately moving away from the kind of novel which *The Rainbow* and *Women in Love* represented towards a more "freewheeling," perhaps more arbitrary kind of novel or "thought adventure." He no longer felt as compelled by the laws of realism or probability as he had before. *Aaron's Rod* and the novels which follow it thus require a necessary adjustment of response for readers or critics of Lawrence. To criticize *Aaron's Rod* exclusively on the basis of the artistic achievement of *Women in Love* or *The Rainbow* is to mistake the nature and artistic intention of *Aaron's Rod,* as well as to employ the wrong critical apparatus for appreciating Lawrence's new kind of fictional endeavor.

Aaron's musicianship and the social privileges which it grants him are two related aspects of the novel which have suffered from misinterpretation due to an insistence upon literal fact or probability. Several incredulous critics have objected to Aaron's swift progress from amateur musician to professional flutist in the orchestra of Covent Garden, dismayed by his apparently easy transition from the primitive society of Beldover and his companions at the "Royal Oak" to the fashionable drawing-rooms of London. The implication of both objections is that Aaron is incapable, musically and socially, of adapting to a sophisticated urban milieu. He is supposedly too coarse or awkward to succeed in "society"; his playing merely the self-taught hobby of a skilled amateur. Kate Millett, with characteristic insensitivity, informs us that

> Aaron's acceptance by the novel's flimsy smart people of the middle classes is instantaneous and utterly fantastic. On his first night of freedom, he gets drunk and stumbles into a party in the house of his employer. Although very recognizably a miner, he is immediately asked to share a bed with his proprietor's son. Noblewomen fall in love with him; however tedious he may be with his put-on dialect, everyone recognizes the natural aristocrat in him, and in his tuxedo he can pass for a gent as well as the rest.[16]

Millett's oversimplifications are transparently inadequate and factually incorrect as well. Graham Hough seems quite bothered by Aaron's musical proficiency and social acceptance:

We begin to be worried, too, by material and social improbabilities. Aaron is represented as an accomplished flute-player, therefore an artist; and this gives him both an *état civil* and an unusual degree of social mobility; but that he should be immediately employed in an operatic orchestra, immediately begin to move freely in monied, more or less artistic, circles rather strains our credulity.[17]

A serious critical problem is raised here in the oversimplifications of both these critics. My objection to both is that like Vivas they continually move beyond the novel *per se,* obviously feeling that every event surrounding Aaron should be referred to the touchstone of their own (supposedly) normal experience of life. It seems to me that, in *Aaron's Rod,* Lawrence has indeed presented us with an artistically valid experience, a stylized rendering or "imitation" of experience, in which the reader is asked to accept certain premises. These constitute the novelist's chosen *donnée,* and are perfectly legitimate on his own terms. Most critics, like those above, mistrust the fiction and the narrator to the extent that they will subordinate the action of the novel to their own idiosyncratic notions of what may or may not be possible in "everyday" life, and what may or may not be the essential "truth" of the novel. But characteristically, Lawrence has also anticipated the incredulous refusal of critics to accept Aaron's acceptance by "society," which is largely provided by his musical gifts and sexual attractiveness.

Both these critics have also failed to read the novel carefully enough, especially the first chapter in which, as startling as it might seem in a village like Beldover, Lawrence clearly establishes for us Aaron's extraordinary musicality. As I stated earlier in a chapter dealing with the music of *Aaron's Rod,* it is mentioned specifically that passers-by stop to listen to Aaron's playing: "He was esteemed a good player: was in request at concerts and dances, also at swell-balls" (17). It is further mentioned in Chapter 2 that Aaron is not only respected but considered rather remarkable by the townsfolk: ". . . Aaron was considered a special man, a man of peculiar understanding, even though as a rule he said little" (28). The description of Cunliffe (one of the earliest and more sensitive critics of the novel) of Aaron as ". . . a man of very exceptional taste and talent for music and philosophy, exceptional not only in his position in life, but in any position"[18] is much to the point.

In the dispute between Lilly and Aaron in Chapter 10, Lawrence has obviously anticipated such incredulous objections to Aaron's social success as those above in providing an answer through Lilly. Just after surviving the crisis of his attack of influenza, Aaron takes up his flute again. Lilly grudgingly foretells the social ease which the flute and Aaron's attractiveness will undoubtedly provide. (126) Lilly's words are echoed later by Sir William Franks in his dispute with Aaron over Providence. In Chapter 12,

"Novara," the narrator interjects to explain Aaron's acceptance by such wealthy circles as Lady Artemis Hooper: "Aaron had the curious knack which belongs to some people of getting into the swim without knowing he was doing it" (151). Further, it is made quite clear in this chapter that Aaron's transition to these fashionable salons is not as easy as many critics would have us believe, certainly not guaranteed; nor is Aaron's acceptance of such patronage completely unqualified. He always realizes eventually that such favors are quite ephemeral.

> So he found London got on his nerves. He felt it rubbed him the wrong way. He was flattered, of course, by his own success — and felt at the same time irritated by it. This state of mind was by no means acceptable. Wherever he was he liked to be given, tacitly, the first place — or a place among the first. Among the musical people he frequented, he found himself on a callow kind of equality with everybody, even the stars and aristocrats, at one moment, and a backstairs outsider the next. It was all just as the moment demanded. There was a certain excitement in slithering up and down the social scale, one minute chattering in a personal tete-à-tete with the most famous, or notorious, of the society beauties: and the next walking in the rain, with his flute in a bag, to his grubby lodging in Bloomsbury. Only the excitement roused all the savage sarcasm that lay at the bottom of his soul, and which burned there like an unhealthy bile. (152)

It should also be pointed out that in addition to possessing musical gifts and sexual attractiveness, Aaron furnishes a certain fascination to the upper classes precisely because he *is* a working-man of lower class origins. In this sense he attracts Jim Bricknell who delights in walking home from Covent Garden having "between his fingers the arm muscles of a working man, one of the common people" (66), while Lady Artemis Hooper takes great satisfaction in noting the similarity between herself and Aaron. Both share a touch of the reckless "modern, social freebooter" (151). Josephine Ford also takes great pleasure in extracting from Aaron the full story of his lower class origins and upbringing. Finally, although there seems virtually no need to establish further the authenticity of Aaron's musical talent, might we not, in reply to Mr. Hough's incredulity, pursue a similarly arbitrary line of argument in order to point out (what anyone with any musical sense at all knows) that one need not be a Jean Pierre Rampal in order to qualify for an opera orchestra! After all, Aaron does himself reveal that he had a friend in the Covent Garden orchestra and has secured his position "through an agent" (70). There seems no reason to mistrust Aaron's word on this point.

Another aspect of the novel which has been open to critical attack because of some critics' insistence upon the supposed limits of realism is Lawrence's treatment of the unusual relationship of Aaron and Lilly, in Chapters 9 and 10, particularly in the famous "massage" scene. The biblical symbolism of these chapters, indeed of the entire relationship of

Aaron and Lilly has already been discussed in detail in an earlier chapter. As I suggested there, critical problems are raised by Lawrence's pervasive allusions to the biblical narrative of Moses and Aaron. The failure to note the biblical symbolism of the scene in which Lilly mysteriously revives Aaron by rubbing him with oil has fostered many naïvely literal interpretations of the relationship between the novel's two central characters. Frequently these oversimplified readings may be traced to critics' oversuspicious reaction and personal distaste for male homosexuality. Millett describes the massage as the novel's "surrogate for sodomy," a grotesque oversimplification, and even goes so far as to state that the incident is a "couvade" and thus follows a typical Lawrencean pattern.[19] In her zealous efforts to castigate what she alleges to be male-chauvinistic or anti-feminine overtones, Millett once again resigns her duty (as a critic) to examine closely the full thematic or symbolic significance of this scene.

George Ford has astutely summed up the pitfalls of assuming too literal an approach to such scenes in Lawrence's fiction:

> For readers such as myself, more readily familiar with all the biographies of Lawrence than with certain passages of Exodus and Leviticus and Numbers, this curious scene seemed significant only in what it tells of an incident in Lawrence's own life, with homosexual overtones, of which Middleton Murry has left an account. Yet readers as familiar with the Bible as Lawrence expected us to be will readily recognize that allusion is being made to God's instructing Moses... "Then thou shalt take the anointing oil, and pour it upon his head, and anoint him."
>
> It is fascinating to speculate about Lawrence's preoccupations with incidents having homosexual overtones, but we miss the core of *Aaron's Rod* if we are sidetracked into overlooking the analogy of the prophet consecrating his chief priest who will fail at times to follow in his footsteps...[20]

It must be observed that Lawrence has not made our task any easier in his insistence upon establishing the external or circumstantial realities of the scene: the use of *camphorated* oil for the anointing; the influenza attack, including the stoppage of the bowels; indeed, the rather shabby naturalistic setting, a cramped flat overlooking Covent Garden Market. Yet Lawrence is asking the reader in this and other such scenes to probe constantly beneath the literal surface of the incident in order to perceive its symbolic significance, the biblical parallel being drawn. At the same time, we must be careful not to lose sight of the "physical features" of the scene or of the special function which the episode performs in relation to the customary requirements of plot, characterization, and so on. Lawrence thus places great demands upon his readers' sensibilities. He expects us to approach such critically challenging episodes with a "dual" vision which simultaneously accommodates both the realistic and symbolic import of the episode.

Further problems of realism have arisen from the efforts of nearly every critic to read *Aaron's Rod* exclusively in terms of Lawrence's own biography. Such approaches are related to the same conviction described above that the novel, especially one by Lawrence, must always be somehow grounded in ordinary "real" life. While no one could dispute that Lawrence's fiction most often grew out of or was at least inspired by the actual events of his life or that, *Aaron's Rod* (as I demonstrated earlier) is firmly connected to Lawrence's experience of people, places and events during the final months of the war and its strange aftermath. But *Aaron's Rod* represents a good deal more than mere undisguised or unassimilated autobiography.

Here is Vivas' approach to the apparent relation between the ordinary events of Lawrence's life and the novel itself.

> The book shows no trace of creative imagination whatever. It is a mere transcription, mere reportage. We do not have to identify the original of Lilly, "the dark, irascible little man," a rootless and drifting writer, and his Norwegian wife. We need not perceive that we are presented here with another version of the couple we are to meet in Lawrence's next novel, whose slight physical changes and new aliases are the merest pretense at concealment. We do not need the key with which his letters and his biographers so generously provide us, in order to realize that the other characters of this flat book are taken directly from life and stuck into the novel. This is not true of his successful novels, but it is of *Aaron's Rod*. In this book the stuff of the drama, whether a faithful record of actual events or sheer invention, lacks that which lifts the matter of experience into the substance of poetry.[21]

No one would deny that the novel contains more or less satiric portraits of a good many of Lawrence's acquaintances of the period. Earlier I suggested that the novel did indeed include certain elements of a *roman à clef,* though ostensibly not written like others of this genre—*Orlando* for example—for a particular circle. Lawrence's mimicry was apparently wickedly accurate enough to provoke the wrath of Norman Douglas, who was strangely "not amused" by Lawrence's jovial caricature. And yet, how can this help our understanding or appreciation of the novel *per se*? Do not these characters, however close their resemblance may have been to actual persons, exist vividly and convincingly within the fictional world of the novel itself? Do not they all perform their own thematic function within the limits of the novel in their relation to aspects of Aaron's continuing "quest"? Contrary to Vivas' statements, the "portraits" are both rich in humor and have been fully incorporated into the scheme of the novel with remarkable success. Such was Lawrence's genius and his amazing powers of objectivity that such characters *do* exist independently within the created universe of the novel, without further reference to the minute details of Lawrencean biography. In *Aaron's Rod* (Vivas' attack notwithstanding), we find a perfect example of the transmutation of the seemingly disjointed events of ordinary life into an extraordinarily unified whole which stands independent of the separate events which merely inspired it and thus commands our attention as critics rather than biographers.

Even Leavis, normally judicious in his inquiries into the autobiographical substance of Lawrence's fiction, seems to have fallen prey to the danger of reducing the novel to the level of thinly disguised autobiography.[22] His treatment of the episode with the Marchesa seems curiously inadequate:

> The affair with the Marchesa forms a major episode in Aaron's Italian adventure. If one asks what significance it has in relation to his specific problem, his 'case,' there doesn't seem to be any very impressive answer to hand. In it, one can say, he confirms his knowledge that he has remained married to Lottie, and that 'any other woman than his wife is a strange woman to him, a violation'; and one can add that, in declining finally to be Antony to the Marchesa's Cleopatra, he has learnt to place the love in which each uses the other as a 'mere magic implement'. . . . But there is no inevitability about the episode as part of Aaron's history. One is convinced, in fact, that it appears there because Lawrence himself had encountered the original of the Marchesa and had been struck by her—been intrigued by her interest as a case. . . .
>
> The whole episode, in fact, is irritatingly unsatisfying because not completely significant.[23]

Leavis has overlooked the important thematic implications of Aaron's relationship with the Marchesa, the way in which Lawrence links her destructive will with that of Lottie and other willful women in the novel. Of course it is inevitable that Aaron in his resistance to Lilly and his incomplete or wrong-headed notions of the sexual relationship should fall prey once more to a wilful woman, should involve himself in a deadly opposition of wills. I shall have more to say later of Leavis' "autobiographical" treatment of the final episode of *Aaron's Rod,* an approach which I find quite unsatisfactory.

It must also be pointed out that in *Aaron's Rod* and elsewhere Lawrence never allows himself to be confined by the limits of everyday credibility, nor by ordinary concepts of realistic presentation. He gives us his own special kind of "realism" which, as R. Draper points out in his profile of Lawrence, goes far beyond the photographic documentation often associated with the term:

> Lawrence is a great realistic novelist, but his conception of what is real goes beyond the photographic recording of appearances and the factual accuracy which realism is usually taken to imply. Even if one adds the shrewd observation of people's actual behavior and motives to be found in the work of a few exceptional realists, Lawrence's realism is still not defined. He has intimations of a deeper level of reality that seems to have a profound effect on human life and is therefore very much the business of the novelist, but which can only be apprehended imaginatively and seems to require therefore the techniques of the poet.[24]

The episodes with the Marchesa illustrate perfectly how ludicrous it would be to read *Aaron's Rod* in terms of strict "photographic" realism:

> Her soul seemed to breathe as a butterfly breathes, as it rests on a leaf and slowly breathes its wings. And for the first time her soul drew in its own deep breath....
> And as in a dream the woman sat, feeling what a joy it was to float and move like a swan in the high air, flying upon the wings of her own spirit. She was as a swan which never before could get its wings open, and so which never could get up into the open where alone it can sing. (299–300)

Here we have another example of Lawrence's "stylized rendering" or imitation of experience, in which as I suggested earlier the reader is presented with certain unalterable facts and asked to accept the premises of the special world which the novel itself creates. As I hinted before, *Aaron's Rod* is a kind of picaresque-romance. Aaron is Lawrence's own approximation of the rogue-heroes of eighteenth or nineteenth century fiction who travel from place to place in search of adventure, fortune, amorous conquests, living largely by their wits or their charm. Just how close Aaron was conceived to be related to this kind of earlier fictional "hero" is made clear by Lawrence's exuberant letter to the Brewsters: "Instead of bringing [Aaron] nearer to heaven, in leaps and bounds, he's misbehaving and putting ten fingers to his nose at everything. Damn heaven. Damn holiness. Damn Nirvana. Damn it all."[25] Of course Aaron's travels and search for fulfillment and self knowledge have their more serious side. In Lawrencean terms Aaron's wandering is a type of spiritual or religious quest for selfhood which incorporates certain Romance elements. During the portions of the novel dealing with Aaron's affair with the Marchesa, Lawrence refers directly to fairy-tale and legend in order to bring out these romance elements of the novel. In an earlier chapter dealing with music in *Aaron's Rod,* I noted in Aaron's rejuvenation of the Marchesa the deliberate parallels with the legend of Siegfried and his awakening of Brünnhilde (itself a version of the Sleeping Beauty story). At another point, the Marchesa's soul-sickness is described in terms of popular fairy-tale:[26]

> She seemed like one who had been kept in a horrible enchanted castle – for years and years. Oh, a horrible enchanted castle, with wet walls of emotions and ponderous chains of feelings and a ghastly atmosphere of must-be. She felt she had seen through the opening door a crack of sunshine, and thin, pure, light outside air, outside, beyond this dank and beastly dungeon of feelings and moral necessity.... She looked at her little husband. Chains of necessity all around him: a little jailor.... If only he would throw away the castle keys. He was a little gnome. Why did he clutch the castle keys so tight for? (267)

Yet the novel is also the tale of Aaron's discovery of himself and, as I suggested in an earlier Chapter 3, shares certain similarities with the traditional *bildungsroman* or "novel of development" albeit in Lawrence's own terms. It is Lawrence's strange combination of aspects of the picaresque, Romance, and *bildungsroman* in his portrayal of Aaron which imparts such a peculiar tone and texture to the novel.

The novel is deliberately made even less realistic by the presence of the narrator who joshes the reader, whimsically comments upon the conventions of fiction ("our story continues by night"), and also plays an important role as translator or interpreter of Aaron's deepest unspoken thoughts. The use of Lawrence of the narrator-device has often been attacked simply as an intrusion. Yudhishtar, however, comments:

> One artistic crime Lawrence is alleged to have committed in *Aaron's Rod* is to have addressed the reader directly. Lawrence's address to the reader is neither a sign of his strength nor of his weakness; it is only an instance of what Lawrence has called the "struggle for verbal consciousness" ("I do but make a translation of the man. He would speak in music. I speak with words")....
> Lawrence did not *need* to make an address to the reader for the purposes of the narrative. Those critics who find this objectionable, approach the novel, it would appear, with some narrow, fixed, arbitrary concepts about the form of a novel...[27]

What many critics fail to observe is that Lawrence is perfectly *aware* of the awkwardness of the device and cannot resist poking fun at those very novels which he is imitating, particularly in the early chapters of the novel. The use of the fussy and sententious narrator ("therefore, behold our hero alighting one night in Novara") is thus simply a humorous parody of other similar yet delightful intrusions of early "narrators" in English fiction — most noticeably in the novels of Fielding, Dickens or Thackeray. The use of the archaic device is also part of Lawrence's satiric attacks upon English notions of what is proper in art as well as life. No doubt the narrator was meant to contribute to the overall effect of the novel being "blameless as Cranford [sic]" as Lawrence described it to Lady Cynthia Asquith.[28] At the same time the device permitted Lawrence's own sneer at "Mrs. Grundy" and her requirement that novels should be suitable for the *jeune fille.*[29]

Critical dissatisfaction with the form or structure of *Aaron's Rod* has been even greater than the quarrel with the "morality" or the "realism" of the novel. Even those critics normally most sympathetic to Lawrence's work and the special demands it places upon the reader seem anxious to reprimand Lawrence for the apparent "formlessness" of the novel. Harry T. Moore, usually an indefatigable defender of Lawrence, criticizes *Aaron's Rod* along with the later novels for "awkward moments, digressions, collapses of theme and structure" not present in the more fully integrated master-works — *The Rainbow* and *Women in Love.*[30] R. P. Draper describes *Aaron's Rod* as "the most formless and disconnected of the novels"[31] while Graham Hough informs us that *Aaron's Rod* is a "short and scrappy" novel with severe "structural lapses."[32] Glancing rather perfunctorily at what seem to him to be the major components of the novel, Hough concludes that "the chance of imposing unity on these heterogeneous materials seems slight."[33] Daleski speaks of the "flabby flesh" of the novel's structure and concludes further that "Lawrence is no longer concerned with form in the novel."[34] F. R. Leavis remarks the "spirit of unabashed tentativeness" of the novel and makes an eccentric though well meaning attempt at accounting for what seems to him to be the peculiar form of the novel:

> We come in fact to recognize in due course that in *Aaron's Rod* we are not reading a work of art of the order of *Women in Love;* there is nothing of that closeness of organization or density of significance, though what we are reading is certainly a most lively novel and a work of genius. The genius is irresistably apparent in the rendering of the various scenes and episodes of Aaron's truancy. There are Sir William and Lady Franks and their house-party at Novara; there are the street-demonstration at Milan, and the meeting with Angus and Francis (Francis, that perfectly observed type of the artistic-intellectual nineteen-twenties in whom we recognize the Rico of *St. Mawr*); there is Aaron's railway journey with this distinguished pair to Florence; and at Florence there is the English-speaking colony, done with that incomparable rightness of touch which is Lawrence's — comedy too intelligent and sensitive and poised for malice or the satirical note (and placing the callowness of Forster's treatment of the theme in *A Room with a View*). And as one goes on recalling the things in which the genius of the novelist especially compels recognition, one realizes that their power is not, as a rule, at the same time some inevitability of significance in relation to the themes of the novel.[35]

Leavis seems to be admiring the novel for the wrong reasons; at least, we might say that he appreciates the novel not as an integrated work of art but simply as a lively novel of social portraiture with a profusion of brilliantly rendered though unrelated incidents. Here is another example of Leavis' curious defence of the novel:

> Lawrence, we feel, would not have been at a loss to substitute things that would have done as well. We recognize, in fact, that what we have here is for the most part recent actual experience of Lawrence's own, directly rendered: it is just because its impact on him is fresh that it plays so large a part in the life of this novel.[36]

We are faced not simply with the recurrent inadequacy of the autobiographical approach but with an inadvertent failure on Leavis' part to appreciate the deeper thematic significance of those very scenes which he applauds for their social observation.

Vivas, as might be expected, is quite harsh in his treatment of such scenes as "pure padding." He further professes to be unable to "find a connection" between "the ideas and the novel":

> In *Aaron's Rod* the values fall apart from their form, from their poetic embodiment; they are added, and one is not able to find a connection between the ideas and the novel. A series of incidents are contrived in order to thrash out a number of ideas defended or attacked by characters who are in no way connected with the ideas put forth.... There is no organic relation between ideas and the characters.[37]

Vivas' criticisms and, to a lesser extent, those of Leavis suggest that both critics have missed the fact that the diverse incidents of the novel, particularly those of the middle chapters, are neither the "merest reportage" nor "padding" but essential thematic units, integrally related to the central concerns of the novel: music, war, the relationship of the sexes, and so on. Indispensable as these scenes must seem in providing us with humorous or diverting social portraiture, nevertheless they must be seen as firmly linked to Lawrence's much deeper thematic purposes. They thus lay the fullest claim to our serious critical attention.

Leavis' misunderstanding may of course be plausibly traced back to his biographical interest in the novel and to his sympathies for Lawrence the man and artist. Vivas' myopia must once again to be attributed to his refusal to penetrate the novel beyond the level of his own superficial moral and tendentious concerns. Glancing back over the novel we could choose any number of incidents (considered hopelessly unrelated by Vivas) in order to establish their subtle and close thematic relationship with the major concerns of the novel. Let us take for example the episode in Novara in which Aaron remains for two nights a guest of the wealthy Franks, an incident which has been praised by critics, at best, merely as penetrating social observation; or at worst, as extraneous — a piece of pure "padding."

As I have suggested before, the conversational skirmishes of Sir William and Aaron are related to Aaron's growing allegiance to Lilly and thematically to the entire concept of a true and separate selfhood. The threat which Aaron's replies pose here to the old knight's self-satisfaction anticipates Aaron's bitter letter to Sir William (in Chapter 28), expressing fully Aaron's terrifying misanthropy at this point as well as revealing the limitations of Aaron's own concept of aloneness, unaided by Lilly's guidance. The pathetic exhibition of Sir William decked out in his war decorations touches upon the larger theme of war, its glorification by false idealists attacked by Lilly throughout the novel. So too the discussion of Sir William's philanthropic war efforts reveals the misguided efforts of the typical industrial magnate to enact an atonement for the perennial exploitation of men and the mechanization of life which had been largely responsible for leading the nations of Europe to war. The recoil of the corrupt love-urge which Lilly speaks of later is clearly demonstrated here, particularly Lilly's remarks concerning the love-whooshing of world politicians on humanity's behalf.

At the same time Lady Franks and her music, as I suggested in an earlier chapter, are subtly connected with the theme of human lust for power or bullying. Her music expresses her unyielding feminine will and links her thematically to the destructive figures of Lottie and the Marchesa. All three women threaten to undermine or destroy Aaron's "sacred self-hood." At the same time, Lawrence uses Lady Franks' moral indignation at his desertion to express the conventional outrage of society, ironically also victimized itself by a decadent code of conduct based upon love or self-sacrifice. Aaron's musical participation in a "Mozart bit" (208), accompanied by Lady Franks, is used thematically to demonstrate the extent to which Aaron may still be lured from his quest for individuality by the temptations of luxury and musical dilettantism. Lady Franks is also linked here to the parade of musical dilettantes winding its way through the many episodes of the novel—Lady Artemis Hooper, Cecil Grey, Francis Dekker, and so on. Lady and Sir William Franks, and the scenes in which they figure, are thus closely related to the major themes of the novel, and the Novara episode, far from being a piece of mere "padding," is organically connected to other scenes of wry social observation, which, on closer examination, disclose a deeper thematic seriousness.

It would be possible to demonstrate just as easily the thematic relevance of the many other scenes which provide the novel with its unusual, variegated texture.[38] The thematic nature and importance of these scenes and their personages has been dealt with in depth in the previous chapters of my study. In brief, Lawrence has presented us with a vast collage of persons and events, all thematically interconnected and, within his assimilation of the picaresque-*bildungsroman,* a part of Aaron's continuing "education" or growing awareness of himself. One might even speak legitimately, in musical terms, of a system of recurrent thematic motifs which underpin and strengthen the novel. Re-examining the novel, we find ourselves shuttling back and forth from one episode to another as we follow up various successive thematic threads. One scene will remind us of yet another in a slightly different "key" and the major themes of the novel are constantly presented in the juxtaposition of one incident with another. Ultimately we realize that we are dealing not with a series of unrelated persons and events but with a highly complex and skillfully organized work of art.

Much criticism has been levelled upon *Aaron's Rod* for what some deem to be an excess of "talk." Anthony Beal sums up his grudge against the novel in this way:

> Lawrence says here nothing that he did not say better elsewhere. What is profound in
> *Women in Love* here becomes superficial or even silly and the tough verbal battles of

that book degenerate into nagging or boring tirades. Much of the novel is in fact at the level of journalism; parts of it, indeed, might be direct transcripts of those pieces that Lawrence wrote "in an hour and a half" for the *Evening News* and *Sunday Dispatch* (and which were reprinted in *Assorted Articles*). It is significant that an early chapter of the book is called "Talk," and the final one "Words." Towards the end of "Talk" we have: " 'Good-bye,' said Tanny. 'I've been awfully bored.' " The reader may well echo the remark.[39]

Of course there is no way of predicting literary tastes but we cannot help noticing in Beal's half-successful attempt to be witty at Lawrence's expense the failure on his part to grasp the full thematic significance of what he deems an excess of "talk." As I noted previously, the preponderance of "talk," whether in arguments, debates or in simple conversation, is symptomatic of the strange malaise of the post-war period. The characters seem hopelessly gripped, like Joyce's Dubliners, by spiritual paralysis, failing to find a proper creative outlet for their restless feelings of dissatisfaction or sublimated hostility. The superficial chit-chat of the dilettantes' world is also portrayed vividly by Lawrence as the thematic illustration of the decadent atmosphere of the post-war period. Lawrence thereby suggests the degree to which Aaron, in being seduced by the attractions of the dilettantes' world, has compromised his "sacred selfhood." Yet with what verve and humor has Lawrence accomplished the tricky feat of making even the most obnoxious "talkers" fascinating to us!

Lawrence has not simply related the various kinds of "talk" to the thematic concerns of *Aaron's Rod,* but has interrelated the various conversations, particularly those of a debating nature, so as to impose a subtle yet strong unity upon the novel. This unity may be perceived if we are able to step back momentarily, as it were, setting aside our notions of what a novel should or should not be, to consider in isolation the scheme of debates which occur throughout the novel.

The novel opens with an implied "debate": a bitter meeting between the working classes (the miners) and their mine bosses. The public wrangling so characteristic, we soon discover, of the unsettled post war climate prepares us for the pub debate in Chapter 2 concerning labor, wages and the common good. To Aaron, however, this debate carries unmistakable overtones of "self-righteous bullying." The "fair wise" words of the doctor and the landlady conceal beneath their "benevolence" something "detestable and murderous" (29). The debate ends in a verbal stalemate with nothing satisfactorily resolved. It has all been mere "words."

In Chapter 6, "Talk," we discover that the atmosphere of restless debate pervades London circles, too, particularly those of young intellectuals and pseudo-bohemians such as the Bricknell set. The conversation in this episode contains a thematically important and revealing debate on love as well as reinvestigating at the same time the earlier speculations in "The Royal Oak" on the labor force, social change. The pseudo-bohemians engage in a round of "bolshy" talk about "bloody revolution," smashing and "pulling down the house." With the shift in class, the political themes of the pub-debate are taken up from a different angle. The pseudo-bohemians are made to appear ludicrous in their ineffectual chatter which Tanny justly finds quite tedious. Nevertheless, the exchange of words between Lilly and Jim over the nature and importance of love—"when you love, your soul breathes in—when your soul breathes out, it's a bloody revolution" (73)—carries us forward to Jim's bitter, violent debates with Lilly in Chapter 8. In this chapter Lilly's censorious "words" directed at Jim's pitiful whinings after love are cut short by a "punch in the wind"—precisely the same kind of petty violence or bullying which has so far been encountered in Lawrence's depiction of the post-war atmosphere.

The two kinds of verbal conflict or "talk"—one expressing marital discord (between Tanny and Lilly), the other a stalemated conflict of ideology which focuses upon Christianity and its ideals—both converge in Chapters 9 and 10 in the constant "talk" of Aaron and Lilly. Lilly specifically recalls his talk with another "Judas," Jim Bricknell. The two chapters contain extensive dialogues on the bullying nature of motherhood, indeed, of the entire female sex, as well as inquiries into the nature of self-possession or "separate-selfhood." The hostility of a good many of these exchanges recalls Lilly's earlier debating with Jim Bricknell, while the thematic substance of Lilly's arguments bears directly upon all subsequent inquiries on Lilly's part into the achievement of intrinsic self-awareness and the special goal which it provides for Aaron's quest. Lilly's harsh condemnation later of Herbertson's feverish "talk" of the "sacrifices" of war looks forward to his talk of the destructive love-urge and the falsity of Christianity's ideals of self-sacrifice. Herbertson's compulsive war reminiscences, as I established earlier, are of serious thematic importance and obviously relate back to Jim's earlier talk of the violent horrors of trench warfare, particularly the excesses of the Japanese troops. Typically, Lilly and Aaron's debate ends once again in a stalemate, with Aaron resisting even more Lilly's authority (specifically Lilly's denunciation of poison gas warfare) and Lilly ordering Aaron to leave his flat.

The thematically significant and prolonged debate between Aaron and Sir William Franks in Novara harks back to a similar "talk" of Lilly and Aaron concerning Aaron's dependence upon charm and fortune. The debate also looks forward to further talks between Aaron and Lilly concerning the duty of oneself to follow the true urgings of the soul rather than the dictates of social convention. Aaron's skirmishes with the self-righteous Lady Franks recall earlier discussions of marriage and the domination of society by the feminine will, while anticipating the symposium in Chapter 17 on love and marriage. The talk later of Sir William and Lady Franks' ill-fated charitable efforts recalls the earlier pub conversation of local workmen about the "common good" and the "improvement of conditions."

In Florence we note that "talk" becomes more prevalent and time-consuming, but ironically, even more speculative and ineffectual. As I suggested before, the characters seem more and more to fall back upon talk for talk's sake, preferring inactive "talk" to the more challenging activity of self-renewal. Obviously the symposium on love and marriage of Chapter 17 held in Argyle's flat is centrally related to the previous dialogue of Aaron and Lilly concerning marriage and subservience to women. The discussion reveals a series of parallels between the various pairs of wrangling or unhappy couples described throughout the novel: Robert and Julia Cunningham; Jim Bricknell and his French wife; Argyle and his estranged wife; and even more important, Lilly and Tanny; Aaron and Lottie; the Marchese and the Marchesa del Torre. The introduction of Lilly's theory of positive aloneness, particularly in reply to Aaron, anticipates Lilly's final summing up of his doctrine of "sacred selfhood" in "Words." The theme of Lilly's remarks to Argyle — himself like Aaron a compulsive seeker for love — is directly linked to Lilly's final exchanges with Aaron, concerning the replacement of the decadent love-urge with the vital power-urge:

> "And you will go on till you die, Argyle?" said Lilly. "Always seeking a friend — and always a new one?"
>
> "If I lose the friend I've got. Ah, my dear fellow, in that case I shall go on seeking. I hope so, I assure you. Something will be very wrong with me, if ever I sit friendless and make no search."
>
> "But, Argyle, there is a time to leave off."
>
> "To leave off what, to leave off what?"
>
> "Having friends: or a friend, rather: or seeking to have one."
>
> "Oh, no! Not at all, my friend. Not at all! Only death can make an end of that, my friend. Only death. And I should say, not even death. Not even death ends a man's search for a friend. That is my belief. You may hang me for it, but I shall never alter."
>
> "Nay," said Lilly. "There is a time to love, and a time to leave off loving."
>
> "All I can say to that is that my time to leave off hasn't come yet," said Argyle, with obstinate feeling.
>
> "Ah, yes, it has. It is only a habit and an idea you stick to." (280)

In Chapter 20, we are again presented with a prolonged debate concerned with the inevitability of socialism and its effect upon Europe. The full implications of the doctrines expressed by Lilly in this particular debate will be later presented, as well as an investigation into the degree of seriousness intended by Lilly. In any case, the "talk" in this chapter is of a highly significant nature and demonstrates not simply the interrelatedness of the different kinds of "talk" or debate but also the pains which Lawrence has manifestly taken to provide the novel with an underlying unity in its continual theoretical or philosophical investigations. Levison's description of anarchical violence during a socialist protest against the imprisonment of one of the railway strikers places the silliness of the pseudo-bohemians' idle "bolshy" talk earlier. At the same time, the description recalls other such scenes of mob violence or political upheaval throughout the novel, most notably the flag incident. Lilly's repudiation of socialism suggests that he too has undergone some change of ideology since the "bolshy" talk after the opera in Chapter 6, has himself advanced beyond the vain aspirations of socialism:

> "*You're* a bit of a socialist though, aren't you?" persisted Levison, now turning to Lilly.
> "No," said Lilly. "I was." (324)

Lilly's anathematising of the mob and mob-authority may be traced directly back to his previous "talk" with Aaron in Chapter 10:

> "Damn all leagues. Damn all masses and groups, anyhow. All I want is to get *myself* out of their horrible heap: to get out of the swarm. The swarm to me is nightmare and nullity—horrible helpless writhing in a dream. I want to get myself awake, out of it all—all that mass-consciousness, all that mass-activity—it's the most horrible nightmare to me. No man is awake and himself. No man who was awake and in possession of himself would use poison gases: no man. His own awake self would scorn such a thing. It's only when the ghastly mob-sleep, the dream helplessness of the mass-psyche overcomes him, that he becomes completely base and obscene." (139)

The café-debate taken as a whole is also related to the pub-debate near the beginning of the novel in which the goal of the workers, the common good and other such topics were discussed among the denizens of "The Royal Oak." Ironically, also, when looking back upon the debate we realize that Lilly's hyperbolic theories of slavery seem indeed the grotesque antithesis of his "Words" to Aaron in the final chapter concerning sacred selfhood and the evils of spiritual bullying.

Before any examination of the effect of this final chapter and Lilly's "Words" to Aaron, the confusion surrounding Lilly's extravagant theorising in the café during this episode must be cleared up. In *The Deed of Life* Julian Moynahan, ordinarily a sensitive reader of Lawrence, has taken Lilly's words very seriously, at least, as virtually the unadorned and quite horrifying doctrine of Lawrence himself. Here is part of Moynahan's extensive analysis of the café debate:

> The level of thinking is perhaps only a little lower than one would expect from one sort of Englishman—or American for that matter—who hung about in Paris, Rome,

Florence, or any of a dozen Mediterranean beach resorts during the nineteen-twenties, pretending to work but actually drinking and eating up an unearned income.[40]

The irrelevant drift of such commentary is quite evident. Moynahan, with his critically unacceptable penchant for extending the novel beyond the limits imposed by Lawrence in order to apply the theoretical content of the novel to subsequent historical developments, has this to say of the nature of the debate:

> Despite the obvious parallels it would be a mistake to identify this colloquy of disaffected bourgeois intellectuals in an Italian café with similar colloquies held in the cafés of Munich, Vienna, and Berlin where disaffected bourgeois intellectuals like Rosenberg and Goebbels practiced the art of philosophico-politico dialectic before taking up careers in the world of *realpolitik* at the end of the decade. Argyle is merely a drunken ass and Lilly may be talking, as he often does, more to make a rhetorical *bella figura* than honestly. Besides, neither is a man of destiny.... A pose of petulant nihilism colored with anti-Semitism struck at this particular time and place (northern Italy, 1920) is a blow struck against the living selves of all Europe. Lilly's bad will and bad faith in humanity are specifically political acts in this context and must be condemned out of hand.[41]

Notice that in admitting that Argyle and Lilly are not "men of destiny" Moynahan inadvertently reveals the inherent flaw in his approach to the café scene, the absurd irrelevance of his parallel, indeed, the curious shortcomings of his entire chapter on *Aaron's Rod*. Moynahan has unwittingly stumbled upon the true dramatic significance of the speeches in this chapter. Ironically, he has chosen to ignore the more interesting implications of his observation, preferring to deliver a tirade as tiresome as those of Lilly which he supposedly deplores. The dramatic context of Lilly's exaggerated statements must not be overlooked. Lilly's extreme position is in part a reply to the violent anarchy of the socialists just previously described by Levinson as well as to the general doctrine of "socialistic inevitability" espoused by Levinson and, it would seem, a great many others at this particular point in Italy. Lilly's replies to Levison are clearly intended as a mock-serious counterpoint to the semi-intoxicated extravagance of Argyle, who speaks facetiously of reinstating a kind of slavery akin to that of the Greeks and Romans. Just as Argyle reacts eccentrically to the tense partisan atmosphere of the cafe with forced gaiety and facetious clap-trap, so Lilly may be seen reacting with customary argumentativeness, playing "devil's advocate" to Levison's theories and generally making a nuisance of himself. Both Argyle's words and Lilly's are seen to be no more than empty air, the only difference being that Lilly perversely leads his listeners to assume that they are witnessing a true declaration of his political *credo*.[42]

However seriously we might at first be tempted to take Lilly's reactionary measures in this scene, we should not fail to observe that his statements are nevertheless challenged and virtually undermined in this episode. One obvious attack comes from Levison himself whose thoughts are revealed by the narrator. The condemnation of Lilly at this point by Levison is intended to function to a certain extent as an echo of the reader's own protests at what seems such an extreme position:

> Here Levison smiled a long, slow, subtle smile of ridicule. It all seemed to him the preposterous pretentiousness of a megalomaniac—one whom, after a while, humanity would probably have the satisfaction of putting into prison, or into a lunatic asylum. And Levison felt strong, overwhelmingly strong, in the huge social power with which he, insignificant as he was, was armed against such criminal-imbecile pretensions as those above set forth. Prison or the lunatic asylum. The face of the fellow gloated in these two inevitable engines of his disapproval. (328)

Lilly himself quickly renounces the harshly reactionary measures which he has with false seriousness just advocated. Here is the full exchange:

> "It will take you some time before you'll get your doctrines accepted," he said.
> "Accepted! I'd be sorry. I don't want a lot of swine snouting and sniffing at me with their acceptance. —Bah, Levison—one can easily make a fool of you. Do you take this as my gospel?"
> "I take it you are speaking seriously."
> Here Lilly broke into that peculiar, gay, whimsical smile.
> "But I should say the blank opposite with just as much fervor," he declared.
> "Do you mean to say you don't *mean* what you've been saying?" said Levison, now really looking angry.
> "Why, I'll tell you the real truth," said Lilly. "I think every man is a sacred and holy individual, *never* to be violated. I think there is only one thing I hate to the verge of madness, and that is *bullying*. To see any living creature *bullied,* in *any* way, almost makes a murderer of me. That is true. Do you believe it—?" (328)

Lilly here reveals the full extent of his capricious yet pugnacious nature. If as readers we are to be annoyed with Lilly—and I am not sure we are really justified in being so—it must be for his perversity in arguing something simply for argument's sake. Lilly is rendered quite ridiculous in his revealed capriciousness. He seems here just as afflicted as the other characters in the café by the restless *malaise* of the *dopoguerra*. Yet Lawrence is careful to provide Lilly with the opportunity of elucidating for us his true *credo*—one which he will elaborate more fully to Aaron in the next chapter. Lilly's further "words" are truncated by the bomb blast which of course provides a reply to Lilly and a fitting conclusion to the ineffectual altercations of the café. The explosion of the anarchists' bomb provides as much a negative answer to Lilly's false-serious theories, with their reliance upon repressive military power—more detestable bullying— as it does an answer to Levison's belief in socialism as the ideal panacea for Europe's political ills.

Lilly's final dialogue with Aaron is preceded by a profound and crucial meditation on Aaron's part which coincidentally registers our reactions to Lilly (and his theorising) up to this point:

> His flute was broken, and broken finally. The bomb had settled it. The bomb had settled it and everything. It was an end, no matter how he tried to patch things up. The only thing he felt was a thread of destiny attaching him to Lilly. The rest had all gone as bare and bald as the dead orb of the moon. So he made up his mind, if he could, to make some plan that would bring his life together with that of his evanescent friend.
>
> Lilly was a peculiar bird. Clever and attractive as he undoubtedly was, he was perhaps the most objectionable person to know. It was stamped on his peculiar face.
>
> Aaron had been through it all. He had started by thinking Lilly a peculiar little freak: gone on to think him a wonderful chap, and a bit pathetic: progressed, and found him generous, but overbearing: then cruel and intolerant, allowing no man to have a soul of his own: then terribly arrogant, throwing a fellow aside like an old glove which is in holes at the finger-ends. And all the time, which was most beastly, seeing through one. All the time, freak and outsider as he was, Lilly *knew*. He knew, and his soul was against the whole world....
>
> If he had to give in to something: if he really had to give in, and it seemed he had: then he would rather give in to the little Lilly than to the beastly people of the world. If he had to give in, then it should be to no woman, and to no social ideal, and to no social institution. No!—if he had to yield his wilful independence, and give himself, then he would rather give himself to the little, individual *man* than to any of the rest. For to tell the truth, in the man was something incomprehensible, which had dominion over him, if he chose to allow it. (335–336)

Aaron's musing is essential for an understanding of his motivations at this point.[43] Lawrence intends us to observe the crucial change in Aaron, one which seems to indicate that he is at last ready to listen to the "words" of Lilly with more acquiescence than hostility or repulsion. We are justified in assuming that with this crucial change of outlook Aaron's quest for self-recognition at least *begins* to resolve itself as he moves closer to Lilly.

Lilly's final "words" to Aaron in Chapter 21 have been a perennial source of critical dismay and confusion, and have more than often been responsible for the prevailing condemnation of the entire novel. While the "open-ending" of the novel does not represent an artistic failure, Lilly's words to Aaron and Aaron's strange position at this point are nevertheless problematic. I offer here a more positive approach to understanding Lawrence's artistic attempts, an interpretation based upon numerous critical rereadings of the novel over several years rather than a series of *ex cathedra* pronouncements on the novel's failure, of which there have been already far too many.

One of the most common errors encountered in commentaries dealing with *Aaron's Rod* stems clearly from critics' reluctance to attend to what the novel is actually saying in its final pages through the dialogue of its two central characters, Lilly and Aaron. Before discussing the critical problems raised by Lilly's doctrines it may be useful to review briefly exactly what essentially Lilly is saying in these final pages.

The dramatic context of Lilly's address cannot be overlooked. Lilly has discovered the morose Aaron lying in bed, ostensibly shattered by the recent loss of his flute. He is clearly in need of much the same comfort as he had been given earlier in Lilly's flat. In fact the incident here is meant to recall to us that previous episode in which Aaron was symbolically anointed and revived through Lilly's ministrations. Lilly's words are dramatically intended here both as balm to Aaron's spiritual wounds and as a means of arousing new life in the despondent flutist. Lawrence thus skilfully provides Lilly with adequate dramatic grounds for an extended "therapeutic" speech to Aaron. The subject of Lilly's address is also revealed early in the episode, even before the two men depart for the country:

> "The grinding of the old millstones of love and God is what ails us, when there's no more grist between the stones. We've ground love very small. Time to forget it. Forget the very words religion, and God, and love—then have a shot at a new mode. But the very words rivet us down and don't let us move. Rivets, and we can't get them out."
> "And where should we be if we could?" said Aaron.
> "We might begin to be ourselves, anyhow."
> "And what does that mean?" said Aaron. "Being yourself—what does it mean?"
> "To me, everything."
> "And to most folks, nothing. They've got to have a goal."
> "There is no goal. I loathe goals more than any other impertinence. Gaols, they are. Bah—jails and jailers, gaols and gaolers— —" (338)

Lilly thus hints at the adoption of a new mode of living at the same time making it clear that external or idealistic goals are really a form of self-destruction. It is also important to note that even here Lilly makes it clear to Aaron that perhaps his solutions may operate only at a personal level. "Well, I didn't make life and society. I can only go my own way" (338). Aaron's reaction to Lilly's claim is particulary interesting. He feels "a deep disappointment...setting over his spirit" (338). These exchanges contain the germ of Lilly's prolonged talk later as well as Aaron's stubborn reactions to Lilly's words.

Before introducing Aaron to his concept of the power-urge which must supplant the love-urge, Lilly neatly disposes of all of what he terms Aaron's "lost illusions." He attacks Aaron's love-urge; his compulsion to surrender himself to the momentary sensations of romatic love:

> "And what are you looking for in love?—A woman whom you can love, and who will love you, out and out and all in all and happy ever after sort of thing?"
> "That's what I started out for, perhaps," laughed Aaron.

"And now you know it's all my eye!" Aaron looked at Lilly, unwilling to admit it. Lilly began to laugh.

"You know it well enough," he said. "It's one of your lost illusions, my boy. Well, then, what next? Is it a God you're after? Do you want a God you can strive to and attain, through love, and live happy ever after, countless millions of eternities, immortality and all that? Is this your little dodge?" (341)

Notice also that Lilly attributes the idealism of striving towards a God of Love to the decadent love urge:

"All right then. You've got a love-urge that urges you to God, have you? Then go and join the Buddhists in Burmah, or the newest fangled Christians in Europe. Go and stick your head in a bush of Nirvana or spiritual perfection. Trot off."

"I won't," said Aaron.

"You must. If you've got a love-urge, then give it its fulfillment."

"I haven't got a love-urge."

"You have. You want to get excited in love. You want to be carried away in love. You want to whoosh off in a nice little love whoosh and love yourself. Don't deny it. I know you do. You want passion to sweep you off on wings of fire till you surpass yourself, and like the swooping eagle swoop right into the sun. I know you, my love-boy." (341)

Lilly's reply to Aaron's objection that he (Aaron) is now filled more with hate than love illustrates Lilly's belief in the poisonous effects of the perverted love-urge, at the same time placing the deeper sources of all the acts of anarchy so far encountered in the novel:

That's the recoil of the same urge. The anarchist, the criminal, the murderer, he is only the extreme lover acting on the recoil. But it is love: only in recoil. It flies back, the love-urge, and becomes a horror. (342)

What Lilly is trying to point out to the stubborn Aaron in this exchange (and indeed, all through the novel) is that man's notions of romantic love; the idealism of a religious quest for a God beyond the self; the Buddhist search for a mystic Nirvana; the "heroic" self-sacrifice of men like Herbertson to the war machine; the anarchist's acts of violence: all of these constitute an utter denial of the sacred responsibility of the individual to his own soul. Lilly establishes clearly that Aaron can never lose himself, and must never abdicate the sacred responsibility of self-knowledge and development:

You can whoosh if you like, and get excited and carried away loving a woman, or humanity or God. Swoop away in the love direction till you lose yourself. But that's where you're had. You can't lose yourself. You can try. But you might just as well try to swallow yourself. You'll only bite your fingers off in the attempt. You can't lose yourself, neither in woman nor humanity nor in God. You've always got yourself on your hands in the end: and a very raw and jaded and humiliated and nervous-neurasthenic self it is, too, in the end. A very nasty thing to wake up to is one's own raw self after an excessive love-whoosh. Look even at President Wilson: he love-whooshed for humanity, and found in the end he'd only got a very sorry self on his hands. (342)

In images of fertilization, gestation and incubation Lilly speaks fervently of Aaron's responsibility never to deny but always to acknowledge the Holy Ghost within him, and to nourish his soul, a kind of Tree of Life within.

It is worth noting that at this point Lilly's doctrine does *not* exclude love or sensual fulfilment. As he says earlier also, the possession of the soul in isolation comes "after a lot of fighting and a lot of sensual fulfilment. And it never does away with the fighting and with the sensual passion. It flowers on top of them" (122). Aaron of course protests, with some justification, that he has never denied that responsibility for his actions must fall upon his own shoulders; and Lilly further elaborates:

> You never said it did. You never accepted. You thought there was something outside, to justify you: God, or a creed, or a prescription. But remember, your soul inside you is your only Godhead. It develops your actions within you as a tree develops its own new cells. And the cells push on into buds and boughs and flowers. And these are your passion and your acts and your thoughts and expressions, your developing consciousness. You don't know before-hand, and you can't. You can only stick to your own soul through thick and thin. (344)

Up to this point we notice that Lilly has gained Aaron's grudging approval of the concept that it is "an imbecility to say that love and love alone must rule" (345). Having established the necessity of man's discovering and obeying the Holy Ghost of his own soul and suggesting that there is a time for change and renewal, Lilly makes a skillful (and to him alone, a logical) transition to the doctrine of power which he is convinced must replace the outworn love-urge.

> But listen. I told you there were two urges—two great life-urges, didn't I? There may be more. But it comes on me so strongly, now, that there are two: love, and power. And we've been trying to work ourselves, at least as individuals, from the love-urge exclusively, hating the power-urge, and repressing it. And now I find we've got to accept the very thing we've hated. (345)

Lilly makes several important qualifying statements by which he brings into sharper focus for Aaron the nature of the power-urge he has in mind:

> It is a vast dark source of life and strength in us now, waiting either to issue into true action, or to burst into cataclysm. ...The will to power—but not in Nietzsche's sense. Not in intellectual power. Not conscious will-power. Not even wisdom. But dark, living, fructifying power. ...

The urge of power does not seek for happiness any more than for any other state. It urges from within, darkly, for the displacing of the old leaves, the inception of the new. It is powerful and self-central, not seeking its centre outside in some God or some beloved, but acting indomitably from within itself. (345-46)

We must notice also that Lilly's doctrine of deep submission of woman to the power urge emphatically is not a submission to any foolish fixed authority, "not to any foolish and arbitrary will," but to "the soul in its dark motion of power and pride." Lilly also emphatically denies that his free submission is to be confused with slavery. In so doing, he distinctly separates what is here his serious creed from his earlier belligerent, mock-serious remarks calculated to annoy Levison, those which seemed for the moment to second the tipsy hyperbole of Argyle with his obnoxious racist theories of enslavement.

Yet at this point Lawrence allows Lilly to become more tentative, even more "uncertain" yet "assertive" (336) than he has previously been when he begins to develop his newly conceived and peculiar notions of submission to a superior soul. Lawrence thus deliberately presents in *dramatic* terms, what has been suspected all through the novel (and has been especially conveyed in the harsh criticism of Lilly by both Tanny and Aaron) namely, that Lilly is here more than ever the victim of his own uncertainties and contradictions. It appears that Lilly himself has become confused in his belief in the necessary surrender of the individual to the "greater soul" of another while advising Aaron to attend only to the sacred promptings of his inner "Holy Ghost." Lawrence skillfully manipulates his presentation of Lilly in order that we may perceive in dramatic terms that Lilly is far from settled in his doctrines and, as Aaron has himself pointed out earlier in the novel, is far from achieving the peace or self sufficiency he would like to assume he has:

"I think a man may come into possession of his own soul at last — as the Buddhists teach — but without ceasing to love, or even to hate. One loves, one hates — but somewhere beyond it all, one understands, and possesses one's soul in patience and in peace — "

"Yes," said Aaron slowly, "while you only stand and talk about it. But when you've got no chance to talk about it — and when you've got to live — you don't possess your soul, neither in patience nor in peace, but any devil that likes possesses you and does what it likes with you, while you fridge yourself and fray yourself out like a worn rag." (122)

Notice also the disturbing, hectoring quality which Lawrence assigns to Lilly's final exhortation:

All men say, they want a leader. Then let them in their souls *submit* to some greater soul than theirs. At present, when they say they want a leader, they mean they want an instrument, like Lloyd George. A mere instrument for their use. But it's more than that. It's the reverse. It's the deep, fathomless submission to the heroic soul in a greater man. You, Aaron, you too have the need to submit. You, too, have the need livingly to yield to a more heroic soul, to give yourself. You know you have. And you know it isn't love. It is life-submission. And you know it. But you kick against the pricks. And perhaps you'd rather die than yield. And so, die you must. It is your affair." (347)

Lilly, still fretting and tentative, is still to some extent playing at "little Jesus" in this episode. A further dramatic point being made in this final scene is Lilly's failure to realize that his own theories, no matter how appropriate to his own peculiar conditions, need not necessarily fit the requirements of others such as Aaron. Aaron in turn feels more than justified at this point in his skepticism. Lilly too has his limitations, for he cannot perceive that his own exhortations and theories also exist outside Aaron and *beyond* the call of his soul, and that, as such they must take their place beside those external voices or creeds which, significantly, Lilly's earlier teaching itself condemns as false or inferior to the true urgings of the individual soul. Thus, according to Lilly's earlier statements Aaron should now reject many of Lilly's theories on the basis that they come from without rather than within Aaron's undeniable soul. It is to Lilly's credit, however, that he goes no further in his bullying than to suggest that Aaron himself is indeed in need of submission, but refuses to name himself as a heroic leader — or anyone else for that matter. Lilly obviously feels rather reluctant to impose any further authority upon Aaron, especially in view of Aaron's growing antagonism.

The novel thus ends rather abruptly in the same mood of doubt or self-questioning which has pervaded it throughout:

> There was a long pause. Then Aaron looked up into Lilly's face. It was dark and remote-seeming. It was like a Byzantine eikon at the moment.
> "And whom shall I submit to?" he said.
> "Your soul will tell you," replied the other. (347)

It is nevertheless ironic that Aaron is too proud or obdurate to perceive that some of Lilly's "words" contain more than a modicum of truth, even if pragmatically unacceptable in a larger social context. At least Lilly's doctrine of the private "Holy Ghost within" offers a plausible alternative to Aaron's self-destructive exile and egocentric "love-whooshing." Dramatically Lawrence presents us with another spiritual stalemate. Lilly, it seems, has only arrived at the beginnings of wisdom. He still overlooks the bullying nature of his urgent assertions, and further destroys the beauty of his *credo* by confusing inadvertently the nature of creative, dark, personal power with an external and quite spurious state-power or leadership.

Aaron, on the other hand, is apparently disillusioned by Lilly's obvious human shortcomings, particularly as he conceives Lilly to be his "mind's hero," and falls back upon the same sullen resistance with which he has met Lilly's offers all through the novel. Part of Aaron's reluctance stems from his misconceiving of Lilly's part in his unfolding destiny. Lilly, like Vergil in the *Divina Commedia*, simply functions as a guide to bring Aaron closer to self-recognition or renewal. Aaron's problem in his attitude towards Lilly is summed up best by an earlier remark dropped casually by the narrator during the railway journey to Florence:

> Mankind loves being impressed. It asks to be impressed. It almost forces those whom it can force to play a role and to make an impression. And afterwards, never forgives. (235)

Aaron mistakenly assumes that Lilly's personal doctrines should be fixed and idealistic and that Lilly is here insisting upon his own superiority as a heroic leader. In fact, Lilly never once states that he is either superior or a heroic leader. He simply lays the final responsibility for Aaron's choice of a leader upon Aaron's own soul and its inviolable rights.

It is particularly significant that Aaron has previously conceived of Lilly simply in terms being his "mind's hero":

> As he lay pondering this over, escaping from the *cul de sac* in which he had been running for so long, by yielding to one of his pursuers: yielding to the peculiar mastery of one man's nature rather than to the quicksands of woman or the stinking bogs of society: yielding, since yield he must, in some direction or other: yielding in a new direction now, to one strange and incalculable little individual: as Aaron lay so relaxing, finding a peculiar delight in giving his soul to his mind's hero, the self-same hero tapped and entered. (336-37)

The impulse which drives Aaron towards Lilly comes not from the soul but from the mind. The Lawrencean distinction between mind and soul is particularly relevant here. Aaron's impulse is also contrary to Lilly's concepts of the preeminence of the soul's own urge. Aaron's half-hearted decision to submit to Lilly is especially revealing, for his submission here, it is clearly suggested, is to be associated with the false idealism of the decadent love-urge, the compulsion for cozy friendship, self-sacrifice or the surrender of oneself to another goal not only outside the self but utterly opposed or foreign to the soul. Aaron's subsequent refusal to acknowledge the truth of Lilly's "diagnosis" of his own failures is connected to Aaron's inability to envision a submission beyond the limits of sexual surrender or ideal friendship.

The final image of the novel in which Lilly's face appears as a

Byzantine eikon [sic], "dark and remote seeming," rather than representing anything "pompous, arrogant, or absurd" is grimly ironic—a strong visual representation of the distorted way in which Aaron views Lilly, not as human but as an idealized rendering of a sacred subject—disembodied and quite incomplete. Lilly is a mere voice to Aaron, an indication of a significant default of understanding on Aaron's part. Just as Lilly fails to move beyond his anxious self-questioning to resolve the incongruities of his doctrine and his approach, so Aaron also fails to note Lilly's true significance as mentor and the ultimate truth of Lilly's observations concerning his failures. The novel ends thus on a doubly ironic note. As Tedlock has pointed out, "Aaron does not reach the Promised Land. Neither does the Lawrencean Moses, Lilly."[44] Like the troubled fisher of *The Waste Land* who stands with the arid plain behind him and with merely the keys to liberation or renewal in his possession, so Aaron remains suspended, having crossed the border line which separates his old life from a possible new one. Whether or not Aaron will ever heed either Lilly's theories either of intrinsic "self-aloneness," obey the true promptings of his soul or ever submit, is all part of a puzzle which Lawrence deliberately leaves unsolved. The inconclusiveness of the "open-ending" is entirely characteristic of a good deal of Lawrence's fiction. The admirable refusal to impose an artistic tyranny upon Aaron in order to bring about his surrender and thus a resolution to the novel reminds us that Lawrence considered the novel to be a living form, not a rigidly contrived set of formulae. The uncertainty and questioning of both Aaron and Lilly also recall vividly the spirit of self-inquiry or restless uncertainty which informed the endings of earlier fictions. Most notably we recall Rupert Birkin's dissatisfaction at the conclusion of *Women in Love*, the uncertainty of his position, as he is left longing for "eternal union with a man too: another kind of love" (473).[45]

No doubt it is the persistent confusion between Lilly and Lawrence—as if the two were interchangeable—which accounts for so many critical attacks upon the concluding pages of *Aaron's Rod*. Most critics in their haste to point out that Lilly's speech is simply a contrived harangue being delivered by Lawrence himself miss the point that Lilly is a dramatic embodiment of a would-be savior whose positions, far from being infallible, are eminently contradictory and uncertain in their direction. Most critics also fail to note that the concluding "words" of Lilly suggest his own struggle to extemporize. Lilly himself is only at the beginnings of articulating his complex theories.

It seems strange that Yudhishtar, in other places quite penetrating in his examination of *Aaron's Rod*, should complain that the conclusion is unsatisfactory because it fails to present the proper challenge to Lilly's torrent of words:

> [I]n handing over nearly all of the last "words" chapter to Lilly, Lawrence, I think, failed to include in the book adequate criticism of Lilly's point of view. This is a serious flaw in *Aaron's Rod*, and in this respect it is probably the weakest of Lawrence's mature novels.[46]

Yudhishtar has missed several important features of the last chapter, including the dramatic device of allowing Lilly as many "words" as he requires to entangle himself and to expose the patent flaws in his argument. The stubborn resistance of Aaron and his repeated questions and cynical challenges in this chapter (and indeed through the entire novel) must surely have been overlooked. And what, we must ask, of Tanny's constant undermining or challenging of Lilly's position? Even when she is not present, her resistance is vividly conveyed to us by Lilly himself. It is clear that Lawrence has intended that Tanny and, to a larger extent, Aaron should function as "devil's-advocates" throughout the novel. In the final scene, as Tedlock points out, Aaron's continuing criticism of Lilly calls up in him "all his powers of self justification."[47] Though Tanny or Aaron really present few alternative ideas or theories to refuse Lilly, they at least present a challenge to Lilly's self-assumed authority and suggest further that Lilly's spiritual bullying will never be accepted by the many.

Leavis complicates the issue with his confusing treatment of the conclusion of the novel as Lawrence's untransmuted autobiography:

> Wherever the centre of interest was in the early part of *Aaron's Rod*, there can be not doubt where it is now. What bearing has Lilly's sufficiently explicit prescription on Aaron's problem? It is not suggested that Aaron is one of the 'greater men,' and it is hardly to be supposed that his submitting to the 'heroic soul' in Lilly will reconcile Lottie, his wife, to forgoing the love he cannot give her. It might of course be suggested that the insolubility of the individual problem while the governing ideas of civilization remain what they are is just the moral. But actually nothing could be plainer than that Aaron is left so in the air because he is now for Lawrence a decidedly minor and subordinate interest — because, in fact, as a case different from Lawrence's own he is just not *there*. ...
>
> That Lawrence should have been able so to slight the situation of his hero, so to ignore the pressures than an actual Aaron must surely have felt, shows how compellingly his own problems must have been pressing upon him when he wrote *Aaron's Rod*, and with how betraying an unawareness, therefore, he could fail to transcend his own personal situation. We have evidence enough that at this time not only was Lilly's kind of preoccupation with 'power,' 'responsibility' and 'submission,' and with the extra-literary implications of such genius as Lawrence's, very much Lawrence's own, but that the preoccupation as it absorbed Lawrence was at the same time a wrestling with the problem of his own most important personal relation — his relation with Frieda.[48]

No one would wish to dispute that *Aaron's Rod* is very much the product of the troubled situation faced by Lawrence during the final months of the war and its disturbing aftermath. It is true also that Lawrence during these years was profoundly stirred by the problems of "power and responsibility and submission." But, we must ask, does all this necessarily mean that Rawdon Lilly is to be that new leader of men, himself possessed of a heroic soul, the kind of leader who, Lawrence was later to prophesy, would emerge from the unsettled climate of post-war Europe?[49]

Surely the whole point of the final episode lies in the dramatic proof that Lilly is neither a hero nor a destined leader but simply a *guide*, possessing some notion of private "sacred-selfhood" or power which he conceives as a viable alternative to the love-whoosh. However, when Lilly begins applying his theories to the larger context of society as a whole and thereby begins to confuse the intrinsic and inviolable power of the soul with military or political power, he goes seriously astray, and within the dramatic form of the episode shows himself to be erring and vulnerable. Yet Aaron's failure to observe the kernal of truth in Lilly's diagnosis of his own special "case" reinforces our impression that Aaron still has some distance to go before completing his quest for true selfhood.

Finally, we have Julian Moynahan's unsuitable approach to the conclusion of the novel in which *Aaron's Rod* is treated as if Lawrence were attempting to place before his readers an actual political treatise. Moynahan obviously considers that the novel is a kind of "tract for the times," and is therefore subject to repudiation by the unforeseen later developments of history:

> With pieces of broken flute in his hands and his sensitive musician's ears still ringing from the blast, Aaron seems indisposed to stir himself over Lilly's prosing about "the deep power-soul in the individual man." The modern reader, blessed with the superior insight of historical hindsight, is stirred in ways that Lawrence could not have anticipated. The bomb casually flung in the café announces an era of social chaos in Italy out of which will soon emerge a power-soul named Mussolini to elicit abject submission from all but the very rich. Furthermore, it is a kind of Viconian thunder-clap ushering in two decades of savagery and folly which will see the rise of Nazism, the collapse of Russian socialism and of the League of Nations, the agony of Spain, the failure of democratic leadership in England and France, and the outbreak of a second world war. Lilly's slender claims to a knowledge of visionary truth are overwhelmed by a nightmare of history. His ethos of anarchic individualism and his insistence on the right to act in a spirit of pure irresponsibility lose their appeal when we see them written large in the revolution of nihilism engineered by master demolitionists like Hitler.[50]

The puzzling inadequacy of Moynahan's chapter on *Aaron's Rod* may be easily traced to his mistaken assumptions about the "type" of novel Lawrence is attempting in *Aaron's Rod*:

Aaron's Rod is a kind of Russian novel written for Anglo-Saxons, a novel in which the questions, "How should one live nowadays?" and "What must one do to be saved?" are kept constantly in view. Unfortunately, the power and authority of such a novel lie in the author's ability to suggest viable answers to his central questions or to suggest that his central characters are serious seekers after the living truth, however absurdly it may be formulated. But Lawrence's answers are not viable and his two main characters, Aaron and Lilly, lack ethical authenticity.[51]

It seems quite impossible to accept Moynahan's notion that Aaron or Lilly are not "serious seekers after the living truth." Lawrence is not writing a "Dostoevsky" kind of novel either, as Moynahan tries to demonstrate. We cannot so classify *Aaron's Rod* without doing an injustice to Lawrence's genius. Like *Kangaroo* (to which Lawrence first applied the term) *Aaron's Rod* can best be described as a "thought adventure." Both words of the description carry an equal weight. No final answers are either discovered, insisted upon or dramatically presented. Examining all of the critical confusion surrounding *Aaron's Rod* we come to the inevitable conclusion that many critics attempt to discredit the novel because it does not conform to their notions of the kind of novel that they feel Lawrence *ought* to have written. The constant evocation of the indisputable artistic triumphs of *The Rainbow* and *Women in Love* suggests also that works like *Aaron's Rod* have been condemned out of hand and consigned to critical neglect simply because they either do not measure up to what most critics consider to be Lawrence's highest level of achievement as a novelist, or because they simply refuse to conform to traditional or arbitrary concepts of what constitutes that most chameleon of all literary forms — the novel.

As a final answer to such perennial critics, we must allow Lawrence the final word. The famous reply to Linati is quite appropriate:

But really, Signor Linati, do you think that books should be sort of toys, nicely built up of observations and sensations, all finished and complete? — I don't. To me, even Synge, whom I admire very much indeed, is a bit too rounded off and, as it were, put on the shelf to be looked at. I can't bear art that you can walk round and admire. A book should be either a bandit or a rebel or a man in a crowd. People should either run for their lives, or come under the colours, or say *How do you do*? I hate the actor-and-the-audience business. An author should be in among the crowd, kicking their shins or cheering on to some mischief or merriment.... You need not complain that I don't subject the intensity of my vision — or whatever it is — to some vast and imposing rhythm — by which you mean, isolate it on a stage, so that you can look down on it like a god who has got a ticket to the show. I never will: and you will never have that satisfaction from me. Stick to Synge, Anatole France, Sophocles: they will never kick the footlights even. But whoever reads me will be in the thick of the scrimmage, and if he doesn't like it — if he wants a safe seat in the audience — let him read somebody else.[52]

By placing us in the veritable "thick of the scrimmage," Lawrence stimulates in us our most intense reactions. He forces us to re-examine our preconceptions of the nature of fiction, and art itself. When, as critics, we come to assess those works such as *Aaron's Rod,* long considered "problematic," Lawrence demands of us a critical sensitivity or awareness which will enable us to deal as completely and honestly as possible with the special challenges his work invariably lays before us.

Appendix

Original Typescript version of "the flag incident", *Aaron's Rod,* Chapter 14 (TS292-99/A232-37) [Numbering of paragraphs mine]

1. As he lay thinking of nothing and feeling nothing except a certain weariness or dreariness, or God-knows-what, he heard a noise of many people and many voices in the street below. Rising he went on to his little balcony. Came up from below the most frightening of all noises: the hoarse chaffered resonance of a mob in uneasy cry. It was men — all men — mostly youths — rather shabby but not particularly poor, wearing the inevitable black hat of the working people. They were all talking, and haranguing with one another, and moving forward in that curious ebbing, revolving, reluctant, motion of an Italian crowd. Dark, they filled the street below with their ebbing, rotatory flood: and the upturned faces seemed pale, and the hands in gesticulation seemed to fly like sparks. They had no flag /293/ or badge: were evidently workmen of some sort: and the mob consisted of little gangs or clotted groups, which clotted groups, pressed more together, formed a serious crowd. But still it had no fixed purpose but seemed to drift desultorily forward, talking and haranguing. Aaron saw a shopman in a white coat hastily fixing up his last shutter, a little ahead: then dart indoors like a white rabbit. And the crash of his down-sliding iron door-front, as he pulled it safe to earth, resounded above the curious swelling, tearing noise of the crowd.

2. Suddenly, however, some one caught sight of the Italian tricolor hanging directly opposite Aaron's hotel, and a shout was lifted. Many voices shouting many things, suddenly swelled in a wave of sound, like a great puff of smoky flame, up past Aaron's face, from the street below. Many faces were lifted pale from the darkness of the mob; many upturned faces, and mouths opening strangely in shouts, away below there. And still there seemed no one uniting emotion in it all. Still there seemed only a jolting, massive discord of voices, as group-voice smote against group voice. They seemed to be exhorting one another — and exhorting themselves. They seemed to be urging a sort of growling, strangled passion into heat and flame. And the passion seemed to bubble and spurt irregularly.

3. The whole crowd had come to a stop immediately below the hotel, and all were now looking up at the green and /294/ white and red tricolor which stirred damply in the early evening light, from under the broad eaves of the house opposite. Aaron looked at the long flag, which drooped almost unmoved from the eaves-shadow, under the sky of light. Then he looked down at the packed black shoulders of the mob below, and the curious clustering pattern of a sea of black hats. He could hardly see anything but hats and shoulders, uneasily moving like boiling pitch away beneath him. But the shouts came up hotter and hotter. The passion was beginning to fuse. It was a terrible noise, unspeakably depressing to the soul, the sound of this mass of men trying to work up a deep, slow, strangled anger to a pitch where it would take fire, and release itself into action. The shouts rose in pitch, and became more

unanimous. The curious hot sound of the rising blood, and that most peculiar prolonged roaring resonance of a really angry mob now began to fill the street. Loud thuds and crashes as men beat and smashed at the great green door of the house. Stones rattled against the green shutters of the closed windows, and clanged against the iron wrought fencing of the little balconies. But the house heeded nothing, and the Italian flag hung heavily drooping. The pale stone house with its green shutters and its balconies beneath each window—balconies with fine wrought iron work on the first floor, with simpler iron-work on the second floor, and only a sort of grille for the /295/ top floor: this rather handsome, oldish, stone house stood utterly unmoved, whilst the black sea at its foot urged and lashed itself towards a frenzy which still would not properly enkindle.

4. Suddenly there was a lull—then shouts,—half encouraging, half derisive. And Aaron saw a smallish-black figure of a youth, clinging like a monkey to the front of the house, and by the help of the heavy stone-work ornamentation climbing up the massive iron grille of the ground-floor windows, up like a black cat on to the projecting upper entablature above this window, clinging like a fly to the stone ornamentation and working himself up, gripping the balcony of the first-floor windows with his hands and swinging himself again like a black monkey upwards. He was on the balcony of the first floor windows. But he did not stay a moment—not a second. On he went, upwards, clambering up the wrought-iron scrolls, and flowers of the fencing, up on to the rail of the balcony, then again, in the same way catching hold of the shutters and inserting his fingers in the lattice and simply working himself upwards, cleaving to the house front [sic] like a black fly, and never for one single instant hesitating or relaxing, but all the time, with strange, non-human quickness wriggling his way upwards to the windows of the second floor. How he did it no one knew, though they watched him with their own eyes.

5. /296/ At first the crowd had shouted, half derisive, [sic] half-cheering. Then they had begun to get excited, as the lad wriggled himself so strangely, up the flat height. Then, as he reached the second floor, the feeling became intense. Voices, distinct, individual voices called to him, apparently giving directions. Sudden strange flashes of passionate exclamation broke out—*Bravo! Bravo!*—and then what was probably the name: *Gino! O-Gi! Gi'i! Gino!* All the time, from below, these sudden flashes of passionate sound, above the deep murmur of the crowd, the deep, slow murmur, that was like the swarming of bees, deep, pleased excitement. The shouts grew fewer after the climber had left the second storey and was working his way, a perilous small black figure cleaving like a black lizard or wall-newt to the house-front, working his way slowly and with great difficulty over the stone copings above the window, towards the balcony of the third floor. If he fell now he would be smashed to pieces. The crowd in the street had stood back from the walls of the house, so as to watch the progress upwards, and so, also, as to be out of the way if he *did* fall. There he was, working his way as it seemed cleaving against the almost overhanging housefront, [sic] high up, working, never still for a second, never for a hairs' [sic] breadth of a second relaxing his grip and his tension of progress. He seemed as if mesmerized—in some trance cleaving his way across the high and beetling house-front.

6. /297/ Till he grasped the topmost balcony. Then a ragged shout of pent-up anxiety and delight burst from the crowd. A wild and ragged shout of mixed feelings. But Aaron could understand no word, except *Bravo! Bravo!* and the reiterated *Gino!* The climber climbed on unheeding, as if he really were some black lizard, oblivious of human sounds. He scrambled on to [sic] the balcony and up the rail and up the shutters, till he grasped the flag-pole itself, which was fitted into a socket under the broad eaves. There he busily undid the ropes. And then, instead of hauling down the flag, he swarmed along the flag-pole, caught hold of the eaving of the roof, and swung himself up on to the roof's edge. There he knelt for a moment,

drawing in the flag-rope from underneath, and the flag with it. And then he stood up, with the tricolor bunched up in one hand, and waved it raggedly at the crowd below.

7. The a roar of delighted excitement went up, a roar, and strange wild whistlings, ear-piercing whistlings and shrillings and great, wild-throated howlings of excitement. It was excitement rather than enthusiasm. Meanwhile Gino suddenly threw down the flag. He threw it well clear, so that it dropped uneasily through the middle air, not far from Aaron's face. He never forgot the red-white-and-green dropping in mid-space before his eyes. And then the up-lifting of innumerable pale, metal-gold hands, snatching, cruel: the clutched intensity of the black central knot of /298/ men, as the flag dripped plunging: the hands, the wrists, like a myriad-headed snake suddenly striking: and the gaudy red-white-and-green flashing for one moment among the hands and wrists, above the black hats, and then coming asunder, like sparks, and then disappearing altogether in the blackness. The crowd surged and swayed as a black water when some great weight has fallen into it: and the roar was of strange anger: strange, strange, unaccountable cold rage.

8. And now the black figure on the roof-edge crouched and began the terrible descent, clinging and swarming down the now bare flag-pole, slithering down with a little smack on to the first balcony. The crowd below heaved, surged, roared, shouted *Bravo!,* worked with many passions. Some heeded, some did not heed the descent of the black climber, as he clutched his most perilous way downwards. Madness was in the street, madness was in the air: the madness of an unresolved desire. What was it, what was it the crowd wanted? Why, why had the youth scaled the housefront [sic]? Neither he nor anyone else really knew. He scrambled his way anxiously over the topmost balcony-rail, as if he wanted now to be down.

9. And suddenly went a new shout through the mob: a new cry: a sharp new cry, part anger, part warning, part fear. /299/ There was a sudden veering movement away from the house. And just as suddenly, as if it had happened by magic, Aaron saw a posse of carabi-neers in the grey-green Italian uniform in the street, quite near. A yell went up, defiance, rage, fear. A great yell, and the air seemed dark. And at the same moment, sudden shots, as the carabineers rushed. And as if shot the climber fell from the house front [sic]. Aaron saw him fall. And yet, when he looked down, there was nothing to be seen in the street but the last vanishing specks of the black crowd. And the street was empty—empty, save for the posse of nervously-advancing carabineers in grey-green uniform. The black mob gone—melted like a dream. Gone—carrying the fallen climber with them. And the carabineers, far from rushing in pursuit, looking round cautiously and holding revolvers ready.

10. Gone!—the street empty! And the sergeant of the carabineers mustering his men, with their revolvers, to march them away. They marched away tentatively—and the street was empty—quite empty. It had gone like a dream. All had passed like a dream. Even the prosaic grey-green carabineers.

Notes

Preface

1. Advertisement, *New York Times Book Review,* 23 April 1922,19.

Chapter 1

1. Harry T. Moore, *The Collected Letters of D. H. Lawrence,* 541. Subsequently cited as *Collected Letters.*

2. For this resumé of Lawrence's activities from late 1917 to 1922, when *Aaron's Rod* was published, I am much indebted to Harry T. Moore's two biographies, *The Life and Works of D. H. Lawrence* and *The Intelligent Heart;* to his travel calendar, *Poste Restante;* and to Edward Nehls' *D. H. Lawrence: A Composite Biography.*

3. Among such critics are Graham Hough and, surprisingly, Warren Roberts, editor of *A Bibliography of D. H. Lawrence.*

4. 27 May 1921, *Collected Letters,* 655.

5. Cited in Harry T. Moore, *The Intelligent Heart,* 235.

6. *Kangaroo,* 252.

7. See *Collected Letters,* 528–30 for further descriptions of wartime London at the time of the Lawrences' arrival from Cornwall.

8. Letter to Cecil Gray, 17 October 1917, *Collected Letters,* 528.

9. The Lawrences occupied this room from 20 October to 14 December (approx.). See Harry T. Moore, *Poste Restante,* 17. It is also interesting to note that the American Dorothy Yorke, known affectionately as "Arabella" (the model for Josephine Ford in *Aaron's Rod*) occupied an attic in the same building. Lawrence later recalled that life at Mecklenburgh Square was all "very jolly." *Intelligent Heart,* 236.

10. The Lawrences resided at the Radfords' cottage until 2 May 1918, when they moved to Middleton, staying at the latter until the end of April 1919. See *Poste Restante,* 48.

11. Letter to Cynthia Asquith, 7 May 1918, *Collected Letters,* 552.

12. In a letter of "Saturday" [?3 November] 1917, Lawrence wrote to Catherine Carswell, "We have got a much more definite plan of going away.... We shall go to the east slope of the Andes, back of Paraguay or Columbia." *Collected Letters,* 530.

13. Letter to S. S. Koteliansky, 16 February 1918, *Collected Letters*, 540.

14. Letter to Cecil Gray, "Thursday" [?7 February 1918], *Collected Letters*, 539.

15. *Collected Letters*, 543.

16. In a letter written to Martin Secker on 12 December 1920 this contrast was apparently in Lawrence's mind: "Probably between *Women in Love* and *The Rainbow* best insert another incensorable [sic] novel—either *Aaron's Rod,* which I have left again, or *Mr. Noon,* which I am doing." *Letters from D. H. Lawrence to Martin Secker,* 37.

17. Moore suggests 17 March 1918 as the probable date of this letter (*Collected Letters,* 549). A certain amount of confusion has arisen over Lawrence's references to an unnamed "novel" in this letter and particularly in the letter to Koteliansky mentioning specifically Mecklenburgh Square. F. R. Leavis incorrectly assumes that this "blameless" novel must be *The Lost Girl.* Since Lawrence had left the earlier manuscript of *The Lost Girl* in Germany before the war, and did not resume work on this novel until February 1920, this reference could not possibly be to *The Lost Girl.* The reference to Mecklenburgh Square, as I suggested earlier, clearly places the earliest origins of *Aaron's Rod* in London, October-December 1917.

18. Letter to Mark Gertler, 21 February 1918, *Collected Letters,* 542.

19. *Collected Letters,* 548.

20. Letter to Cynthia Asquith, 28 January 1918, *Collected Letters,* 537.

21. *Collected Letters,* 553.

22. See Harry T. Moore, *The Intelligent Heart,* 243.

23. See Aldous Huxley, *The Letters of D. H. Lawrence,* 467. Keith Sagar's chronology is most useful: "The text was revised in April 1919 (*Collected Letters,* 585) and a new chapter was added on Italian Unification in November 1920 (*Collected Letters,* 636). An epilogue was added in September 1924 (*Collected Letters,* 810)." See Keith Sagar, *The Art of D. H. Lawrence,* 99.

24. See Harry T. Moore, *The Intelligent Heart,* 246.

25. Ernest Tedlock Jr., *The Frieda Lawrence Collection of Manuscripts,* 94.

26. *Collected Letters,* 570.

27. See Harry T. Moore, *Poste Restante,* 50.

28. Letters to Katherine Mansfield, 27 December 1918, *Collected Letters,* 571.

29. Lawrence stayed at Becker's estate from Saturday 15 November to Monday 17 November, 1919. *Poste Restante,* 56. See William Becker's own account of the visit in Edward Nehls, *D. H. Lawrence: A Composite Biography,* II, 12-13, cited by Norman Douglas to support his own attack on Lawrence's supposed ingratitude and "bad manners."

30. Letter to Cecily Lambert Minchin, 9 January 1920, *Collected Letters,* 607.

31. The Lawrences were in Capri from 23 December 1919 to 26 February 1920. *Poste Restante,* 57.

32. Letter to Cynthia Asquith, 25 January 1920, *Collected Letters,* 617.

33. In a letter to Huebsch on 29 January 1920, Lawrence promised to send "six little essays on Freudian Unconscious". *Collected Letters,* 618.

34. Ernest Tedlock Jr., *The Frieda Lawrence Collection,* 90.

35. 31 May 1920, *Letters from D. H. Lawrence to Martin Secker,* 27.

36. Ibid., 31.

37. *Fantasia of the Unconscious,* 9.

38. Ibid.

39. *Letters from D. H. Lawrence to Martin Secker,* 31. See also *Poste Restante,* 60.

40. 7 October 1920, cited in Harry T. Moore, *The Intelligent Heart,* 274.

41. 10 November 1920, *Letters from D. H. Lawrence to Martin Secker,* 35.

42. 4 April 1921, *Letters from D. H. Lawrence to Martin Secker,* 38.

43. 9 April 1921. See *Poste Restante,* 62.

44. Earl and Achsah Brewster, *D. H. Lawrence: Reminiscences and Correspondence,* 243.

45. [?8 May 1921], *Collected Letters,* 653.

46. *Letters from D. H. Lawrence to Martin Secker,* 40.

47. *Collected Letters,* 655.

48. *Letters from D. H. Lawrence to Martin Secker,* 41.

49. Ibid., 42; and *Collected Letters,* 656.

50. *Collected Letters,* 655.

51. 10 November 1921, *Letters from D. H. Lawrence to Martin Secker,* 44.

52. Ernest Tedlock, Jr., *The Frieda Lawrence Collection,* 93.

53. Ibid., 94.

54. *Collected Letters,* 676.

55. Ibid., 678.

56. *Letters from D. H. Lawrence to Martin Secker,* 45.

57. 24 January 1922, *Collected Letters,* 687.

58. *Letters of D. H. Lawrence to Martin Secker,* 45.

59. 7 July 1921, *Collected Letters,* 659.

60. 26 January 1922, *Collected Letters,* 689.

61. Ibid.

62. See the main entry for *Aaron's Rod* in Warren Roberts, *A Bibliography of D. H. Lawrence,* 56.

63. Reprinted in R. Draper, *D. H. Lawrence: The Critical Heritage,* 177–80.

64. Rebecca West, "Notes on Novels," *The New Statesman,* 8 July 1922, 388.

Chapter 2

1. *Collected Letters,* 689.

2. *Letters from D. H. Lawrence to Martin Secker,* 32.

3. To avoid confusion throughout this chapter in citing passages for close comparison between the typescript and final versions of the novel I have used a system of double reference, supplying references to both the typescript and American first-edition (abbreviated "A"). Later I have also used the abbreviation "E" (followed by a page reference) in my comparison of the American and English editions of the novel.

4. *Fantasia* had been completed by July 1921, and was published by Seltzer, 23 October 1922. See Keith Sagar, *The Art of D. H. Lawrence,* 100.

5. The villa of Sir Walter Becker who "sat" for Lawrence's portrait of Sir William Franks was actually located at Val Salice just outside Turin. On 18 November 1919 Lawrence wrote Lady Cynthia Asquith that he had "stayed two nights in Turin with rich English people...." See *Collected Letters,* 598.

6. "Anthony" was no doubt later corrected to "Antony" by the house of Heinemann (to whom Secker sold his rights to Lawrence's works during the 1930's) to read "Antony." The Viking Compass edition which reproduces Heinemann's text also prints "Antony."

7. The typescript reveals that Lawrence earlier employed the less colourful "flying" before amending this to the final "fluttering," another minor example of how Lawrence has heightened the original version of the episode.

8. Richard Aldington, "Introduction" to *Kangaroo,* 8.

9. In the American printed version Algy's reply to Argyle, "Then there ought to be a good deal of it about" (A253), hardly makes sense to us at all without the previous statements of Argyle, unfortunately censored. The English version omits Algy's reply altogether. See the comparison of American and English editions of *Aaron's Rod* later in this chapter.

10. This is the final American version of the passage:
    "And again, this night as before, she seemed strangely small and clinging in his arms. And this night he felt his passion drawn from him as if a long, live nerve were drawn out from his body, a long live thread of electric fire, a long, living nerve finely extracted from him, from the very roots of his soul. A long fine discharge of pure, bluish fire, from the core of his soul. It was an excruciating, but also an intensely gratifying sensation.
    This night he slept with a greater obliviousness than before. But ah, as it grew towards morning how he wished he could be alone." (A317)
    The final English version cuts even more of the original passage:
    "And again, this night as before, she seemed strangely small and clinging in his arms. And this night he felt his passion drawn from him as if a long, live nerve were drawn out from his body, a long, live thread of electric fire.
    This night he slept with a deeper obliviousness than before. But ah, as it grew towards morning, how he wished he could be alone." (E263-64)

11. The American and English printed version of these passages are censored in the same way:
    "He was aware of the strength and beauty and godlikeness that his breast was then to her—the magic. But himself, he stood far off, like Moses' sister Miriam. She could drink the one drop of his innermost heart's blood, and he would be carrion. As Cleopatra killed her lovers in the morning. Surely they knew that death was their just climax. They had approached the climax. Accept then." (A318-E265)

12. *Collected Letters,* 689.

13. "I was very glad to get two copies of *Aaron's Rod* this morning — beautifully typed and bound." *Collected Letters,* 659.

14. Nicholas Joost and Alvin Sullivan, *D. H. Lawrence and the* Dial, 225, n. 7.

Chapter 3

1. *Phoenix,* 301–02.

2. *Apocalypse,* 3–4.

3. George H. Ford, *Double Measure,* 136.

4. Ibid., 135.

5. Letter of [?26 April 1917], *Collected Letters,* 510.

6. See Keith Sagar, *The Art of D. H. Lawrence,* 18.

7. *The Complete Poems,* 207.

8. Ibid., 235.

9. *The Rainbow,* 205.

10. Throughout this portion of my chapter dealing specifically with parallels and allusions to the biblical narrative of Moses and Aaron, I have employed Aaron Sisson's surname in order to avoid needless confusion with his biblical namesake.

11. The entire episode may also be part of an elaborate parody of the Nativity story particularly of the shepherds at Bethlehem who stood amazed, and "sore afraid" at "the glory of the Lord" which "shone round about them" (Luke 2:9). The shepherds of the popular Nativity story are recalled earlier in the novel in the carollers' dissonant rendition of "While Shepherds Watched Their Flocks" (14).

12. The specific mention of Egypt as a great source of the "power-urge" must seem rather curious in the face of the pervasive Biblical allusions throughout the novel to the liberation of the tribes of Israel from their Egyptian oppressors, and to the mission of Aaron and Moses to lead their people to the Promised Land. I would suggest that Lawrence is thinking of another more noble and powerful Egypt, a kingdom quite different from the later dynasties which oppressed Israel — biblical historians usually place Exodus around 1320 B.C. The Marchesa is identified with Cleopatra in the novel and Sisson's affair with the Marchesa is clearly a soul-destroying step away from the path which leads to Lilly and a philosophy of inner power. Lilly's doctrine of power and self-possession is thus connected in Lawrence's mind with a more "positive" ancient Egypt. (Compare the references to Birkin as a Pharaoh in "Excurse," *Women in Love.*) Other forms of oppression or counterfeiting such as the unmistakable *nouveau riche* splendor of the Franks' estate or the distasteful, sham *Aïda* are all associated by Lawrence with the internal decay of the *later* Egyptian dynasties.

13. Perhaps there is an added suggestion of the Queen of Sheba in the Marchesa's temptress aspects and Lawrence's descriptions of her. The association of Egypt and Sheba must have been intriguing for Lawrence.

14. The earlier version of this passage as it appears in the typescript contains a stronger hint of a symbolic "death-by-water" process which Aaron must undergo as a means to spirit-

ual rebirth or new life under the aegis of Lilly. Lilly's reply to Sisson's comment alluding to his biblical namesake, "There goes Aaron's rod, then," is followed by the reply "It had better take root afresh, under the water."

The suggestion of receiving a death blow is also more pronounced in the typescript version: "Here was a blow he had not expected" originally read "Here was his way of life finished, with a vengeance." Lilly's important, qualifying "meanwhile" (in "You'll have to live without a rod, meanwhile") was also a later addition by Lawrence. The adverb undoubtedly makes Aaron's predicament seem less final and carries with it the suggestion that Aaron may turn towards Lilly in his search for new direction or purpose for his life.

Chapter 4

1. Ada Lawrence and Stuart Gelder, *Early Life of D. H. Lawrence,* 49-50. Ada also recalled Bert's flair for dancing: "All the girls loved to dance with Bert. His movements were so light" (43).

2. "Then he decided he would learn to play the piano. He could read music easily and thought he could master the rest as easily as he painted and wrote. I remember how he shut himself up in the front room and for an hour and a half or so we heard him labouring with simple scales and exercises. Then came a loud crash of keys and an exasperated young man stalked into the kitchen. His patience was exhausted and he refused to strum his fingers off over the 'beastly scales' any longer. He never tried again and was content to sit with me and hum and sing." *Early Life,* 50.

3. Edward Nehls, *D. H. Lawrence: A Composite Biogrpahy,* I, 48.

4. E. T. [Jessie Chambers], *D. H. Lawrence: A Personal Record,* 54. Like Jessie and her brother, May Chambers Holbrook later recalls not only that Lawrence spent many happy musical moments at the Chambers' home, but also her frequent resentment at "some criticism repeated to me of some member of our family or our way of life from Mrs. Lawrence." See Nehls, *A Composite Biography,* III, 607.

5. E. T., *D. H. Lawrence: A Personal Record,* 80-81.

6. James T. Boulton, ed., *Lawrence in Love: Letters to Louie Burrows,* 14.

7. Ibid., 64.

8. Ibid., 78.

9. Ibid., 88.

10. Herbert B. McCartney was himself Helen Corke's violin teacher and a professional violinist with the Carl Rosa Opera Company. His suicide took place in the summer of 1909. See Harry T. Moore, *D. H. Lawrence: His Life and Works,* 70.

11. Nehls, *A Composite Biography,* II, 151-52.

12. *Collected Letters,* 434.

13. See Nehls, *A Composite Biography,* I, 424.

14. Catherine Carswell, *The Savage Pilgrimage,* 96-97.

15. Cynthia Asquith, *Haply I May Remember,* 106. Cited in Nehls, *A Composite Biography,* I, 441.

16. *Collected Letters,* 539.

17. Brigit Patmore, *My Friends When Young,* 81.

18. Nehls, *A Composite Biography,* I, 497.

19. For these additional "musical" reminiscences see Nehls, *A Composite Biography,* I, 455; II, 124, 344.

20. Nehls, *A Composite Biography,* III, 166.

21. *Collected Letters,* 1213.

22. Ibid., 941.

23. Joseph Foster, *Lawrence in Taos,* 51.

24. *The Trespasser,* 158.

25. It is interesting that most of the disgust which Lawrence obviously must have felt at the original performance of *Aïda* which inspired this fictional version, has been passed on to Josephine Ford, while Lilly, generally thought to be the "Lawrence figure" of the incident, remains detached and unruffled. He is obviously neither impressed nor duped by the sham spectacle, yet he calmly advises the excitable Josephine in so many words to adopt his own indifference: " 'You shouldn't look so closely,' he said. But he took it calmly, easily, whilst she felt floods of burning disgust, a longing to destroy it all" (56).

26. Nehls, *A Composite Biography,* I, 440.

27. Boulton, *Lawrence in Love,* 88–89.

28. Nehls, *A Composite Biography,* I, 424.

29. Lawrence's views on the music of Bach were apparently quite unorthodox, as this reminiscence by Mme Ivy Low Litvinoff (who visited the Lawrences in Lerici in 1914) aptly demonstrates:
    "Lawrence got me down by telling me that I was somehow *unmusically* musical, that I chose pieces that really have no music in them, not beause I liked them—nobody could have!—but because I was suspicious of simple melody. 'Cultivated people,' it appeared simply didn't know what they liked. They had to say they like Bach, but they didn't really. It was just the way they were brought up." Nehls, *A Composite Biography,* I, 219.
    Note the emphasis upon "simple melody," as well as Lawrence's notion of what constituted false music and false musical devotion.

30. Catherine Carswell, *The Savage Pilgrimage,* 147.

31. F. R. Leavis, *D. H. Lawrence: Novelist,* 32.

32. On another notable occasion the sensitivity of Aaron's flute is demonstrated when it refuses to "blossom" in hostile or uncomfortable surroundings. Once arrived in Florence, and deserted by his new acquaintances, Aaron tries his flute in the rather spartan atmosphere of his *pensione,* but "his flute was too sensitive, it winced from the new strange surroundings, and would not blossom" (246).

33. When asked for a tune, Aaron had informed Algy that he had not brought his flute along, not wanting "to arrive with a little bag" (260).

34. *Collected Letters,* 41.

35. Helen Corke, *D. H. Lawrence: The Croydon Years,* 4–5.

36. It is interesting that most of the operas Lawrence objects to in these formative years were associated with Covent Garden. Perhaps this suggests that Lawrence's dislikes were not for purely musical reasons and that this strain of inverse snobbery and so on was beginning to manifest itself in his reactions to Grand Opera.

37. Boulton, *Lawrence in Love,* 44.

38. Ibid., 88.

39. Ibid., 149.

40. One quite interesting reference to Lawrence's experience of Wagner's music-dramas may be found in his description in *Sea and Sardinia* (1921) of an exciting puppet show: "The dragon was splendid: I have seen dragons in Wagner at Covent Garden and at the Prinz-Regenten Theatre at Munich, and they were ridiculous. But this dragon simply frightened me with his leaping and twisting. And when he seized the knight by the leg, my blood ran cold." See *Sea and Sardinia,* 202–03.

41. *Phoenix,* 174.

42. Ibid., 176.

43. *Collected Letters,* 132.

44. Lawrence also spoke of Cornwall in terms of the Tristan legend, referring to the Cornish landscape as "Celtic," "pre-Christian," "going back to Tristan" and so on. See *Collected Letters,* 409–15.

45. *Phoenix,* 154.

46. "The Reality of Peace", *Phoenix,* 684.

47. With its emphasis upon strong emotions, merging and sensual fulfilment, the works of Wagner could not but stir the imagination of the young Lorenzo. Consider the similar *liebestod* effects in his early poem, "Love On the Farm":

> And down his mouth comes on my mouth! and down
> His bright eyes come over me, like a hood
> Upon my mind! his lips meet mine, and a flood
> Of sweet fire sweeps across me, so I drown
> Against him, kiss, and find death good.
>
> *The Complete Poems,*43

48. See my later discussion of fairy-tale elements, in Chapter 7.

49. Professor William Blissett has also described the heroes and heroines of Wagner's music dramas as "great passionate somnambulistic creatures,...mindless 'columns of blood' ." The description obviously applies to *Tristan* more appropriately than to Brünnhilde's role in the *Ring*. See William Blissett, "D. H. Lawrence and D'Annunzio, Wagner," 44.

50. William Blissett, "D. H. Lawrence, D'Annunzio, Wagner," 44. Professor Blissett has summed up well Lawrence's debt to Wagner, at the same time suggesting a fundamental difference between Joyce and Lawrence's uses of Wagnerism: "In contrast to that other mythmaker, Joyce, who learned from Wagner how to plan and to build, Lawrence learned from Wagner how to feel, to sustain feeling, to sustain the flow of feeling. 'Flow' is a key word and concept for Lawrence". See "D. H. Lawrence, D'Annunzio, Wagner," 43.

51. *The Dark Sun,* 17.

52. The censored portions of the passage contained in the typescript version, contribute even further to the effect of incantation:
"There, as in her incantations she used him to curl herself up against, and he knew he was apart. And he looked back over the whole mystery of their love-contact, and his soul saw himself, saw his own phallic God-and-victim self there lying, with her on his breast. Only his soul stood apart." (TS448)
Notice that the short, deliberate final sentence of the passage suggests the "click of awareness"—as Lawrence earlier describes it—on Aaron's part. The rhythm thus provides an obvious contrast to the incantatory flow of the passage immediately preceding, and suggests Aaron's psychological return to daylight and ordinary life—to what Wagner refers to in *Tristan* as the world of "tückischer Tag" opposed to that of "heilige Nacht."

Chapter 5

1. Neil Myers, "Lawrence and the War," *Criticism,* 4 (Winter 1962), 44-58.

2. George H. Ford, *Double Measure,* 176.

3. Neil Myers, "Lawrence and the War," 57.

4. The English edition of the novel prints the comma. The sentence seems to me to make more sense when punctuated by a comma, and I have hereafter used this version of the sentence.

5. Keith Sagar, *The Art of D. H. Lawrence,* 106-07.

6. Ibid.

7. Neil Myers, "D. H. Lawrence and the War," 44.

8. Letter of 4 September 1916, *Quest for Rananim,* ed. George J. Zytaruk, 91.

9. *Collected Letters,* 541.

10. Ibid., 542.

11. Ibid., 542-43.

12. Ibid., 557-58.

13. *Kangaroo,* 220.

14. *Collected Letters,* 487.

15. Ibid., 558. Note that this letter was written soon after the nostalgic letter to Mary Cannan cited above.

16. *Collected Letters,* 545.

17. George M. Trevelyan, *Garibaldi and the Making of Italy,* 292.

18. Herbert L. Matthews, *The Fruits of Fascism,* 66-67. Somers' vivid description of this struggle in his conversation with Struthers in Chapter 11 of *Kangaroo* indicates clearly that Lawrence was quite aware of Italy's changing political climate, and of the Socialists' failure to seize control. Somers informs Struthers, "Why, when I left Europe it seemed to me socialism was losing ground everywhere—in Italy especially. In 1920 it was quite a

living, exciting thing, in Italy. It made people insolent, usually, but it lifted them up as well. Then it sort of fizzled down, and last year there was only the smoke of it: and a nasty sort of disappointment and disillusion, a grating sort of irritation. Florence, Siena—hateful! The Fascisti risen up and taking on airs, all just out of a sort of spite. The Dante festival at Florence, and the King there, for example. Just set your teeth on edge, ugh!—with their 'Savoia!' All false and out of spite"....."I think the Socialists didn't *quite* believe in their own socialism, so everybody felt let down. In Italy, particularly, it seemed to me they were on the brink of a revolution. And the King was ready to abdicate, and the Church was ready to make away with its possessions: I know that. Everything ready for a flight. And then the Socialists funked. They just funked. They daren't make a revolution, because then they'd be responsible for the country. And they *daren't*. And so the Fascisti, seeing the Socialists in a funk, got up and began to try to kick their behinds" (197).

19. Herman Finer, *Musolini's Italy,* 127. In a letter to Rosalind Baynes (7? October 1920), Lawrence spoke of "more and more bolshy scare here—not in Venice, but in the Romagna." Edward Nehls, *A Composite Biography,* II, 50.

20. Finer, 127–28.

21. "...Lawrence went to Naples, Amalfi, Fiuggi (then called Anticoli), Rome, Florence, and various parts of northern Italy. As he reported on September 12 [1920] to Amy Lowell from near Florence: "I have been wandering around Lake Como and Venice, and now am here for a while in an explosion-shattered villa which a friend has lent me" —the friend being Rosalind Baynes (who is now Mrs. E. A. Popham), who had been the Lawrence's hostess at Pangbourne the preceding summer. The windows of the villa she was renting in the hills above Florence had been blown out by an explosion at a nearby ammunition dump. She moved higher up, to Fiesole, where Lawrence used to go for tea or dinner on her terrace during the weeks he stayed in the windowless villa." Harry T. Moore, *The Intelligent Heart,* 273.

22. Frank Kermode's illuminating comments on the strange, blighted post-war atmosphere (in his brief study of Lawrence, published after my chapter on war and *Aaron's Rod* was written) are much to the point:
"The book is rooted in the war, but contemplates a post-war Europe cheapened and debilitated—still at the end of an epoch rather than a beginning. Everything is tainted, from sexual relations down to food and drink. If the servants are dead so are their masters. The bohemian intelligentsia Aaron meets in London play with the idea of bloody revolution, or believe, in a trivial way, that Love can make them well again. The world is like a shell-shocked soldier, unhurt but wounded somewhere 'deeper than the brain'." *Lawrence,* 78. Compare this with Graham Hough's peculiar, unsatisfactory description of Aaron's experience of post-war Italy: "And blowing throughout it all is the cold and windy exhilaration of being free of [in?] Europe again after the war." *The Dark Sun,* 100.

23. Yudhishtar, *Conflict in the Novels of D. H. Lawrence,* 210.

24. *Women in Love,* 98–99.

25. George Bernard Shaw, *Heartbreak House,* 794.

26. "Preface" to *Heartbreak House,* 382.

27. Keith Myers, "Lawrence and the War," 46.

28. George H. Ford, *Double Measure,* 180–81.

Chapter 6

1. See Chapter 2 of this study.

2. This does not imply that such heroes should be construed as mere mouthpieces of Lawrencean dogma as so many critics have frequently assumed. On the contrary the theories or positions of these various "Lawrence-figures" are frequently undercut savagely or called greatly into question by the other characters of the novels in which they appear.

3. Aaron appears in all but one of the thirty-one chapters of the novel, this exception being "A Punch in the Wind." It could be said that Aaron is even present there "by implication," since his later resistance to Lilly is clearly a parallel to that of Jim Bricknell in this particular chapter. Lilly appears in but eight chapters and in at least two of these he merely puts in a perfunctory appearance at a social gathering (Chapters 5 and 19).

4. *The Rainbow,* 9.

5. Aaron's handsome features particularly suggest this curious mixture to Lilly: "Rather beautiful the bones of the countenance: but the skull much too small for such a heavy jaw and rather coarse mouth" (107).

6. *The Rainbow,* 15–16.

7. Ibid., 97.

8. Ibid., 26–27.

9. "I don't want my Fate or my Providence to treat me well. I don't want kindness or love. I don't believe in harmony and people loving one another. I believe in the fight and in nothing else. . . . And if it is a question of the world, I believe in fighting it and having it hate me, even if breaks my legs. I want the world to hate me, because I can't bear the thought that it might love me. For of all things love is the most deadly to me, and especially from such a repulsive world as I think this is. . ." (308). In spite of his misanthropic resolve at this particular point, Aaron ironically continues in the perilous course of the love-urge and its destructiveness.

10. See however Keith Sagar's illuminating analysis of "The Man Who Loved Islands" (1927), in *The Art of D. H. Lawrence,* 176.

11. F. Scott Fitzgerald, *The Great Gatsby* (Scribner Library Paperback Edition), 36.

12. It is interesting to note that the imagery of the invisible black dog was all later added by Lawrence to the earlier typescript version of *Aaron's Rod,* no doubt in order to strengthen further the reader's impression of Aaron's cynical remoteness and misanthropy, even in this early episode.

13. D. H. Lawrence, "Foreword" to *Women in Love,* viii.

14. Earl and Achsah Brewster, *D. H. Lawrence: Reminiscences and Correspondence,* 243.

15. In her *Catalogue of D. H. Lawrence's Reading from Childhood,* Rose Marie Burwell cites the letter of ?8 May 1921 (*Collected Letters,* 652) as proof that Lawrence knew *The Invisible Man* by May 1921. No one could dispute this, but my guess is that Lawrence knew that novel much earlier, had even read it years before, when he had also read *Tono-Bungay* and *The War of the Worlds,* in May 1909 (see *Collected Letters,* 54). In any case the letter written in May 1921 at least confirms for us that *The Invisible Man* was very much in Lawrence's mind at the time he was completing *Aaron's Rod* "sitting

away in the woods," as he informed Koteliansky a week or two later. See *Collected Letters,* 655.

16. Matthew 6:28.

17. In his paraphrase Lawrence has deliberately turned his attention away from the "moment's lull" following the dalliance. Here is the full text of Whitman's poem:

> Skirting the river road, (my forenoon walk, my rest,)
> Skyward in air a sudden muffled sound, the dalliance of the eagles,
> The rushing amorous contact high in space together,
> The clinching interlocking claws, a living, fierce, gyrating wheel,
> Four beating wings, two beaks, a swirling mass tight grappling,
> In tumbling turning clustering loops, straight downward falling,
> Till o'er the river pois'd, the twain yet one, a moment's lull,
> A motionless still balance in the air, then parting, talons loosing,
> Upward again on slow-firm pinions slanting, their separate diverse flight,
> She hers, he his, pursuing.

Choosing to emphasize the "intensification of oneness" and the violence of the consummation Lawrence builds to a splendid *crescendo.* His idiosyncratic concept of the "splendid love way" (which the paraphrase was meant to embody) was obviously to some extent at odds with the slackening of passion but the division into separateness as each resumes his solitary flight seems quite in keeping with Birkin's and Lilly's love ethic.

18. Ernest Tedlock has some difficulty assigning a definite date to Lawrence's poetic essay, "David," which first appeared posthumously in *Phoenix.* He suggests that the essay might have been written in 1919 and was likely inspired in November, as a postcard written to Catherine Carswell (mentioning the heavy rains and curious postwar atmosphere) seems to confirm. The problem is further complicated by the fact that Lawrence visited Florence on several other occasions, most notably in September 1920, when he stayed at Villa Canovaia. It was at this time that he witnessed the strange XX Settembre proceedings, elements of which he incorporated into Chapter 14 of *Aaron's Rod.* In any case, Pritchard is oversimplifying the matter when he refers to the essay as the "kernel of the novel" especially since he gives no account of how he arrives at the earlier date for "David." Tedlock also mentions that Lawrence also referred to the heavy rain in Florence much later in 1926. If this later date is accepted as that of "David," than the descriptive commentary in *Aaron's Rod* would seem rather to be the "kernel" of the essay. See E. Tedlock, *The Frieda Lawrence Collection,* 180, and R. E. Pritchard, *Body of Darkness,* 135–36.

19. *Phoenix,* 63–64.

20. See however R. E. Pritchard's more detailed account of the dream sequence in his *D. H. Lawrence: Body of Darkness,* 139–40. Although I discovered Pritchard's account after I had initially conceived this chapter, I am nevertheless grateful for his account and pleased that many of my ideas, (indeed much of my overall interpretation of the dream sequence), agree with his.

21. I am indebted to my colleague Sam Solecki for the suggestion that one source of Aaron's dream vision might be Wells' *The Time Machine.* Lawrence was, of course, familiar with many of Wells' works from an early age and there is no reason to doubt that he would also have been familiar with *The Time Machine* by the time he was completing *Aaron's Rod.*

22. See also R. E. Pritchard, *D. H. Lawrence,* 139.

23. *The Complete Poems of D. H. Lawrence,* 334–40.

24. This is made quite clear in an exchange which occurs shortly after Aaron has made his firm decision never to make love to the Marchesa again. At the café Argyle asks why he (and Lilly's circle) has not seen Aaron for a week ("Been going to the dogs, eh?") to which Aaron replies wryly, "Or the bitches" (322).

25. See Rose Marie Burwell, *A Catalogue of D. H. Lawrence's Reading,* for an indication of the scope of Lawrence's early reading of authors who had employed the device of the double.

26. Albert J. Guerard, *Stories of the Double,* 3.

27. Ibid., 4.

28. Cited in *Stories of the Double,* 4.

29. John Middleton Murry, *Son of Woman,* 205, 213.

30. Ibid., 213.

31. Ibid., 212.

32. Harry T. Moore, *D. H. Lawrence: His Life and Works,* 169.

33. F. R. Leavis, *D. H. Lawrence: Novelist,* 40.

34. Ibid.

35. Kate Millett, *Sexual Politics,* 269.

36. Sandra Berry, "Singularity of Two: The Plurality of One," 36.

37. Patricia Merivale, *Pan the Goat-God,* 194.

38. *Phoenix,* 31.

39. Merivale, 215–16.

40. "Aaron thought of Lilly's dark, ugly face, which had something that lurked in it as a creature under leaves. Then he thought of the wide-apart eyes, with their curious candour and surety." See *Aaron's Rod,* 335.
It is interesting that the description above might easily apply to Lawrence himself. Certainly Dorothy Brett thought of him both as a Pan and a Christ figure, portraying him as such in several of her more "fantastic" paintings. It is also interesting to recall that in the poetic-essay "David," Lawrence clearly thinks of Pan-David-Christ-Dionysus as a kind of mythic continuum. See *Phoenix,* 61–62.

41. *Phoenix,* 27.

42. Ibid., 31.

Chapter 7

1. Eliseo Vivas, *The Failure and the Triumph of Art,* 23.

2. It is not the business of this book to speculate upon Vivas' deeper motives in producing such a narrowly negative study or to deal extensively with his overall treatment of Lawrence. Kingsley Widmer's recent assessment of Vivas' study is worth noting:
"A rather anachronistic example of formalist-moralist criticism in the 1960's is Eliseo

Vivas, D. H. LAWRENCE, THE TRIUMPH AND THE FAILURE OF ART [sic]. While this has some small merits as tendentious criticism, the exaggerated insistence on Lawrence's failure, falsity and dangerousness raises the larger question: why did a conservative moralist like Vivas, with an insistent distaste for Lawrence's views of sex and passionate individuality—and just about everything else—bother writing such a book? ... Vivas, not ordinarily a detailed critic, and certainly far from knowledgeable about Lawrence (or the writings on Lawrence), seemed determined to reduce and neutralize the most essential qualities of Lawrence with homiletics disguised as aesthetics."
See Kingsley Widmer, "Notes on the Literary Institutionalization of D. H. Lawrence," *Paunch,* No. 26 (April 1966), 6.

3. Vivas, 24.

4. Ibid., 31.

5. Ibid., 29.

6. F. R. Leavis, *D. H. Lawrence: Novelist,* 35.

7. Vivas, 30.

8. Ibid., 24.

9. The limits to which Vivas pushes his over-literal readings of Lawrence's work may be seen in his account of the quarrel in "Excurse" (*Women in Love*) between Ursula and Birkin. See Vivas, 30.

10. Leavis observes that the "whole evocation of Aaron Sisson *en famille* has a marvellous reality," commenting further upon "the power with which the peculiar domestic tone is evoked: the domesticity without warmth; the Christmas festivity that brings no sympathetic flow and does nothing to soften the suggestion of hostile will; and prevailing undersense of grudge." See Leavis, *D. H. Lawrence: Novelist,* 34–35.

11. Daleski acutely sums up the thematic significance of the episode in this way: "[W]e take it on trust that [Lottie's] continual and resentful carping has stiffened [Aaron] to the breaking-point. We realize, however that what he is stolidly resisting is her possessiveness, that her ranting at him is a kindred manifestation of the 'curious, irritating possession' with which their daughter Millicent 'cleaves' to the ornaments for the Christmas tree." *The Forked Flame,* 191.

12. If we wished to adopt the viewpoint of the social moralist as Vivas does we might argue that it is rather to Aaron's credit that he should be capable of such disarming honesty in recognizing and accepting his share of the blame for the failure of his marriage to Lottie.

13. Vivas, 26.

14. Ibid.

15. Aaron is of course the "cad" and a "villain." Most readers of Lawrence's fiction would be surprised to learn that Constance Chatterley and Mellors are "stinkers" and that Ursula and Skrebensky are reduced to mere animality in their state of sexual arousal! See Vivas, 27, 43, 123.

16. Kate Millett, *Sexual Politics,* 270.

17. Graham Hough, *The Dark Sun,* 96.

18. J. W. Cunliffe, *English Literature in the Twentieth Century,* 220.

19. Millett, 271.
Far from discovering such a "typical pattern" in Lawrence's works, I find no evidence whatsoever for a couvade. Perhaps Millett confuses this scene with the later one, after the breaking of the flute, in which Lilly finds Aaron in bed, supposedly "like a woman who's had a baby" (337)?

20. George Ford, *Double Measure,* 135–36.

21. Vivas, 22.

22. See particularly Leavis, 38–40.

23. Leavis, 48–49.

24. R. Draper, *Profiles in Literature: D. H. Lawrence,* 73.

25. Letter of 8 May 1921, *Collected Letters,* 653. Compare also Achsah Brewster's reminiscence about a conversation with Lawrence (in Capri) over what to do with Aaron. See Chapter 6 of this study.

26. It is not possible to "pin down" the fairy tale allusions to any one narrative. Lawrence is of course thinking of *The Sleeping Beauty* but may also be alluding indirectly to *Repunzel* or *Rumpelstiltskin.*

27. Yudhishtar, *Conflict in the Novels of D. H. Lawrence,* 231.

28. See *Collected Letters,* 549.

29. "Seltzer sent me a clean typed copy of the book, begging for the alterations for the sake of the 'general public' (he didn't say *jeune fille*)." 26 January 1922, *Collected Letters,* 689.

30. Harry T. Moore, *D. H. Lawrence: His Life and Works,* 171.

31. R. P. Draper, *D. H. Lawrence,* 92.

32. Graham Hough, *The Dark Sun,* 95, 175.

33. Ibid., 95.

34. Herman M. Daleski, *The Forked Flame,* 211.

35. F. R. Leavis, 32.

36. Ibid., 32–33.

37. Vivas, 34–35.

38. The visit of Jim Bricknell to the Lillys' cottage, the episode of Herbertson's visit, the flag-incident, the male symposium, are but a few such scenes.

39. Anthony Beal, *D. H. Lawrence,* 65.

40. Julian Moynahan, *The Deed of Life,* 99.

41. Ibid., 100.

42. It should be pointed out that most of the uglier anti-Semitic or racist statements uttered during this "colloquium" have been mistakenly attributed entirely to Lilly. A great deal

of the offensive tone of the conversation must be traced back to Argyle and his drunken humour.

43. It should be recalled that the typescript reveals even more of Aaron's curiously ambivalent attitude to Lilly at this point. Lilly is described there as "the devilish little Lilly" whereas in the final printed version he is "the little Lilly" (TS473-A336). See my earlier chapter dealing with differences between the typescript and printed versions of the novel.

44. E. W. Tedlock Jr., *D. H. Lawrence: Artist and Rebel,* 154.

45. Graham Hough at least observes preceptively that the novel concludes with "a mere hint of a new philosophy," and that "Lawrence is doing what he so often does, ending a book with the foretaste of what is to come." *The Dark Sun,* 103.

46. Yudhishtar, 230.

47. Tedlock, 154.

48. Leavis, 43–44.

49. In 1924 Lawrence wrote a prophetic epilogue to his *Movements in European History* in which he spoke of such a new kind of leader as "one great chosen figure, some hero who can lead a great war, as well as administer a wide peace...one figure, who is supreme over the will of the people...[and] responsible to God alone."

50. Moynahan, 100–101

51. Ibid., 96–97.

52. *Collected Letters,* 22 January 1925, 827.

Selected Bibliography

Works by D. H. Lawrence

Fiction

The Trespasser [1912]. London: Heinemann Phoenix Edition, 1955.
Sons and Lovers [1913]. London: Heinemann Phoenix Edition, 1955.
The Rainbow [1915]. London: Heinemann Phoenix Edition, 1955.
Women in Love [1920]. London: Heinemann Phoenix Edition, 1954.
"Foreword" to *Women in Love.* New York: Modern Library, 1950.
The Lost Girl [1920]. London: Heinemann Phoenix Edition, 1955.
Aaron's Rod. Corrected Typescript. Humanities Research Center Library, University of Texas.
Aaron's Rod. New York: Thomas Seltzer, 1922.
Aaron's Rod. London: Martin Secker, 1922.
Aaron's Rod. London: Heinemann Phoenix Edition, 1954.
Aaron's Rod. New York: Viking Compass Edition, 1961.
Kangaroo [1923]. London: Heinemann Phoenix Edition, 1955.
The Plumed Serpent [1926]. London: Heinemann Phoenix Edition, 1955.
Lady Chatterley's Lover [1928]. Unexpurgated version, New York: 1959. Rpt. with an Afterword by Harry T. Moore. New York: The New York American Library of World Literature, 1959.
The Complete Short Stories of D. H. Lawrence. 3 vols. London: Heinemann, 1955.
The Short Novels. 2 vols. London: Heinemann, 1955.

Non-Fiction

Twilight in Italy [1916]. London: Heinemann Phoenix Edition, 1956.
Movements in European History [under pseudonym Lawrence H. Davison]. London: Oxford University Press, 1921.
Psychoanalysis and the Unconscious [1921]. London: Heinemann Phoenix Edition, 1961.
Sea and Sardinia [1921]. London: Heinemann Phoenix Edition, 1956.
Fantasia of the Unconscious [1922]. London: Heinemann Phoenix Edition, 1961.
Apocalypse. 1931. Rpt. New York: Viking Press, 1932.
Phoenix: The Posthumous Papers of D. H. Lawrence. Ed. with an Introduction by Edward D. MacDonald. New York: The Viking Press, 1936.
Phoenix II. Ed. Warren Roberts and Harry T. Moore. New York: Viking, 1968.
The Complete Plays of D. H. Lawrence. London: Heinemann, 1965.
The Complete Poems of D. H. Lawrence. Ed. Vivien de Sola Pinto and Warren Roberts. 2 vols. New York: Viking Press.

Letters

The Letters of D. H. Lawrence. Ed. with an Introduction Aldous Huxley. London: 1932.
The Collected Letters of D. H. Lawrence. 2 vols. Ed. Harry T. Moore. New York: Viking Press, 1962.
Lawrence in Love: Letters to Louie Burrows. Ed. James T. Boulton. Carbondale: Southern Illinois University Press, 1969.
The Quest for Rananim: D. H. Lawrence's Letters to S. S. Koteliansky, 1914 to 1930. Ed. George J. Zytaruk. Montreal: McGill-Queen's University Press, 1970.
Letters from D. H. Lawrence to Martin Secker, 1911–1930. ed. Martin Secker. Bridgefoot, Iver, Buckinghamshire: Privately Published, 1970.
Letters to Thomas and Adele Seltzer. Ed. Gerald M. Lacy. Los Angeles: Black Sparrow Press, 1976.
The Letters of D. H. Lawrence, vol. 1: 1901–1913. Ed. James Cowan. New York: Cambridge University Press, 1979.
————, *vol. 2: 1913–1916.* Ed. George Zytaruk. Cambridge University Press, 1981.

Other Works

Albright, Daniel. *Personality and Impersonality: Lawrence, Woolf, and Mann.* Chicago: University of Chicago Press, 1978.
Aldington, Richard. *Portrait of a Genius, But...* London: Heinemann, 1950.
————. *Pinorman: Personal Recollections of Norman Douglas, Pino Orioli and Charles Prentice.* London: Heinemann, 1954.
Aldritt, Keith. *The Visual Imagination of D. H. Lawrence.* London: Edward Arnold, 1971.
Anon. Review of *Aaron's Rod,* D. H. Lawrence. *Times Literary Supplement,* 22 June 1922, 411.
Anon. Review of *Aaron's Rod,* D. H. Lawrence. *Spectator,* 1 July 1922, 23.
Barry, Sandra. "Singularity of Two: The Plurality of One." *Paunch,* 26 (April 1966), 34–39.
Beal, Anthony. *D. H. Lawrence.* London: Oliver and Boyd, 1961.
Beards, Richard D. and Barbara Willens. "D. H. Lawrence: Criticism; September, 1968–December, 1969." *D. H. Lawrence Review,* 3 (Spring 1970), 70–86.
Beebe, Maurice and Anthony Tommasi. Criticism of D. H. Lawrence: A Selected Checklist. *Modern Fiction Studies,* 5 (Spring 1959), 83–98.
Blissett, William. "George Moore and Literary Wagnerism." *Comparative Literature,* 1 (Winter 1961), 52–71.
————. "Wagnerian Fiction in English." *Criticism,* 3 (Summer 1963), 239–60.
————. "D. H. Lawrence and D'Annunzio, Wagner." *Wisconsin Studies in Contemporary Literature,* 7 (Winter-Spring 1966), 21–46.
Boynton, H. W. "Some British Seekers." Review of *Aaron's Rod,* D. H. Lawrence. *The Independent,* 27 May 1922, 489–91.
Brewster, Earl and Achsah. *D. H. Lawrence: Reminiscences and Correspondence.* London: Secker, 1934.
Burwell, Rose Marie. *A Catalogue of D. H. Lawrence's Reading From Early Childhood.* *D. H. Lawrence Review,* 3 (Fall 1970), 193–324.
Carswell, Catherine. *The Savage Pilgrimage: A Narrative of D. H. Lawrence.* Revised Edition. London: Secker, 1932.
Cavitch, David. *D. H. Lawrence and the New World.* New York: Oxford University Press, 1969.

Corke, Helen. *D. H. Lawrence: The Croydon Years.* Austin, Texas: University of Texas Press, 1965.

Cunliffe, J. W. *English Literature in the Twentieth Century.* New York: Macmillan, 1933.

Daiches, David. *The Novel and the Modern World.* Chicago: University of Chicago Press, 1960.

Daleski, Herman M. *The Forked Flame: A Study of D. H. Lawrence.* Evanston, Illinois: Northwestern University Press, 1965.

Delany, Paul. *D. H. Lawrence's Nightmare.* New York: Basic Books, 1978.

Douglas, Norman. *D. H. Lawrence and Maurice Magnus: A Plea for Better Manners.* Privately Printed, 1924.

——————. *Experiments.* London: Chapman and Hall, 1925.

Draper, Ronald P. *D. H. Lawrence.* Twayne's English Author Series, No. 7. New York: Twayne, 1964.

——————. *D. H. Lawrence.* Profiles in Literature Series. London: Routledge and Kegan Paul, 1969.

——————. *D. H. Lawrence: The Critical Heritage.* New York: Barnes and Noble, 1970.

Eisenstein, Samuel A. *Boarding the Ship of Death: D. H. Lawrence's Questor Heroes.* The Hague: Mouton, 1974.

Field, L. M. Review of *Aaron's Rod,* D. H. Lawrence. *New York Times Book Review,* 30 April 1922, 14.

Finer, Herman. *Mussolini's Italy.* Hamden, Connecticut: Archon Books, 1964.

Ford, George H. *Double Measure: A Study of the Novels and the Stories of D. H. Lawrence.* New York: Holt, Rinehart and Winston, 1965.

Foster, Joseph. *D. H. Lawrence in Taos.* Albuquerque: University of New Mexico Press, 1972.

Freeman, Mary. *D. H. Lawrence: A Basic Study of His Ideas.* Gainesville: University of Florida Press, 1955.

Goodheart, Eugene. *The Utopian Vision of D. H. Lawrence.* Chicago: University of Chicago Press, 1963.

Gregory, Horace. *D. H. Lawrence: Pilgrim of the Apocalypse.* New York: Viking Press, 1933. Rpt. New York: Grove Press, 1957.

Hochman, Baruch. *Another Ego: The Changing View of Self and Society in the Work of D. H. Lawrence.* Columbia, South Carolina: University of South Carolina Press, 1970.

Howe, Marguerite Beebe. *The Art of the Self in D. H. Lawrence.* Athens, Ohio: Ohio University Press, 1977.

Hough, Graham. *The Dark Sun: A Study of D. H. Lawrence.* New York: Macmillan, 1957.

Jarrett-Kerr, Martin ["Father William Tiverton"]. *D. H. Lawrence and Human Existence.* London: Rockliff, 1951.

Joost, Nicholas, and Alvin Sullivan. *D. H. Lawrence and the Dial.* Carbondale, Illinois: Southern Illinois University Press, 1970.

Kermode, Frank. *Lawrence.* Fontana Modern Mastern Series. Bungay, Suffolk: Richard Clay (The Chaucer Press), 1973.

Klein, Holger. *The First World War in Fiction.* London: Macmillan, 1976.

Krutch, Joseph W. "Love's Exasperations." Review of *Aaron's Rod,* D. H. Lawrence. *The Nation,* 2970 (7 June 1922), 696.

Lawrence, Ada, and G. Stuart Gelder. *Early Life of D. H. Lawrence.* London: Secker, 1932.

Lawrence, Frieda. *Not I, But the Wind.* New York: Viking, 1934.

——————. *Frieda Lawrence: The Memoirs and Correspondence.* ed. E. W. Tedlock, Jr. London: Heinemann, 1961.

Leavis, F. R. *D. H. Lawrence: Novelist.* London: Chatto and Windus, 1955.

——————. *Thought, Words, and Creativity: Art and Thought in D. H. Lawrence.* New York: Oxford University Press, 1976.

MacDonald, Edward D. *A Bibliography of the Writings of D. H. Lawrence.* Philadelphia: Centaur Bookshop, 1925.

Matthews, Herbert L. *The Fruits of Fascism.* New York: Harcourt, Brace, 1943.

Merivale, Patricia. *Pan the Goat-God: His Myth in Modern Times.* Cambridge: Harvard University Press, 1969.

Miller, Henry. *The World of Lawrence.* Santa Barbara, California: Capra Press, 1980.

——————. Notes on "Aaron's Rod." Ed. by Seamus Cooney. Santa Barbara, California. Black Sparrow Press, 1980.

Millett, Kate. *Sexual Politics.* Garden City, New York: Doubleday, 1970.

Moore, Harry T. *The Life and Works of D. H. Lawrence.* Revised Edition. New York: Twayne Publishers, 1964.

——————. *The Intelligent Heart: The Story of D. H. Lawrence.* New York: Farrar, Staus and Young, 1954.

——————. *Priest of Love.* London: William Heinemann, 1980.

——————. *Poste Restante: A Lawrence Travel Calendar.* Introduction by Mark Schorer. Berkeley: University of California Press, 1956.

——————, ed. *A D. H. Lawrence Miscellany.* Carbondale, Illinois: Southern Illinois University Press, 1959.

Moynahan, Julian. *The Deed of Life: The Novels and Tales of D. H. Lawrence.* Princeton, New Jersey: Princeton University Press, 1963.

Murry, John Middleton. *Son of Woman: The Story of D. H. Lawrence.* London: Jonathan Cape, 1931.

——————. *Reminiscences of D. H. Lawrence.* London: Jonathan Cape, 1933.

Myers, Neil. "Lawrence and the War." *Criticism,* 4 (Winter 1962), 44–58.

Nehls, Edward. *D. H. Lawrence: A Composite Biography.* 3 vols. Madison: University of Wisconsin Press, 1957–1959.

Niven, Alastair. *D. H. Lawrence: The Novels.* Cambridge: Cambridge University Press, 1978.

Panichas, George A. *Adventure in Consciousness: The Meaning of D. H. Lawrence's Religious Quest.* Studies in English Literature, III. The Hague: Moulton, 1964.

Patmore, Brigit. *My Friends When Young: The Memoirs of Brigit Patmore.* Ed., with an Introduction by Derek Patmore. London: Heinemann, 1968.

Pritchard, R. E. *D. H. Lawrence: Body of Darkness.* Hutchinson University Library, No. 161. London: Hutchinson, 1971.

Roberts, Warren. *A Bibliography of D. H. Lawrence.* Soho Bibliographies. London: Rupert Hart-Davis, 1963.

Sagar, Keith. *The Art of D. H. Lawrence.* Cambridge: Cambridge University Press, 1966.

——————. *D. H. Lawrence: A Calendar of His Works.* Manchester: Manchester University Press, 1979. (Includes L. Vasey, *Updated Checklist of Manuscripts of D. H. Lawrence.*)

——————. *The Life of D. H. Lawrence.* New York: Pantheon Books, 1980.

Sanders, Scott. *D. H. Lawrence. The World of the Five Major Novels.* New York: Viking Press, 1973.

Secker, Martin. *Letters from a Publisher: Martin Secker to D. H. Lawrence and Others, 1911-1929.* London: Enitharmon Press, 1970.

Shanks, Edward. Review of *Aaron's Rod,* D. H. Lawrence. London Mercury, 6 (October 1922), 655–57. Rpt. in R. P. Draper, ed. *D. H. Lawrence: The Critical Heritage.* New York: Barnes and Noble, 1970, 181–83.

Shaw, George Bernard. *Heartbreak House. The Complete Plays of Bernard Shaw.* London: Paul Hamlyn, 1965.

—————. Preface to *Heartbreak House. The Complete Prefaces of Bernard Shaw.* London: Paul Hamlyn, 1965.

Slade, Tony. *D. H. Lawrence.* Arco Literary Critiques Series. New York: Arco, 1970.

Spilka, Mark. *The Love Ethic of D. H. Lawrence.* Bloomington: Indiana University Press, 1955.

Stewart, J. I. M. *Eight Modern Writers.* Oxford History of English Literature, Vol. 12. New York: Oxford University Press, 1963.

Stoll, John E. *The Novels of D. H. Lawrence.* Columbia, Missouri: University of Missouri Press, 1971.

"T., E." [Jessie Chambers]. *D. H. Lawrence: A Personal Record.* Ed. J. D. Chambers. 2nd edition. New York: Barnes and Noble, 1965.

Tedlock, E. W., Jr. *The Frieda Lawrence Collection of Manuscripts: A Descriptive Bibliography.* Albuquerque: University of New Mexico Press, 1948.

—————. *D. H. Lawrence, Artist and Rebel: A Study of Lawrence's Fiction.* Albuquerque: University of New Mexico Press, 1963.

Trevelyan, George M. *Garibaldi and the Making of Italy.* London: Longmans, Green and Co., 1914.

Vickery, John B. *The Literary Impact of "The Golden Bough."* Princeton: Princeton University Press, 1973.

Vivas, Eliseo. *D. H. Lawrence: The Failure and the Triumph of Art.* Evanston, Illinois: Northwestern University Press, 1960.

West, Rebecca. "Notes on Novels." Review of *Aaron's Rod,* D. H. Lawrence. *The New Statesman,* 8 July 1922, 388–89.

Widmer, Kingsley. "Notes on the Literary Institutionalization of D. H. Lawrence: An Anti-Review of the Current State of Lawrence Studies." *Paunch,* 26 (April 1966), 5–13.

Worthen, John. *D. H. Lawrence and the Idea of the Novel.* London: Macmillan, 1979.

Yudhishtar. *Conflict in the Novels of D. H. Lawrence.* Edinburgh: Oliver and Boyd, 1969.

Index